Relational Economics and Organization Governance

This interdisciplinary book series examines recent developments concerning the "relational view" in economics. While the relational research perspective primarily has roots in philosophy, sociology and economic geography, this series offers contributions to the relational view from such diverse fields as institutional and organisational economics, management, organisational theory, and mathematics. Focusing on a relational approach to contracts and governance, leadership, rents, global cooperation, intersectoral cooperation and civil society, the series welcomes theoretical and empirical research on relational structures in market theory, institutional and organisational economics, the resource-based view of the firm, organisational studies, behavioural economics and economic sociology. Within this range of fields, researchers are invited to contribute to the further development of a relational view in economics.

More information about this series at http://www.springer.com/series/16570

Josef Wieland

Relational Economics

A Political Economy

Springer

Josef Wieland
Zeppelin University
Friedrichshafen, Germany

ISSN 2662-9852 ISSN 2662-9860 (electronic)
Relational Economics and Organization Governance
ISBN 978-3-030-45111-0 ISBN 978-3-030-45112-7 (eBook)
https://doi.org/10.1007/978-3-030-45112-7

English translation: Matthew Fentem, gonative language solutions (www.gonative.de)

Translation from the German language edition: Relational Economics—Ökonomische Theorie der Governance wirtschaftlicher Transaktionen, © 2018. Published by Metropolis-Verlag Marburg. All Rights Reserved.

This Springer imprint is published by the registered company Springer Nature Switzerland AG
The registered company address is: Gewerbestrasse 11, 6330 Cham, Switzerland

Preface

This book analyses the mechanisms of the relational economy of modern societies and global value creation chains. It is a translated, revised and significantly extended version of the book Relational Economics—Ökonomische Theorie der Governance wirtschaftlicher Transaktionen, published in 2018. The book develops a taxonomy of categories that are suitable and necessary for analysing relational economics. Lastly, it represents the product of a research agenda that I have pursued for a considerable time, one that chiefly focuses on the question of how relational norms—like moral values; integrity; conformity with legal regulations, human rights and social standards; and the sustainable use of natural resources—can be reintegrated into the economic theory of governance. Nevertheless it is still work in progress.

The impressions and outcomes of countless discussions with colleagues, collaborators, students and participants of public events are inarguably one of the most essential ingredients for expanding and transforming ideas and lines of argumentation into the book you now hold in your hands. In this regard, I would especially like to thank two colleagues: on the occasion of my 60th birthday, Birger P. Priddat told me in no uncertain terms that I should write this book. In turn, Michael Schramm helped me recognise how my long-standing interest in Alfred N. Whitehead's process philosophy and its social scientific consequences could contribute to this theory.

In closing, I would like to thank Isabel Jandeisek and Lennart Brand, but also and especially Dominik Fischer, my colleagues at the Leadership Excellence Institute Zeppelin (LEIZ) and my wife Géraldine Kortmann, who tirelessly supported me with the literature research, creating and formatting the manuscript and who shared their critical questions on the argumentation presented therein. My thanks also go to Ricarda Nopper for her help in preparing the manuscript. I am also grateful to Matthew Fentem for his tireless engagement and accurate translation, who made it possible to transfer a rather complex German text into the English language.

Konstanz, Germany — Josef Wieland
Spring 2020

Contents

About the Author

Josef Wieland is professor of institutional economics, organizational governance, integrity management and transcultural leadership at the Zeppelin University in Friedrichshafen and director of the Leadership Excellence Institute Zeppelin (LEIZ). He is the initiator and president of the German Forum Compliance and Integrity (FCI). He served as the former chairman of the German Network of Business Ethics (DNWE) and currently as the chairman of DNWE's advisory board. He is a member of the National CSR Forum of the BMAS (German Federal Ministry of Labour and Social Affairs) and serves on the jury board for the "CSR Prize" of the German government. He received the Max Weber Prize for Business Ethics of the BDI (Federation of German Industries) in 1999. In 2014, he received the highly estimated State Research Prize for Applied Research from the State of Baden-Württemberg, Germany. Since 2017, he is Vice-President (Research) of Zeppelin University, Friedrichshafen, Germany.

Chapter 1
Introduction: Relational Economy and Economic Theory

1.1 Space and Economic Process

This book discusses the value-creation processes of modern and global economic systems, as well as the challenges they pose for economic theory-building.

Since its earliest beginnings, economic theory-building has always been linked to a spatial conception of society. The *oikonomia* in the Greek poli, the household economy in the Middle Ages and the national economy in the modern era are all based on a social, political and cultural space that provides a comparatively stable environment for the system of economic transactions. This distinction between system and environment, in turn, has made the economy and society mutual sources of external positive and negative effects: the economy is an engine for societal development, concerning both material prosperity and the sustainability of living conditions. Conversely, society defines the political and cultural prerequisites and conditions for any and all economic services. But how is the connection between economic transactions and the societal space to be understood in a global economy in which the idea of a global society that is separate from the global economic system is, to date, at least, hard to imagine?

One way of dealing with this question from a theory-building standpoint consists in endogenising the system/environment difference and in viewing society as an event in the execution of economic transactions. But that means at the same time, that economy is an event in the execution of social and societal interactions. More generally speaking, society exists in the relations of its interactions; it is a relational society. In the following, I will explore the range and scope of this theoretical option in terms of developing an economic theory for the global economy. In this regard, the focus will be on deterritorialisation and especially on the development of global production and value-creation networks and the constitutive political and cultural diversity of global transactions—in terms of both their practical and especially their theoretical consequences.

In contrast to national economies, I will not approach the global economy as a space, or as a politically or administratively integrated unit. In keeping with my

J. Wieland, *Relational Economics*, Relational Economics and Organization Governance,
https://doi.org/10.1007/978-3-030-45112-7_1

theoretical approach, I instead see it as a network of transactions on the part of individual and collective actors from various areas of society, especially from the economy, politics and civil society. Though these actors are in competition with one another, they are nonetheless potentially also cooperating economic, political and civil-society actors—either individual or collective. Viewed in this light, the global economy becomes a network of regional, national, transnational and international economic interactions between actors, who dock their respective decision logics to transactions. Accordingly, economic transactions become attractors of societal interaction. In this context, globalisation is by no means a homogeneous phenomenon: though economic value creation and the standardisation of consumer preferences are to a large extent driven by a logic of global processes, nevertheless politics and culture remain predominantly, albeit not exclusively, national. That means the concrete, practical lives (life-worlds) of the actors are still regionally anchored and will remain that way for the foreseeable future. Consequently, the societal challenge posed by globalisation is not because, as globalisation progresses, all other social spaces will eventually be replaced by an overarching whole of some sort; rather, the challenge consists in the fact that the continuous dynamic and complexity of interaction between regional, national, transnational and international transactions must be furnished with a governance structure that delivers value creation and which is productive and mutually advantageous for all stakeholders involved. With regard to this process, firms—which, as collective actors, enable and facilitate the cooperation of individual actors—play an essential part and not merely in terms of their revenues and the costs of value creation, but also in terms of the societal legitimation for their existence.

In a world that continues to be characterised by sovereign and independent nation-states that, as Burton (1972, p. 28) astutely noted, are mutually demarcated entities interacting like colliding billiard balls, interpreting the relationship between economic systems and the world society can't readily be done at the spatial level. It seems far more promising to conduct the analysis at the level of collaborative events, such as between scientific findings and ethical values, trade and production and of individuals and the organisation. Accordingly, here globalisation is understood as a network of events, initiated by cooperating actors and resource owners. Under competitive conditions, these actors temporarily and fragmentarily relate to each other by organising specific transactions for their mutual benefit. Relationalisation amounts to a productive proportioning, a means of viewing events in dynamic and unfolding relations to one another. By employing it, I endorse Burton's suggestion to not use systems or actors as the basic unit for analysing the global society or global economy, but instead "transactions and links that exist" (ibid., p. 35). Viewed in this light, approaching the global economy no longer simply means 'adding up' the various national economies, but instead consists in identifying, grasping and shaping collaborative and transactional relations. The question of whether these cooperative networks—or *atopian societies* (Willke, 2001), will lead, as Mau (2007) assumes, to the creation of *condensed social spaces* (cf. ibid., p. 38) and therefore to new forms of transnational society formation, is one we need not discuss here. For our purposes, it suffices to assume that the socialisation of global networks is a result of the respective transactions and their interconnections.

In response to the growing despatialisation of modern economies, the sociologist Latour (2014) has suggested viewing the economy as *what counts* (cf. ibid., p. 629), as practices of accountability, value measurement and calculation used to codify events. For Latour, economically speaking the focus is only on "commitment, organisation, distribution and morality" (ibid., p. 624), in short, on the formation of dynamic collaborative relationships whose idiosyncratic rationality is "woven from more than one thread" [own translation] (ibid., p. 625).[1] From this perspective, globalisation is a process: not one of functional de-differentiation, but rather of the growth and intensification of structural couplings between various areas of society and their respective decision-making premises. In the following, the chief characteristics of this fundamental aspect of modern economies will be referred to as *polycontextuality*, *polycontexturality* and *polylingualism*.

1.2 Governance and Private Ordering

When we apply the discussed findings from political science and sociology to globalisation in the context of economic theory-building, we then speak about the forms of governance of economic transactions. According to Oliver E. Williamson (cf. Tadelis & Williamson, 2013; Williamson, 1979), the economics of governance differentiates between the market and hierarchy on one hand and hybrid forms like global supply chains, strategic alliances and networks of firms in general on the other. An economic theory of governance, Williamson (2005) maintains, seeks to analyse these three modes of control (cf. Williamson, 1979) in terms of *good order*, *workable arrangements* and the *continuity* of cooperative relationships as a source of transaction-cost-optimised economic value creation. When *public regulation* fails—which is the systematic point of departure for governance economics, which links it to the social scientific discussion on globalisation precisely here, the focus then shifts to *private ordering* on the part of NGOs like civil society organisations or by firms, based on contracts.

> The application of the lens of contract/private ordering/governance leads naturally into the reconceptualization of the firm not as a production function in the science of choice tradition, but instead as a governance structure. (Williamson, 2002, p. 191)

Approaching governance as a form of private ordering to support economic transactions concerns, at least according to the underlying thesis of this book, not only firms but organisations of all kinds, those in politics, civil society, law and so on. As a consequence, not only the market but also various forms of organisational governance and their connections to firms' day-to-day business are of critical importance

---

[1]On the genesis of this discussion in Wittgenstein and Deleuze, as well as its significance for the ethics of governance, cf. Schramm (2008).

in the process of private and public value creation. From this relational standpoint and with regard to specific transactions, the firm itself becomes a multi-stakeholder agent for the productive, value-creating proportioning of available and invested resources. This categorial redefinition of the firm as a nexus of stakeholders and their resources is another basic premise of my analysis. The *Relational Economics* discussed here is both based in and refers to governance economics. That being said, it also generalises the latter's theoretical framework, applying it to organisations of all kinds and their contributions to private and societal value creation. Consequently, relational economics is from the outset informed by and interested in, social theory. This connection is intrinsic; the just briefly described functional mechanisms of social, political and economic globalisation have produced their fair share of impacts on what is referred to as the categories *market*, *firm* and *hybrid* organisational forms in conventional economic standard theory, as explained in the following section.

1.3 Forms of Governance and Economic Theory Building

With regard to the governance structure *market*, the digitalisation and globalisation of value creation are primarily driving its transformation (for an overview cf. Goldfarb, Greenstein, & Tucker, 2015; Greenstein, Goldfarb, & Tucker, 2013). When, thanks to digital products, the distribution of information and knowledge is no longer limited by the borders of the nation-state and involves virtually no marginal costs, in other words, when additional information has no price and can essentially be provided free of charge, it has consequences not only for property rights, taxation and consumer behaviour but also for the quantification of value creation (cf. Wallsten, 2015) and the calculation of a given country's gross national product. For example, Greenstein and Nagle (2014) have estimated that the amount of value creation for a certain type of software in the digital economy of the USA, which is not reflected by the statistical and measurements instruments of conventional economics, was anywhere between two and twelve billion dollars. The research into and development of said software by a network of governments, universities, firms and non-governmental organisations (NGOs) would lead, at least hopefully, to economic growth, albeit a type of growth that was completely ignored by the categories of traditional economics.

> *Digital dark matter* can serve as the phrase for these digital goods and services that are non-pecuniary and effectively limitless, and serve as inputs into production. They are hybrids of public goods and private investments. (ibid., p. 623)

The findings on value creation in global and *hybrid* networks point in a similar direction. Though I'll return to this point in Chap. 6, for the time being, a few brief comments will suffice: strategic alliances, joint ventures, innovation platforms and multi-stakeholder forums for establishing economic and social standards combine economic, political and social interests to form *Global Value Chains*. The UNCTAD (2013) has estimated that because the figures were and continue to be recorded only incompletely roughly 80% whereas the OECD (2018) estimates 70% of what we now refer to as *international trade* doesn't take place on the market, but in the form of intra- and inter-firm collaborations, and that, as a result, roughly a quarter of international trade is effectively recorded twice. The economic, legal, and social as well as moral risks that these collaborations entail for firms—supply chain discontinuity, corruption and the violation of social, environmental as well as human rights standards—are endogenously linked to this form of global value creation. The following conclusion, drawn by Sony Kapoor, reveals the resulting challenges for economic theory-building:

> To sum up, the Dynamic Stochastic General Equilibrium (DSGE) models and other traditional approaches to modelling the global economy are increasingly inadequate and inaccurate in capturing the rising complexity of the global economy. (OECD, 2017, p. 54)

The *firm* as a form of governance is also undergoing a dynamic transformation. Nevertheless, economic theory-building continues to view the market as the point of reference and has shown little interest in exploring what Coase (1937) dubbed *The Nature of the Firm*. Though there have been significant theoretical advances in the areas industrial organisation (cf. for example Willig & Schmalensee, 1989), transaction cost theory and organisation economy (cf. for example Gibbons & Roberts, 2013), the economy of 'Two-Sided Markets' (Rochet & Tirole, 2003; Rysman, 2009) and multi-sided platforms (Evans & Schmalensee, 2016) in economic theory the firm is viewed as a purely economic entity; the social forces driving it and the effects it produces, are completely ignored.

The theory-based choice to ignore these aspects is only possible at a price: namely, that real phenomena can no longer be reflected in the categories used. Accordingly, as Evans and Schmalensee (2016) have noted quite frankly:

> Let's be clear: ignoring the interdependence of matchmakers' demand was a big mistake. Economics textbooks and business school courses made claims that just didn't apply to a large and growing part of the economy. (ibid., p. 3. Similar ideas can be found on pp. 5, 28 and so on)

What they have recognised is that the assumption of 'single-sided markets' that has been in place since Adam Smith and Neoclassicism no longer applies to highly relevant segments of the modern economy. However, they themselves remain biased by a market paradigm that relegates everything beyond its horizons to the status of externalities and is essentially only interested in whether said externalities have a positive or negative effect on value creation.

As such, though Evans and Schmalensee recognise the fundamental importance of standards of conduct for the actors in connection with the value-creation performance of multisided platforms, they characterise them as "behavioral externalities", so as to set them apart from direct and indirect network externalities. They assume that the enforcement of integrity and prevention of opportunism can be achieved by the law, a shared Code of Conduct and the threat of being banned from the platform (Evans & Schmalensee, 2016, p. 136 ff.). Though surely not wrong, this view fails to take into account the positive productive and value creating logic of the platform actors' morally appropriate conduct. And the omission appears to be intentional, since the two authors rightly identify the realisation of sociality and cooperation as the core of the platform economy: "Multisided platforms are communities, too. Their whole reason for being is to provide a place for participants to get together" (ibid., p. 137).

In an era of globalisation and network economy, this practically and theoretically inadequate perspective is, I believe, the cause of the largely undeveloped economic analysis when it comes to trans-sectoral stakeholder management, the management of social normativity and responsibility and their significance for

1. open and social innovation management,
2. interactive marketing,
3. global market penetration, together with its economic, legal and political risks,
4. the required supply-chain and partner management,
5. the internalisation of negative external effects via sustainability strategies,
6. the integrity and responsibility of the business model of a given organisation and its leadership, as well as,
7. the constitutive transculturality of global transactional networks.

And this is the case despite the fact that these aspects' relevance for private and public value creation is now largely undisputed. This can be seen for example in the global acceptance of the UN's Sustainable Development Goals (SDGs) and the agenda of the 2018 and 2019 World Economic Forum, both of which revolve around the idea of social growth through the relationalisation of stakeholder interests and resources.

Though this applies, as mentioned above, to both theory and practice, the learning processes are progressing only slowly. Empirical studies released by the Leadership Excellence Institute Zeppelin (cf. Wieland & Heck, 2013; Wieland, Baumann Montecinos, Heck, Jandeisek, & Möhrer, 2017) indicate that, at the German firms surveyed, the costs of these multi-stakeholder strategies are only selectively and incompletely reflected in cost accounting systems, because the systems were never designed to accommodate them. Whereas 62.8% of the firms surveyed recorded their cost accounting systems expenses in connection with fulfilling corporate social responsibility (CSR) obligations for the stakeholder group *employees*, only 15.3% did so for *society*, 7.1% for *partners* and 1.9% for *investors* (cf. Wieland et al., 2017, p. 40). And Michael Porter's industrial economic proposal for a corporate strategy of *Creating Shared Value* (cf. Porter & Kramer, 2011) points in the same direction because he provides only general, intuitively plausible arguments regarding its connection to costs and benefits. The phenomena of the relational economy not only stem from the categories of conventional economics, but also from corporate cost accounting.

Here, too, an OECD guideline for responsible corporate behaviour sums up the point aptly:

> Business relationships include relationships with business partners (any kind of business partner whether through a contractual or commercial relationship or some other kind of relationship, including a cascade of relationships), [...] and any other non-State or State entity directly linked to its business operations, products or services. (OECD, 2016, p. 3)

I will seek to further develop the relational view of the firm as a nexus of stakeholder interests, expressed above and to refine and concentrate it into a texture of multiple rationalities. In this regard, one fundamental aspect is the previously mentioned, growing complexity of the global economy, which can be seen in the difference between a given firm and its polycontextual environment. In practical terms, it concerns the challenge of integrating economic, political, cultural, social and ecological events from that environment into the guidelines and procedures of regionally, nationally, transnationally and internationally operating firms. Once again, we see that this cannot be achieved by the economics of governance without societal reflection, which, in the age of globalisation, is always also transcultural reflection.

The challenges that arise with regard to using conventional categories to analyse modern economies, briefly outlined above, are primarily of interest to us in connection with the governance form of the *firm*. Its nature, I argue, goes far beyond short-term and long-term contractual relationships between economic actors or actors with exclusively economic interests; in fact, it has far more to do with analysing a network of productive resources, the owners of which can in principle hail from all social contexts, view economic matters from their own perspectives and employ different and distinct decision logics in order to pursue their interests. The previously mentioned polycontexturality[2] of the actors relevant to twenty-first century economics has led to a differentiation of the required forms of relational collaborations and contracts—and, consequently, has also led to the question of how the factor incomes and especially the above-average profits from these trans-sectoral transactions, which we will refer to as rent, are to be distributed. As such, we have now arrived at the classical questions concerning the political economy of private and social value creation.

1.4 Pluralism and Taxonomy

This tendency of certain phenomena from the real economy to "disappear" from the architectures of established economic theory can be responded to in one of two ways.

On the one hand, we could seek to achieve, on the basis of empirical studies, a reformulation and expansion of conventional research areas, combined with the establishment of new ones. This would address the previously identified increase in complexity and the resultant failure to consider certain relevant economic factors and would add new research focus areas to an increasingly differentiated framework of economics, one that can barely still be integrated. This type of pluralisation, in addition to being advantageous, is already taking place on several levels, for example in Behavioural Economics, Digital Economics, Organisational Economics, Stakeholder Theory of the Firm and relational Contract Theory, to name but a few.

On the other, we could work under the assumption that the increasing vanishing of economic 'facts' from economic theory has less to do with the factual complexity

[2]For the epistemological side of this distinction cf. Günther (1979, 1980).

of the transactions and much more to do with the categories used to cover, evaluate and process them. Categories have both an experiential and, accordingly, an expectational component (cf. Koselleck, 1979), which produce attention, interpretation and a normative source of orientation for one's actions. Consequently, it could also prove interesting to change the basic unit of economic analysis, so as to arrive at a new categorical taxonomy. As a first step, the goal would have to consist in developing categories for a generalisable political economy regarding the governance of economic transactions. Further, its explanatory power for other areas of economic research, such as financial and capital markets or the role of the state, as well as its refinement and formalisation, would have to be tested and pursued in theoretical and empirical studies. With this book I would like to take a first step in this direction, beginning with an empirically informed discussion on the categorical taxonomy of relational economics—here the goal being less deductive and more explorative in nature.

In this regard, one fundamental concern is the explanation and structuring of private and social economic value creation, achieved through the successfully continued relationalisation of productive but socially diverse stakeholder resources.

To date, there have been very few studies that have explicitly contributed to this discussion. For example, in a working paper entitled Towards a Relational Economics: Methodological Comments on Intellectual Property Strategy, Industrial Organisation and Economics, Binenbaum (2005) proposed a meta-model for the relationalisation of relations, by means of which the various logics that influence how organisations carry out transactions can be viewed in relation to one another and, accordingly, can be integrated in their decision-making processes. In the model, said logics are represented by various approaches to economic theory-building; as a result, the model ultimately involves the relationalisation of different approaches to economic research. Further, in *The Relational Economy: Geographies of Knowing and Learning*, Bathelt and Glückler (2011) characterise economic behaviour that involves values, interpretive frameworks and path- and context-dependent institutions as being relational (cf. Bathelt & Glückler, 2011, pp. 6 f., 235 ff.). Process and randomness are, according to the authors' theoretical assumptions, further hallmarks of relational economics. In turn, Gilles, Lazarova, and Ruys (2015) view networks as value-generating sets of socioeconomic relations, the relational complexity of which is stabilised by institutions.

In his Essays on the Historicity of Capital, Herscovici (2019), building on the works of Grossman and Stiglitz, presented a well-founded dogma-historical analysis in which he criticised the intrinsic value theory of the neoclassical Scientific Research Program as being substantivistic and objectivistic. Value, he claims, is not some fundamental, intrinsic quality of goods or commodities. Rather, economic value is produced by the interaction of actors, especially by the asymmetry of information available to the respective actors, their mimetic behaviour and, in a very general sense, their ex-post behaviour. Consequently, it is historicity and not the assumptions of the rational expectation paradigm regarding isolated actors, that becomes the pivotal aspect of relational economic analysis.

> "Relational Economics highlights the fact that asset value is the result of interactions between individuals" (ibid., p. 76) and later "I will qualify such approach as Relational Economics to the extent that it primarily studies the nature of generalized interdependency of economic agents and its implications [...]." (ibid., p. 143)

The theory of Relational Economics presented in this book argues in the same direction, though it also expands the range of value-creating relations to encompass events of all kinds and elucidates the implications of doing so.

1.5 Polyvalent Transactions and Organisation

That being said, this book suggests a different approach. In Parts I and II, this study on Relational Economics calls for replacing the *exchange (exchange transaction)* with the *transaction (relational transaction)* and for replacing the *market* with *relational governance*, as the basic units of economic analysis. I will show that the category of discrete, market-mediated dyadic exchange is responsible for producing the biased view of modern economic analysis. In this context, adopting the category of transaction as an attractor for multiple actors and polyvalent events is intended to restore access to the analysis of economic interactions. In keeping with the philosophy of Whitehead (1929, 1941, 1967, 1968), a society of events is polyvalent when it uses multiple language games and system references to depict economic matters and uses decisions to establish their relations to one another. In the economy, these relational transactions necessarily take the form of relational contracts and the respective forms of governance used for them must be tailored accordingly.

This process, the polyvalent processing of economic transactions, can work efficiently and effectively at the organisational level, but not at the level of the market. Accordingly, the economic organisation as a form and process of relations is the point of reference for the theoretical architecture of Relational Economics. In this regard, the term 'relation' is not limited to the interpersonal, social and trust-based side of dyadic and discrete economic behaviour; rather, a relation in relational economics refers to the successful integration of multiple rationalities in an adaptive governance structure for the dynamic processing and development of specific economic transactions. Accordingly, the successful continuation of cooperative relations on the part of an organisation is what determines the performance level of a relational economy and that of its actors.

In this regard, the governance structure must be capable of flexibly adapting to social norms and coping with different but interacting, polycontextual decision logics. These refer for example to the logics of economic, legal and moral rationality, which, as Latour (cf. Latour, 2014, Chapter 16) has observed, can only process the rationality of reasonable logics as an intertwined relation. In this world, values—which also, but not exclusively, include moral values—aren't stable entities that actors can use as ultimate points of orientation for their decisions; rather, they are dynamic events as defined in Whitehead's process philosophy, which must be made more concrete ("conresance") and conceptually captured ("prehension") and which require adaptive micro-mechanisms of governance in order to be operationalised (cf. Wieland, 2017, p. 325).

How these mechanisms of global relation building can be effectively and efficiently designed, particularly in the corporate areas stakeholder management, polycontextual governance, leadership and transculturality, is a question we'll explore in Part III of this book. It is at precisely this level of analysis that the various intertwined "threads of reason" (to use Latour's terms) come together, in the form of structures for the micro-governance of global economic transactions. And here is where we can also succeed in operationalizing the seemingly insurmountable complexity, together with its resulting trade-offs, in the form of guidelines and procedures; by doing so, it can be made 'processable', which is simply another way of saying that it can be applied to collaborative and productive value creation. Though the areas just mentioned above provide constitutive factors of relational value creation, they are currently receiving insufficient attention in economic theory-building. Their significance for the relational economy and relational economics stem from the nature of the firm as a stakeholder relation, which must be an attractive one in terms of resource investment, while also capable of efficiently and effectively managing resources from various parts of society. In this regard, relational leadership, understood as the outcome of a social exchange process at all levels of the network, is a success-critical resource, primarily due to its ability to pave the way to economic success via transcultural actors. The requisite individual resources and abilities, as well as the corresponding micro-political governance expertise, will be extensively analysed on the basis of empirical findings and further developed from both a theoretical and practical standpoint. Here, the adaptivity of governance, the uncertainty, specificity and productivity of the resources and the actors' abilities and standards of conduct are essential components.

Lastly, Part IV addresses questions on the conditions for establishing stable and productive collaborative relations and for the distribution of the factor incomes and rents produced by those relations. Here it will become apparent that a specifically conditioned mechanism, consisting of the individual and organisational willingness and ability to cooperate, determines the opportunities for cooperation that are available to a given firm and accordingly, the level of private and social value creation. This discussion will also, at least that is my hope, help to clarify not only the theoretical categories of relational economics as a political economy for the governance of economic transactions but also the practical challenges for the relational economy.

1.6 Epistemological and Methodological Assumptions

The development of relational economics as a categorical taxonomy of a political economy for the governance of economic transactions depends on certain social theoretical and epistemological preconditions that it cannot establish on its own. Accordingly, in this section I will briefly discuss a number of central concepts that are essential to the chain of argumentation; this discussion will be resumed in the conclusion.

To a considerable extent, this work draws on the system theory put forward by Niklas Luhmann,[3] though it does not fully accept and integrate its premises and conclusions. It does, however, agree on the assumption that modern societies are functionally differentiated and that functional systems like the economy, law and politics are mutually autonomous. In other words, these systems are operatively closed and perform their functions by assessing events using binary codes and guiding differences. Further, they apply different decision logics, which are determined by these codes and differences. However, the systems are also communicatively open and consequently capable of structural coupling and therefore being in relations with other systems. At its core, this system theory is based on a distinction between the system and its environment, autonomy and relationality.

Moreover I, like Luhmann, will differentiate between functional, organisational and psychic systems, to which the above-mentioned properties apply. Accordingly, the term *polycontextuality* will be used to describe the fact that modern societies consist of multiple systems that serve as environments, existential and operational conditions for one another. For example, the political system and its organisations offer an environment for the organisational systems of the economy (for example firms) and there are structural couplings between the two; however, there is no relation of 'embeddedness' or hierarchy. Difference is what defines the relation between system and environment. Further, polycontextuality refers to the constitutive need for and ability of economic actors to connect and act in various social contexts. In my analysis, this particularly applies to the concept of the firm as a nexus of stakeholder resources and interests, which, from an operative standpoint, requires the management of stakeholder groups and therefore methodologically precludes viewing the firm as a purely economic actor.

The concept of polycontextuality is not to be confused with that of *polycontexturality*, which, as previously mentioned, stems from the works of the philosopher Gotthard Günther and will be used in this book to refer to the interlinking and intertwining of a given system's various rationalities and decision logics. Polycontexturality plays an essential part in the analysis of structural coupling between different and potentially conflicting system logics, which are themselves relevant in the exploration of relational transactions—an aspect that will prove extremely important with regard to the governance of polycontexturality, e.g. managing transculturality. In this regard, we will follow on Luhmann's comment that modern society is a polycontextural system "[…] the complexity of which can be described in myriad ways. Accordingly, research can hardly be expected to impose a monocontextural description on society" [own translation] (Luhmann, 1997, p. 36 f.).

In Luhmann's social theory, social systems are formed by and consist of communication; they emerge from and are maintained by communication. Accordingly, modes of speech play an important part in our investigations. Functional systems, like the market, are constitutively monolingual, which means the market assesses

[3]On the methodological terminology see Luhmann (1987, p. 15 ff.; 1997, p. 36 ff.).

and communicates on all internal and external events in the form of prices, in contrast to organisations and psychic systems, which are polylingual. *Polylingualism* is a communicative ability and means that a given system or actor can use different language games and decision logics to authentically (i.e., accurately) reconstruct, understand and communicate on an event or transaction. Moreover, polylingualism means that systems can compare such reconstructed events with their own guiding differences and integrate them in their decision-making processes so as to produce new communication patterns. Business Ethics, for example, is a comparatively new and distinct communication pattern for moral-economic events that consists of more than just "business plus/minus ethics".

Corporate Business Ethics programmes address precisely those events in the economy that neither business nor ethics can process on its own in a value-creating manner, because they cannot apply their traditional codes and logics to these events without prohibitive losses of information. We will further develop this idea as the 'unity of difference' on the basis of various examples, such as child labour, anti-corruption efforts and charitable work. System, polycontextuality, polycontexturality and polylingualism are theoretical concepts that will shape the relational research design of the analysis. Further, these concepts will be revisited in the respective chapters, where their implications for economic value creation will be discussed. From time to time, alternative terms (for example area, sector, intersectorality or transculturality) will also be used, especially when applying or discussing theoretical approaches in which these terms are commonly used. On the one hand, this serves to simplify the discussion; on the other, it adds a certain degree of terminological variety.

It is self-evident that there is a connection between the diversity of contexts, their decision logics and language games. The basic system-theoretical distinction between system and environment (polycontextuality) implies that a given system's diverse range of environmental contexts is characterised by a higher level of complexity than the system itself. This poses a constant challenge for the system: to remain open to communicating this environmental complexity, while simultaneously reducing that complexity so that it is communicatively accessible and can be processed. Achieving this requires the structural coupling of different decision logics (polycontexturality) as the unity of difference of system and environment. As a result, structural coupling involves the categorical relationalisation of various logics (binary codes, guiding differences) and their corresponding language modes (polylingualism). In the course of the argumentation developed in this book, we will repeatedly explore the new possibilities and challenges for economic theory-building that this insight entails.

Polycontextuality, Polycontexturality and Polylingualism are essential characteristics of a relational society which is the social theoretical foundation[4] of Relational Economics as a Political Economy. With these terms, Relational Economics internalises and operationalises those matters that conventional economics characterises as externalities.

[4]For a sociological discussion see Donati (2010), and Gottlieb (1983).

References

Bathelt, H., & Glückler, J. (2011). *The relational economy: Geographies of knowing and learning*. Oxford, UK: Oxford University Press.

Binenbaum, E. (2005). *Towards a relational economics: Methodological comments on intellectual property strategy, industrial organisation, and economics* (Working Paper 2005-04). Adelaide: University of Adelaide.

Burton, J. W. (1972). *World society*. Cambridge, UK: Cambridge University Press.

Coase, R. H. (1937). The nature of the firm. *Economica, 4*(16), 386–405.

Donati, P. (2010). *Birth and development of the relational theory of society: A journey looking for a deep 'relational sociology'*. Retrieved January 22, 2020, from https://www.relationalstudies.net/uploads/2/3/1/5/2315313/donati_birth_and_development_of_the_relational_theory_of_society.pdf.

Evans, D. S., & Schmalensee, R. (2016). *Matchmakers: The new economics of multisided platforms*. Boston: Harvard Business Review Press.

Gibbons, R., & Roberts, J. (Eds.). (2013). *The handbook of organizational economics*. Princeton, NJ: Princeton University Press.

Gilles, R. P., Lazarova, E. A., & Ruys, P. H. M. (2015). Stability in a network economy: The role of institutions. *Journal of Economic Behavior & Organization, 119*, 375–399.

Goldfarb, A., Greenstein, S., & Tucker, C. (Eds.). (2015). *Economic analysis of the digital economy*. Chicago, IL: University of Chicago Press.

Gottlieb, G. (1983). Relationism: Legal theory for a relational society. *The University of Chicago Law Review, 50*(2), 567–612.

Greenstein, S., Goldfarb, A., & Tucker, C. (Eds.). (2013). *The economics of digitization*. Northampton, MA: Edward Elgar.

Greenstein, S., & Nagle, F. (2014). Digital dark matter and the economic contribution of Apache. *Research Policy, 43*(4), 623–631.

Günther, G. (1979). *Beiträge zur Grundlegung einer operationsfähigen Dialektik* (Band 2). Hamburg: Meiner.

Günther, G. (1980). *Das Problem einer trans-klassischen Logik. In Beiträge zur Grundlegung einer operationsfähigen Dialektik* (Band 3). Hamburg: Meiner.

Herscovici, A. (2019). *Essays on the historicity of capital*. Cham: Palgrave Macmillan.

Koselleck, R. (1979). *Vergangene Zukunft: Zur Semantik geschichtlicher Zeiten*. Frankfurt a. M.: Suhrkamp.

Latour, B. (2014). *Existenzweisen: Eine Anthropologie der Modernen*. Berlin: Suhrkamp.

Luhmann, N. (1987). *Soziale Systeme. Grundriß einer allgemeinen Theorie*. Frankfurt a. M.: Suhrkamp.

Luhmann, N. (1997). *Die Gesellschaft der Gesellschaft* (Band 1). Frankfurt a. M.: Suhrkamp.

Mau, S. (2007). *Transnationale Vergesellschaftung: Die Entgrenzung sozialer Lebenswelten*. Frankfurt a. M.: Campus Verlag.

OECD. (2016). *Public consultation: OECD due diligence guidance for responsible business conduct (draft 2.1): Implementing the due diligence recommendations of the OECD guidelines for multinational enterprises*. Paris: OECD.

OECD. (2017). *Debate the issues: Complexity and policy making*. Paris: OECD.

OECD. (2018). *Trade policy brief: Trade policy implications of global value chains*. Retrieved January 27, 2020, from https://www.oecd.org/trade/topics/global-value-chains-and-trade/.

Porter, M. E., & Kramer, M. R. (2011). Creating shared value. *Harvard Business Review, 89*(1/2), 62–77.

Rochet, J. C., & Tirole, J. (2003). Platform competition in two-sided markets. *Journal of the European Economic Association, 1*(4), 990–1029.

Rysman, M. (2009). The economics of two-sided markets. *Journal of Economic Perspectives, 23*(3), 125–143.

Schramm, M. (2008). Transaktions-Rhizome. Ontologie und Ethik eines mikroanalytischen Stakeholder-Managements. In J. Wieland (Ed.), *Die Stakeholder-Gesellschaft und ihre Governance. Management, Netzwerke, Diskurse* (pp. 39–64). Marburg: Metropolis.

Tadelis, S., & Williamson, O. E. (2013). Transaction cost economics. In R. Gibbons & J. Roberts (Eds.), *Handbook of organizational economics* (pp. 159–189). Princeton, NJ: Princeton University Press.

UNCTAD. (2013). *Global value chains and development: Investment and value added trade in the global economy*. Geneva: United Nations.

Wallsten, S. (2015). What are we not doing when we are online? In A. Goldfarb, S. Greenstein, & C. Tucker (Eds.), *Economic analysis of the digital economy* (pp. 55–88). Chicago, IL: University of Chicago Press.

Whitehead, A. N. (1929). *Process and reality: An essay in cosmology*. New York, NY: MacMillan.

Whitehead, A. N. (1941). *Process and reality*. New York, NY: The Free Press.

Whitehead, A. N. (1967). *Science and the modern world*. New York, NY: The Free Press.

Whitehead, A. N. (1968). *Modes of thought*. New York, NY: The Free Press.

Wieland, J. (2017). Unternehmung und Gesellschaft. Notizen. In FUGO—Forschungsgruppe Unternehmen und gesellschaftliche Organisation (Ed.), *Unternehmen der Gesellschaft* (pp. 313–336). Marburg: Metropolis.

Wieland, J., Baumann Montecinos, J., Heck, A. E., Jandeisek, I., & Möhrer, M. (Eds.). (2017). *CSR performance: Managen und messen*. Marburg: Metropolis.

Wieland, J., & Heck, A. E. (2013). *Shared value durch stakeholder governance*. Marburg: Metropolis.

Williamson, O. E. (1979). Transaction-cost economics: The governance of contractual relations. *The Journal of Law and Economics, 22*(2), 233–261.

Williamson, O. E. (2002). The theory of the firm as governance structure: From choice to contract. *Journal of Economic Perspectives, 16*(3), 171–195.

Williamson, O. E. (2005). Transaction cost economics. In C. Menard & M. M. Shirley (Eds.), *Handbook of new institutional economics* (pp. 41–65). New York, NY: Springer.

Willig, R., & Schmalensee, R. (1989). *Handbook of industrial organization*. Amsterdam: Elsevier Science.

Willke, H. (2001). *Atopia. Studien zur atopischen Gesellschaft*. Frankfurt a. M.: Suhrkamp.

Part I
Transaction and Contract

Chapter 2
Discrete Exchanges and Relational Transactions

2.1 Goods and Commodity

Let's begin with something ostensibly simple. Economic goods are products or services with specific characteristics. Producing these goods entails certain costs (the investment of resources, no matter which kind); in turn, they produce specific benefits for consumers. If one good is directly exchanged for another, we refer to both as bartered goods; if they are exchanged via the market, they become commodities, that is, they are assigned prices and become subject to scarcity. In this context, scarcity does not necessarily mean a given commodity is hard to come by; rather, it describes the relation between supply and demand in the price system.

A transaction is a process of transfer; in the economy this can refer, for example, to the transfer of goods, commodities, property rights, or rights to use something. Transactions can take a variety of forms, for example, gift- or market-mediated equivalent exchanges, contracts or organisational processes. We refer to the first category as Exchange Transactions and to the second as Relational Transactions. In both cases, attention must be paid to the difference between and the simultaneity of form and process.

2.2 Dyadic and Discrete Exchange

The paradigmatic basic unit in the neoclassical theory of economics is the dyadic exchange of commodities via a market. Each exchange is a discrete event in the economic system of society. Discrete means that every exchange is an isolated act between two individual or collective actors, one in which only the economic aspect—in other words, the supply of and demand for the commodity's subjective use value (utility) and/or its exchange value (quantity of value), which is expressed in the form of a price that is paid—must be taken into consideration. The cycle of the economic system 'market' is the outcome of countless discrete exchanges that utilise

J. Wieland, *Relational Economics*, Relational Economics and Organization Governance,
https://doi.org/10.1007/978-3-030-45112-7_2

the medium of money, that is, payment. The resulting balance, it is assumed, leads to a self-organising and self-stabilising, static equilibrium. Self-organising markets run efficiently, that's the assumption, provided they are not disturbed by other logics, especially political or ethical logics. This represents the concisely formulated and normative—because natural—basis of the system of discrete exchange according to Smith (1776): "The quantity of every commodity brought to market naturally suits itself to the effectual demand" (WN I.vii.12).

If we choose to equate a given society's economy with the functional system 'market', since the nineteenth century at the latest, the despatialisation of the economy has represented the point of departure for neoclassical theory-building. For Jevons (1871/1911, p. 86), the market is a "community of knowledge", a process of "close communication" (p. 85) that is not bound to any specific place or location.

> Thus the common expression *Money Market* denotes no locality: it is applied to the aggregate of those bankers, capitalists, and other trades who lend and borrow money, and who constantly exchange information concerning the course of business. (ibid., p. 85)

I will use this definition of the market as a community of information, knowledge and its communication throughout this book. That being said, a given society's economy consists not only of discrete market transactions, but also of transactions between organisations like firms and individual actors. It is this interaction of market, organisation and individual that defines the economy of a society and which neoclassical standard economics caused to disappear from the epistemological focus of the business sciences, producing consequences that can still be felt today.

Yet at the analytical level, neoclassical economists are interested in neither the concrete utility of a product or service nor the identity of the actor. The benefit is identical to the prevailed preferences, willingness and ability to pay on the part of the actor, whose identity disappears in the behavioural assumptions of methodological individualism and rational economic maximisation strategies. This act is an event within an economic system intended to be functionally independent and one that exclusively obeys its own decision logic. Viewed through this lens, the environment of the exchange, its connections to societal, cultural, political, legal and other events completely fade out. The same is true for the influences of decision-making algorithms codified in other forms, for example law, ethics and politics, which, in the context of an exchange, may place certain external constraints on the actor's decisions, or shape his/her individual preferences. In this way, they may manifest in the form of a good or quality, which, in the case of a moral good (cf. Wieland, 1996), only has an influence on a commodity's exchange value if there is a corresponding preference and willingness to pay on the part of the buyer. In other words: it is reflected in the market system's binary code of "payment/non-payment". This closed cycle of discrete exchanges is a process we will hereafter refer to as Exchange Transaction (ET).

In a monetary economy and under conditions of complete competition, the supply of a given good (Sg) and the demand for payments (Dp) are simultaneous, while said demand (Dp) in turn simultaneously generates a supply of payments (Sp). This supply corresponds to a demand for goods (Dg), which is also the supply of payments (Sp) for the next Exchange Transaction and so on.

$$ET = f(Sg/Dp-Sp/Dg);\ (Sp/Dg-Sg/Dp\ldots)$$

This process takes place at two levels: that of the goods or services (supply and demand based on use value) and that of the resulting prices and payments (supply and demand based on commodities or exchange value). It is characterised by:

1. the double difference of goods (g) and payments (p) in each act of individual exchange;
2. the simultaneity of all events in an exchange, which are conveyed and expressed using prices;
3. the temporalisation of the events, their coming into existence and ceasing to exist at a specific and isolated point in time t_1; and
4. their particularity: their inhomogeneity with regard to events and logics outside the economic system.

2.3 Exchange Transactions

In his essay, *The Nature of the Firm*, the previously mentioned Coase (1937) differentiates between *transactions* in and between collaborative projects and "exchange transactions co-ordinated through the price mechanism" (p. 393). Subsequently, Williamson (1985), referring to the work of John R. Commons, declared the transaction to be the basic unit of economic theory-building, which is to say, of transaction cost theory and governance economics (cf. Williamson, 1975, 1979, 1985). Yet unlike Commons (1950), whose deliberations he partly draws on, Williamson makes no distinction between transactions and exchanges. In his *Economics of Collective Action*, Commons (1950) states that "business economics has more or less clearly distinguished between a 'transaction' and an 'exchange'" (p. 45). Whereas an exchange, he claims, describes the physical process involved in the mutual provision of objects, a bargaining transaction is the process of negotiating and concluding contractual agreements for the purposes of "transfer [of] ownership under the 'operation of law'" (ibid.).

Accordingly, at least five potential actors can be involved in a transaction, namely two competing buyers and two competing sellers, as well as a legal actor as third party enforcement for the conclusion of the contract; whereas an exchange, as a discrete event, involves only two actors. However, it should be noted that, through competition, the transaction becomes connected to the market. As such, the economic logic of the transaction manifests not only in the decision logics of the actors but also in their connection to the logic of the market, against which they must judge their own logics. Transactions are constitutively polycontextural and polylingual; in other words, various social systems and their decision logics (market, law, ethics) are essential to their completion. This is made unequivocally clear in the well-known definition from *Institutional Economics*:

> Thus, the ultimate unit of activity, which correlates law, economics and ethics, must contain in itself the three principles of conflict, dependence, and order. This unit is a transaction. A transaction, with its participants, is the smallest unit of institutional economics. (Commons, 1934/1990, p. 58)

An economic transaction is formed by the integration of various decision logics (law, economics, ethics) and multiple actors, who succeed, within the framework of their mutual dependencies, to productively—because they do so in an organised manner—reconcile and employ said logics. In his *Legal Foundations of Capitalism*, Commons (1924) supplements the definition of the transaction as the ultimate unit:

> It is the ultimate but complex relationship, the social electrolysis, that makes possible [...] association [...] and other going concerns. (ibid., p. 68)

Yet the transition from exchange to transaction doesn't simply entail an increase in the level of complexity (cf. Commons, 1950, p. 51); rather, the transaction itself is a relation of multivalent, social interactions between actors and events, which ultimately lead to the formation of economic organisations. Consequently, unlike for Coase or Williamson, for Commons (1950) the relations between multivalent actors and resources and not transaction-cost advantages, are what constitute the nature of the firm. That is, as he goes on to explain, the difference between

> individual economics and institutional economics, and between static economics and dynamic economics. (ibid., p. 52)

Further, since interactions take place over time, it can also be said that a transaction is an interaction between "two or more persons looking towards the future" (Commons, 1924, p. 4). It is the addition of time, of future and, with it, of a process (ibid., p. 8), that—by relationalising various behavioural contexts and multiple language games as the preconditions for completing organised economic transactions—allows us to address uncertainties and contingencies of all kinds as rationally as possible in the context of institutional economics.

> In fact, transactions have become the meeting place of economics, physics, psychology, ethics, jurisprudence and politics. (ibid., p. 5)

With regard to theory-building, the aspects mentioned above necessitate interdisciplinarity and an approach that can accommodate and integrate various epistemological sectors. Trans-sectoralism and polylingualism have a shared point of reference, namely, multivalent value creation as an outcome of the transaction. Expressed somewhat more directly, relational transactions are attractors for material and non-material value creation:

> A transaction is thus a compendium of psychological value, real value and nominal value. (Commons, 1924, p. 9)

At a higher level, the diversity in terms of the context, communication and value creation leads to the formation of collective actors, to the birth of the firm from the continuity of transactions, namely as a "going concern existing in its transactions" (Commons, 1934/1990, p. 53). Yet this *going concern* is a form that provides continuity for perpetual change:

> The distinguishing character of a perfected going concern is its capacity to continue with changing personalities and changing principles, not depending upon any particular person or any particular principle. (ibid., p. 750)

The firm as a going concern that emerges from the process of transactions and which transpires in and is preserved by each transaction the organisation completes; the firm as an abstract object, which is generated, preserved and 'perishes' in the process of its real-world transactions, clearly reflects the epistemological embeddedness of Commons' economics in the process philosophy of Alfred N. Whitehead (for a detailed analysis cf. Wieland, 2016, 2017). In fact, with regard to his concept of the going concern, Commons directly mentions Whitehead:

> But the mechanism itself is 'organic' in that it is a kind of prolonged interweaving of changing events, having as Whitehead says, a past, a present realization, and a future life in its present events. (Commons, 1934/1990, p. 619)

These processes are a relation of *events* or *actual entities*, whose relations to a nexus Whitehead refers to as *societies* and represent a form of social order (cf. Whitehead, 1929/1941, pp. 50, 619 ff.). Relations are self-enfolding forms in which and together with which processes take place; within these forms, nothing is lost, while new things constantly form and fade again.

> In the philosophy of organism it is not 'substance' which is permanent, but 'form'. Forms suffer changing relations; actual entities 'perpetually perish' subjectively, but [are] immortal objectively. (Whitehead, 1929/1941, p. 44)

To stop and take stock for a moment, what we have determined so far is the following: the basic paradigmatic unit of relational economics is the transaction as relation, that is, the transaction as an attractor of polyvalent contexts, decision logics and sources of value creation. Transactions are the focal point in a complex system. Accordingly, the characteristics of the transactions and the form of their relationalisation determine the networks' performance. The paradigm of the discrete exchange eliminates this complexity because it views the system's performance and behaviour merely as the addition of all individual exchanges. In contrast, by applying the paradigm of the Relational Transaction, relational economics draws on the institutional economics tradition. In keeping with Commons, Relational Transactions are events and at the same time represent a relation of events: supply, demand, utility, value, individual rational maximisation strategies, legally binding contracts, moral principles, aesthetic sensibilities, technologies, innovations and so on are events with regard to and in relation to a transaction. That being said, in this methodological context, economic transactions are not embedded in an antecedent or hierarchical society; rather, they attract and combine a host of interactions between societal institutions and organisations and their corresponding, respective decision logics, between which there is, with regard to the transaction, no *ex-ante* fixed hierarchy. Relational Transactions are polycontextual, polycontextural and therefore polylingual relations of interaction in which, for the purposes of a specific transaction, a prioritising order is temporarily and fragmentarily created and subsequently ceases to exist. Priddat (2016) has correctly indicated that the transaction is "only the site of the juxtaposition, the momentary convergence" [own translation] (p. 208)—and not just of two actors, it should be added, but also of logics, emotions, perceptions, convictions and a theoretically unlimited number of additional events (cf. also Priddat, 2018). As such, they are principally equally valid, but not equally valuable, in terms of their contribution to a local transaction. The epistemological world of the relational economy is flat, but not holistic.

2.4 Society and Relational Transactions

In order to make multivalent transactions accessible for economic analysis, the problem of holism, that is, of the potentially infinite trade-offs between events and relations, must be solved, which will be accomplished in two main steps in this chapter: firstly, relational economics isn't concerned with all transactions, but instead with specific economic transactions and their contributions to value creation. That means, it requires the social theory-based attribution of a given transaction (T) to the previously outlined and binary-code-based functional system 'market' as a never-ending sequence of Exchange Transactions (ETs) involving goods and services and their monolingual evaluation via prices, which produces a code of 'payment – non-payment'. All transactions that involve a price and generate a payment are economic transactions.

Secondly, the relation between these discrete Exchange Transactions (ET) and polyvalent (polycontextual, polycontextural, polylingual) Relational Transactions (RT) must be depicted and operationalised. This is achieved by introducing distinct decision logics into the analysis, which we attribute to the following levels: individual actors (I), organisational actors (O) and societal institutions (SI). Individual and collective actors alike can and must reconstruct and assess economic transactions in various contexts and decision logics, for example with regard to rational considerations based on their benefits, legal or ethical norms, technical feasibility, aesthetic preferences, cultural values and so on. The resulting trade-offs are assessed at two of the three levels using the guiding economic code 'earnings – costs'. In other words: individual and organisational economic actors make their decisions based on the positive, value-creating aspects of this guiding difference. In a given timeframe, for every rational actor, the earnings or revenues from his or her resources must be greater than the costs associated with them. Further, this applies not to each of his or her decisions at a specific point in time t_1. With regard to a specific transaction, individual and collective economic actors can, at t_1, choose to apply organisational, technical, ethical, legal or aesthetic logic and choose not to apply economic logic, provided the economic earnings are greater than the costs in a certain timeframe ($t_1 \ldots t_n$). Otherwise, disruptive innovations and strategic investments under uncertainty could not be theoretically integrated as endogenous economic events. This does not imply that the costs involved are irrelevant for the decision; rather, at t_1 they simply do not determine said decision.

A further factor to consider: societal informal institutions like religion, culture or commonly held values and norms, as well as formal institutions like the law or general, socially codified and enforceable rules continually evaluate every economic act using the guiding difference 'conformity – nonconformity'. In the normal course of things, it suffices to comply with these standards, which can only produce an explicit event if they are violated. Here, too, the costs involved in adhering to this guiding difference for individuals and organisations are certainly not meaningless, yet they do not determine the decision made at t_1. No one can, based on cost considerations, systematically choose not to comply with legal and moral norms without facing any costly consequences; otherwise, compliance management systems and efforts to promote social responsibility would not be endogenous of and constitutive for economic transactions; rather, they would be exogenous, externally imposed limitations. Consequently, Relational Transactions can be formally expressed as follows:

$$RT = f(I, O, SI)$$

An economic transaction is relational if more than two individual or collective actors and polycontextual and polylingual decision logics (for example, earnings – costs, conformity – nonconformity) are constitutive for the conclusion of the transaction. This in turn tells us that the monolingual and operatively closed functional system of the discrete Exchange Transaction, which is to say, the market or the maximisation strategy of an individual, cannot be the fundamental analytical point of reference for relational economics. Rather, the organisation—as a system for processing and allocating different logics, which is to say, the *enterprise* or the organisation of another functional system and as a collective actor—is the factual and logical point of reference for relational economics. An organisation is "a structure composed of positions in relation, not persons in relation" (Coleman, 1990, p. 427). This is applicable to organisations' internal and external relations alike, which involve individual persons, collective persons and societal institutions. Institutions are forms of societal and economic normativity that have their own behavioural consequences for actors. The market—which, from the standpoint of the firm or any other organisation, is a societal institution that greatly influences its environment—initially reflects said organisation's Relational Transactions in terms of their 'conformity – nonconformity' with market-mediated 'supplies – demands' and simultaneously classifies them as Exchange Transactions with prices. Figure 2.1 represents the codifying events in a Relational Transaction.

Parameter	Guiding difference for the decision
Individual (I)	Earnings – Costs
Organisation (O)	Earnings – Costs
Societal institution (SI)	Conformity – Non-conformity

Fig. 2.1 Parameters of relational economic transactions

2.5 Exchange Transactions and Relational Transactions

In this way, Relational Transactions are structurally linked with the market of Exchange Transactions. Through their guiding codes 'earnings – costs' and 'conformity – nonconformity', the events Dg, Dp, Sg and Sp, that is, the supply and the demand for goods and the payments they generate, are coupled with the market's price system. Through this coupling with price-based Exchange Transactions, they influence the market and are at the same time communicatively linked to its monolingual decision logic. The binary market code 'payment – non-payment' and the firm's guiding code 'earnings – costs' are in a relationship of mutual causality. Successfully combining the two is the life's blood of the economy, whose continual flow links all organisations in a society to the economic system. It is the economic side of organisational continuity, which is recursively linked to its societal side, cooperation. In other words, each side is the condition for the other's continuing existence, yet neither is an exclusive decision-making criterion. If the supply (Sg) of a given T-shirt was produced in a socially responsible manner and therefore simultaneously generates a demand for an appropriate payment from consumers (Dp), there may nevertheless be little or no demand for the good (Dg) and therefore little willingness to pay on the part of consumers (Sp). In the former case, the Relational Transaction is not successfully transferred to the system of the market; in the latter, the difference 'earnings – costs' is negatively influenced.

Because this structural coupling always takes place at t_1, the scenario described above by no means implies that the provider has to completely abandon the production and sale of socially responsible T-shirts. They can improve the product, reduce their costs, change their communication strategy and so on and subsidise these measures using cross-financing or organisational slack; in other words, they can use other resources to buy time for an additional event at t_1. Here, too, we see that, though the market reflects the activities of individual actors and organisations and evaluates them in the form of prices, this aspect needn't determine the decisions of the two actors at t_1. Nonconformity with market signals is one event in a bundle of events and can—over a certain length of time and viewed in a specific context—become a decisive event, but it is not systematically decisive from the outset, nor in every Relational Transaction. This aspect broadens not only the decision-making options for individual and collective actors but also the options for analysing and explaining economic transactions. To review, the process of coupling and decoupling between Exchange and Relational Transactions is shaped by:

1. the different contexts of individual and collective actors and the market, which represent non-determining decision-making environments for one another;
2. the different decision logics and language games in these environments, in other words, monolingualism versus polycontexturality and polylingualism; and
3. the different time metrics, that is, the market horizon, which is limited to the present (t_1), versus the process horizon of individual and collective actors from the past – present – future ($t_0 - t_1 - t_n$).

By distinguishing between Exchange Transactions and Relational Transactions, the possibility of their decoupling—which is to say, of the transition from market exchanges to intra- and inter-organisational or civil society transactions—is theoretically endogenised. This is of fundamental importance to understanding modern network economies and the productivity of global value-creation chains with their various levels of value creation. The difference between structural coupling and decoupling is then ultimately merely a question of the relationalisation of societal logics during the execution of economic transactions, which can be based on economic, political, societal or other considerations.

In this regard, too, from an economic theory-building perspective, it is essential that the range of potential trade-offs should be strictly limited. The point of departure is the assumption that, for the specific governance of Relational Transactions and their coupling and decoupling, the following factors are essential and effective:

1. the ability of Relational Transactions to couple with Exchange Transactions through context-, communication- and time-adaptive governance structures;
2. the situational and personal degree of informational and expectational certainty, which are closely tied to the limited rationality, values and norms of the actors in various sectors and systems of society;
3. the specificity of the resources required for a Relational Transaction and, consequently, the relation between the contribution to value creation on the one hand and the risk of opportunistic exploitation on the other;
4. the productivity of a specific Relational Transaction and its contribution to private and societal value creation; as well as
5. the existence of workable mechanisms for attributing value creation to and distributing it among the resource-investing stakeholders.

In the course of the following chapters, I will return to these aspects—which are essential to the analysis—time and time again, partly in order to better explain the characteristics of Relational Transactions.

References

Coase, R. H. (1937). The nature of the firm. *Economica, 4*(16), 386–405.

Coleman, J. S. (1990). *Foundations of social theory*. Cambridge, MA: Harvard University Press.

Commons, J. R. (1924). *Legal foundations of capitalism*. New York, NY: MacMillan.

Commons, J. R. (1934). *Institutional economics: Its place in political economy* [Reprint: 1990]. New Brunswick/London: Transaction Publishers.

Commons, J. R. (1950). *The economics of collective action*. New York, NY: MacMillan.

Jevons, W. S. (1871/1911). *The theory of political economy*. London: Macmillan.

Priddat, B. P. (2016). Die Transaktion als Juxtaposition und als Kooperation. Differente Interpretationen des Marktes. In H.-C. Schmidt am Busch (Ed.), *Die Philosophie des Marktes* (pp. 207–226). Hamburg: Meiner.

Priddat, B. P. (2018). *Vertrag als Kooperation. Über die implizite Ethik der Transaktion* (Unpublished manuscript).

Smith, A. (1776). *An inquiry into the nature and causes of the wealth of nations*. Carmel, IN: Liberty Fund.

Whitehead, A. N. (1929). *Process and reality: An essay in cosmology*. New York, NY: MacMillan.

Wieland, J. (1996). *Ökonomische Organisation, Allokation und Status*. Tübingen: Mohr Siebeck.

Wieland, J. (2016). Philosophie der Firma. Eine Skizze. In W. D. Enkelmann & B. P. Priddat (Eds.), *Was ist? Wirtschaftsphilosophische Erkundungen. Definitionen, Ansätze, Methoden, Erkenntnisse, Wirkungen* (pp. 285–314). Marburg: Metropolis.

Wieland, J. (2017). Unternehmung und Gesellschaft—Notizen. In FUGO—Forschungsgruppe Unternehmen und gesellschaftliche Organisation (Ed.), *Unternehmen der Gesellschaft. Interdisziplinäre Beiträge zu einer kritischen Theorie des Unternehmens* (pp. 313–336). Marburg: Metropolis.

Williamson, O. E. (1975). *Markets and hierarchies, analysis and antitrust implications*. New York, NY: The Free Press.

Williamson, O. E. (1979). Transaction-cost economics: The governance of contractual relations. *The Journal of Law & Economics, 22*(2), 233–261.

Williamson, O. E. (1985). *The economic institutions of capitalism*. New York, NY: The Free Press.

Chapter 3
Relational Contracts and Goods

3.1 Coordination and Cooperation

The governance of economic transactions can involve the coordination or cooperation of events. The two aspects, coordination and cooperation, are linked by a relation of interaction. In the paradigm of standard economics, no distinction is made between a given form of governance's coordination performance and cooperation performance. The assumption is that in efficient competitive markets, the two aspects coincide and as such, they are generally considered to be identical. However, when the market and organisation are viewed as different forms of governance for the relationalisation of events, it also has consequences for the theoretical architecture.

Coordination requires a form of governance that attributes *ex-post* services to existing demands or rules. Coordination is a thing-to-thing relation, a type of regulating procedure. In contrast, cooperation should be understood as a form of governance in which the individual and collective actors agree to *ex-ante* rules on the provision of a service and upholding that agreement—in terms of the rules and the service—can become problematic *ex-post*. Cooperation is an actor-to-actor relation and a fragile process for the relationalisation of societal actors. Markets, organisational charts and methods are all forms of coordination in which the actors' characteristics are irrelevant. Organisations in their diverse manifestations are examples of forms that enable, require and delimit cooperation between actors and in which the individual and collective actors' characteristics are significant events. Transactions can be completed in the mode of coordinating competition (Exchange Transactions), or that of organising cooperation (Relational Transactions). Relational economics initially reflects this distinction by means of different contractual forms for market and organisational relations; in this regard, it follows in the footsteps of institutional and governance economics. The classical and neoclassical contract is based on one-time or repeated, long-term market transactions (Exchange Transactions), in which the actors' characteristics are not taken into consideration. Transactions within and

J. Wieland, *Relational Economics*, Relational Economics and Organization Governance,
https://doi.org/10.1007/978-3-030-45112-7_3

between organisations cooperating in the long term are based on relational and societal contracts (Relational Transactions), in which the actors' traits—for example, their trustworthiness, moral integrity, or opportunism—are highly relevant.

Consequently, relational contracts play a fundamental part in the on-going discourse on organisational economics (cf. Gibbons & Roberts, 2013) and in two different senses: on the one hand, with regard to the actors' expected and actual conformity with their respective roles and the contract; on the other, with regard to the corresponding cooperation rent that can be achieved for all actors involved.

> We therefore focus on relational contracts – roughly, understandings that the parties share about their roles in and rewards from cooperating together, but understandings so rooted in the details of the parties' relationship that they cannot be shared with a court. (Gibbons & Henderson, 2013, p. 681)

Accordingly, from an economic perspective, the fundamental purpose of a relational contract is always to generate a shared value for all participating actors. "[T]he parties must have a rent from continuing their relationship" and "that rent must exist" (Malcomson, 2013, p. 1057). This rent comes in the form of a supernormal profit, which refers to the difference between the individual or organisational resource revenues that can be achieved in the cooperation relation and those that can be achieved in the next-best cooperation or market relation and which must be distributed by means of relational or exchange contracts. This is an aspect I'll discuss in more depth in Chap. 11.

Relational contracts are systematically incomplete—and intentionally incomplete, because they have to offer sufficient flexibility to permit continual economic rent generation and accommodate the contingencies in the actors' interactions that it unavoidably entails. In other words, they are characterised by unavoidable situational or individual behavioural uncertainty and the contingencies of continual interactions and must be equipped with adaptation and enforcement mechanisms outside of the law, whether they be of an economic, societal or moral nature (revenues, costs, reputation, trust, trustworthiness and so on) (Macaulay, 1963, pointed out this aspect quite early on. For the status quo cf. Baker & Choi, 2015).

From this perspective, they are "informal agreements sustained by the value of future relationships" (Baker, Gibbons, & Murphy, 2002, p. 39) or societal informal institutions (SII), without whose focused efficacy economic value creation can only reach a Pareto-suboptimal level. As such, informal institutions represent an essential form of governance for prospective contingencies, which are capable of coupling with transactions.

I will cover this form in more detail in the next chapter. For the sake of the current discussion, it suffices to say that, as a rule, informal cooperation mechanisms are related to formal coordination mechanisms. In order to be efficient and effective, moral or cultural standards must be coupled with a formal monitoring or conflict-resolution process—and vice versa. Although these relations have received insufficient attention in the discussion of relational contracts in organisational economics to date, they are the most intrinsic subject matter for relational economics.

3.2 Discrete and Relational Transactions

In modern economies with their networks and global value-creation chains, which are characterised by the transition from *international trade* to *relational exchange*, relational contracts are the predominant tool for shaping cooperative relations that continue over the timeframe $t_1 \ldots t_n$ and in which, consequently, the traits of the actors are relevant. At any rate, that is the central premise in the works of Ian R. Macneil (cf. above all Macneil, 1974, 1978, 1985, 2000), who, following on the works of Stewart Macaulay (for a list of principles regarding relational contracts cf. Macaulay, 1963, pp. 65–68), founded the field of Relational Contract Theory, which has since become essential to economic research. In his famous article *The Many Futures of Contracts* from 1974, Macneil states that:

> The major premise of this essay is the prevalence of relation in the post-industrial socioeconomic world. [...] relational economic behavior is on the increase (p. 694 f.). Increasingly the dominant mode of economic organization is the relation and not the discrete transaction. (p. 757)

The discrete transaction is the basis of the classical contract; in turn, the classical contract represents a promise that either party can be legally forced to honour. Williamson (1973, 2005) has, following up on Commons and Macneil, made the distinction between classical, neoclassical and relational contracts fruitful for transaction-cost theory and governance economics—albeit, in the paradigm of discrete structural alternatives, only with two decision logics, namely those of the economy and the law. Accordingly, for the purposes of this work, it would seem appropriate to develop the concept and nature of the relational contract on the basis of Macneil's deliberations.

Unlike economic contract theory, Macneil takes Durkheim's (1930/2013) observation that "in a contract, not everything is contractual" (Durkheim, 2013, p. 165) at face value. What Durkheim had in mind was the fact that, in every contract, there are additional, implicit contractual obligations that emanate from its social character. Accordingly, they do not stem from the free will of the competing or cooperating parties, but from the rules of society: "We co-operate because we have wished to do so, but our voluntary co-operation creates for us duties that we have not desired" (ibid., p. 168).

These implicit duties permit voluntary contracts to be constantly adjusted to situational contingencies and serve to reduce transaction costs. In Durkheim's view, purely legal—which is to say, classical—contracts are extremely rare events, as they require complete information and stable social processes.

> Summing up, therefore, the contract is not sufficient by itself, but is only possible because of the regulation of contracts, which is of social origin. (ibid., p. 169)

For the legal scholar Macneil, it is precisely this insight that forms the social-theoretical perspective and point of departure for his Relational Contract Theory. In his view, a relational contract theory is—and this should also be a key aspect for the contemporary discussion—unthinkable without social theory. Therefore, Macneil's works also and, in my opinion, first and foremost represent a critical contribution to legal theory; one from the perspective of behavioural theory and systemic social theory and drawing on Durkheim and especially Talcott Parsons. This is an aspect that we should bear in mind in the pages that follow (cf. Macneil, 1974, p. 710).

Earlier in the book, I made the suggestion, with regard to Relational Economics, to no longer approach society as a distinct context in which the economy operates or is embedded, but instead, to always view the execution of relational transactions as also being the execution of a temporalised and fragmented society. From a contract-theoretical perspective, doing so has certain unavoidable consequences for the social contract, which, since Hobbes, Locke and Rousseau, has been seen as a moral and legal bond between the actors in a society. Macneil (1979) depicts these consequences by reformulating the traditional concept as a New Social Contract:

> So too, the New Social Contract is social in two important senses. It contains its own internal social relations, and it is society's basic socioeconomic tool in both Western and developed socialist states. (ibid., p. xiii)

Accordingly, the execution of society through its transactions is, from a contract-theoretical standpoint, based on two assumptions: that modern societies organise their interactions via contracts; and that these contracts must reflect and take into account the multiple logics of the respective society, which is to say, law, economics, ethics, politics and so on, which are relevant for a given transaction. Precisely this point is the most fundamental definition of the relational contract. Consequently, when, in the remainder of the book, we discuss social contracts, say, between a firm and its interactions with civil society or political organisations, it should be understood as being in the sense developed here, namely as a form of relational contract, which is the essence of a relational society (cf., Donati, 2010; Gottlieb, 1983).

For Macneil (1974), the behaviour of economic actors takes place on an axis between two poles: discrete transactions and relational contracts (ibid., pp. 696 and 738–740). These poles are defined by the different qualities of their contractual promises (ibid., pp. 715–718); by the specificity of the service, the unequivocal way in which it is communicated and the quantifiable reciprocity of services at the pole 'discrete transactions'; and by the motivation to cooperate, the acceptance of the partners' interdependence and a preference for continuing the relation at the pole 'relational contracts' (Fig. 3.1).

The y-axis shows various characteristics of discrete transactions (D = performance specification, clear communications, measurable reciprocity), while the x-axis indicates those of relational transactions (R = motivation, dependence, continuity). Point a_1 represents a purely discrete transaction and Point a_4 depicts a purely relational transaction; at these two points, the aforementioned criteria are perfectly fulfilled. Given that both forms are theoretical ideals, their practical relevance is fairly limited. The points a_2 and a_3 represent mixed forms in which either discrete (a_2) or relational (a_3) elements, which form the basis of neoclassical and relational contracts, respectively, are predominant.

Classical contracts are a means of coordinating interests, while neoclassical and relational contracts allow those interests to be pursued through cooperation. The line

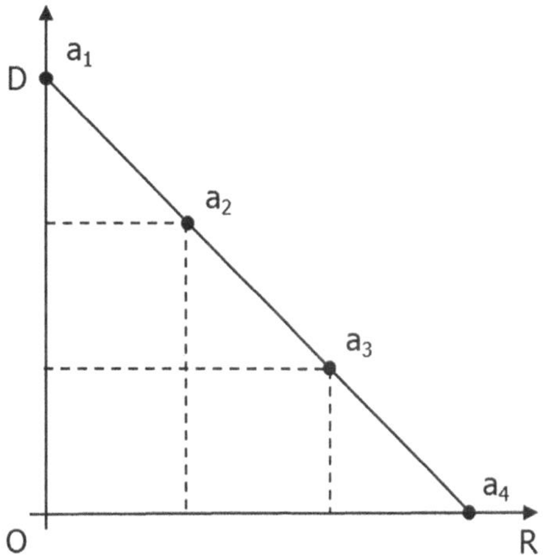

Fig. 3.1 Continuity of exchange–relation–exchange

connecting the poles D and R, between coordination and cooperation, represents a continuum on which the real-world manifestations of a broad range of mixed forms can be depicted. As we move from left to right on the x-axis, motivational factors and language take on increasing importance; that being said, Macneil has principally argued for "the primal role in contract of language" for the majority of all contracts (ibid., p. 711).

Whereas the language of the law and of the economy are dominant in classical contracts for exchange transactions, which tend to be short-term and of limited scope, in relational transactions we find "person[al] relations, [...] communication by a variety of modes [...] non-economic values, personal satisfaction" (ibid., p. 723)—in short, polycontexturality and polylingualism. Stopping on the motorway to fill your car with petrol during a road trip would seem to be the perfect example of a communicatively limited classical contract ('Sharp in, sharp out', ibid., p. 750), a theoretically unlimited-term contract that, with its contingent mixture of economic, legal, political and moral logics, is an example of a relational contract. The different ways of viewing these economic events in relation to one another, the process of relationalisation, the relation as form, is a force of economic production in its own right:

> Relations, unlike promise transactions, have internal capacities for growth and change, capacities absolutely essential for the successful completion of any enterprise not capable of specific and complete planning ab initio. (ibid., p. 765 f.)

That being the case, relations are forms of growth for private and societal capital and prosperity (ibid., p. 790) and a type of social capital, as Coleman has recognised (cf. Coleman, 1988, p. 98; 1990, p. 302). Whereas the past, present and future coincide in discrete transactions and their respective advantages and disadvantages are distributed to both parties *ex-ante* (according to a classical contract), relational transactions require *ex-ante* extensive mutual planning with regard to the desired long-term economic relations and the distribution of the resultant, jointly produced rents. While classical contract law is largely axiomatic, deductive, static and standardised, relational contracts are open, dynamic and individual, making them poorly suited to purely legal analysis (cf. Eisenberg, 2000). Each relational transaction is, as defined by Whitehead, a *mini society* with a range of applicable norms (cf. Macneil, 1978, p. 901, the passage is cited from Williamson, 1979, p. 238, with consent) and in which problems and conflicts are bound to arise—"trouble is expected in a relation" (Macneil, 1974, p. 805). Accordingly, management systems for resolving these conflicts and reconciling the interests of different stakeholders, as well as shared moral values—concerning, for example, distributive justice, freedom, human dignity, social equality and inequality and procedural justice—are vital (cf. Macneil, 1978, p. 898; see also the relevant literature on psychological contracts, Wieland, 2010). Leadership, both as a conflict resolution mechanism and as a form of representing moral values in a relation, is also an essential component in the governance of relational transactions.

I will return to these three aspects of relational governance—the management of stakeholder interests, transculturalism in relations and relational leadership—in the following chapters. For relational economics, they represent fundamental events—which are necessarily ignored by the standard economy of discrete transactions—in private and societal value creation. Here it should also become clear what theoretical and practical consequences it has when exchanges are replaced by transactions as the basic unit of analysis. In this regard, we can draw on Macneil's deliberations (cf. Macneil, 1980, 1981, 1983, 2000, as well as Paulin, Perrien, & Ferguson, 1997) on the generalised behavioural expectations and norms of relational contract theory, which should, in turn, be operationalised in the form of corresponding adaptive governance structures.

According to Macneil (cf. Macneil, 1980, 1983), the collective behavioural patterns for successful relational contracts are:

- Role integrity
- Reciprocity
- Planned implementation
- Following through on consensus-based decisions
- Flexibility
- Solidarity in the contractual relation
- Restitution, reliance and expectation interests
- Creation and restraint of power
- Propriety of means
- Harmonisation with the social matrix.

In turn, for Macneil the individual behavioural norms or uppermost behavioural goals for successful relational contracts are (for the behavioural patterns summarised here cf. Macneil, 1980, 1981, 1983, 2000, as well as Paulin et al., 1997):

- Role integrity
- Preservation of the relation
- Harmonisation of conflicts

- Propriety of means
- Adhering to societal norms (supracontractual norms).

It is readily apparent that the behavioural requirements put forward by Macneil do not provide a particularly high degree of discriminatory power. However, transferring them into a *values matrix for relational contracts* and linking them to corresponding performance values, communication values, cooperation and moral values puts them in a form that permits and is an essential prerequisite (for the concept of the values matrix cf. Wieland, 1999, 2011) for the systematic management of these values—both individually and the interaction of all four forms—and can, therefore, prove useful. The classification of the four forms of value is based on the Aristotelian distinction between ethical and dianoetic (determined by reason) virtuous behaviour. In this regard, moral virtues like justice, honesty and integrity are chiefly motivational in nature; in contrast, intellectual virtues focus more on skills, like being successful and useful thanks to competitiveness. In this tradition, virtue refers to actors' readiness (motivation) and ability to understand the ideals of a given social group and, through suitable actions on the part of individual and collective actors, to grasp said ideals in their proportionality and in this way, to implement them excellently (cf. the articles on virtue in Ritter, Gründer, & Gabriel, 1998 and in Blackburn, 2005) (Fig. 3.2).

As the values matrix clearly shows, one of the key factors in relational transactions, namely successful communication, is wholly ignored in Macneil's analyses, despite the fact that he expressly underscores the importance of language. Moreover, a fundamental aspect in the adaptivity of relational contracts is whether the communication between cooperation partners is based on constant pressure and the threat

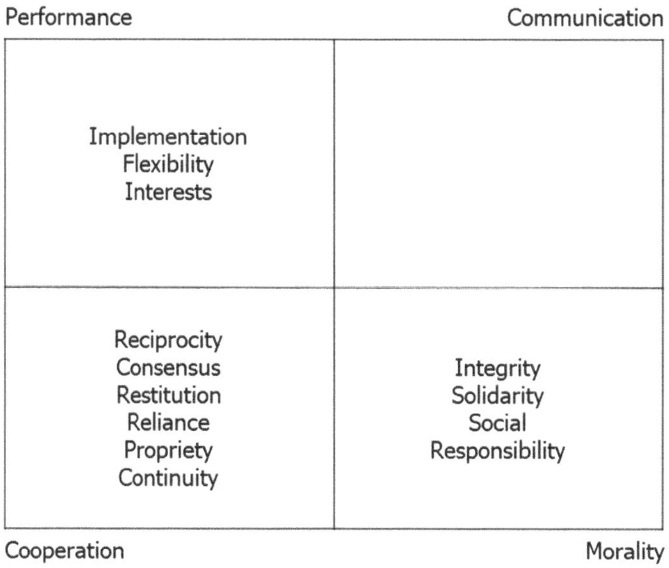

Fig. 3.2 Values matrix for relational contracts

of legal consequences, or on shared convictions and a dialogue amongst equals. In this regard, Artz and Brush (2000, p. 345) have suggested the distinction "coercive or non-coercive communication" (cf. also Blackburn, 2005, p. 345).

Without suitable communication, relation management is doomed to fail. The theoretical and practical challenge lies in the need for polylingual communication regarding the relations in relational contracts, a topic we'll be examining in more detail later in the book. What interests us now is a different aspect: thanks to the structural and individual behavioural requirements for relational cooperation projects as situational cooperative events, the explanatory power of using a behavioural assumption based on rational opportunism, as described in Williamson's transaction cost theory, is extremely limited. Macneil is well aware of this problem; however, instead of simply refuting the assumption, he replaces it with a behavioural description. Naturally, he claims, there is opportunism in relational interactions, which consists precisely in pursuing one's own interests at the expense of relational principles (cf. Macneil, 1981, p. 1024). But in his eyes, societal actors are "entirely selfish and entirely social creatures [...] at the same time" (Macneil, 1983, p. 348). For relational economics, we wish to employ a behavioural assumption based on the prosocial abilities of individual actors, which tells us that anthropologically speaking, human beings are neither good nor evil; these are merely two empirically observed behavioural options whose effectiveness (fostering or blocking) chiefly depends on the effectiveness of the governance structure used for a given transaction. We'll return to this point later.

Replacing behavioural assumptions with behavioural options not only avoids the problematic aspect of using untenable anthropological generalisations (on the current state of the discussion cf. Tomasello, 2016) and approaches the effectiveness of opportunism as the product of bounded rationality in the pursuit of individual interests, which, depending on the form of governance, causes transaction costs to rise or fall (on the evolution of this view cf. Foss & Weber, 2016. For the discussion see also Wieland, 1996, p. 119). At the same time, it avoids overly optimistic expectations regarding the productivity of relational behavioural norms like integrity and trust. The comment that "trust not only binds, but also *blinds* parties" (Poppo, Zhou, & Zenger, 2008, p. 1197) is accurate, given the fact that, as previously mentioned, relational transactions are also characterised by resource specificity and by uncertainty regarding the quantification and attribution of the respective stakeholders' contributions to value creation (for fundamental information on the inseparability of the production function in teams cf. Alchian & Demsetz, 1972). This is where the efficiency and effectiveness of relational governance come into play. The following chapter explores the governance of relational transactions in light of the foregoing discussion.

3.3 Economics and Relational Goods

However, we must first address a further consequence of replacing the exchange with the transaction as the basic unit of theoretical analysis, one that goes far beyond contractual theoretical interpretation. In the neoclassical exchange, the concrete utility or benefit of a good or service—not to mention the identities of the actors—are of no explicit relevance, while the buyer's preference for a commodity, expressed in their willingness to pay for it, is taken as a given. Standard economics essentially shows us a purified 'thing-to-thing' world, in which there are no actor-to-actor relations.

Over the past several years, the discussion on relational goods (cf. Bruni, 2013; Gui, 2005; Uhlaner, 1989), which is to say, on the 'goods' quality of commodities created by personal interaction, has provided ample material for debate. Relational goods are intangible goods that are produced and communicated through interaction in groups. They are simultaneously produced and consumed and they are inextricably linked to the interaction in relations. In other words, it is the social relation itself that creates the benefit, though it does not assume the form of a commodity.

Accordingly, Gui (2005) considers relational goods to be intangible valuable entities (p. 49), which are produced by the communicative-affective aspect of every exchange between persons, while Uhlaner (1989) is more interested in their *local public goods* character (p. 254), which can also be expressed in the "desire to be recognized or accepted by others" (p. 255). In a previous work (Wieland, 1996), I have defined them as *moral goods* and analysed them in detail; this, too, is an aspect we will revisit later in the book.

Bruni (2013, p. 176 ff.) summarises the fundamental characteristics of relational goods using seven main factors, namely the (i) identities of the actors, (ii) reciprocity of the interaction, (iii) simultaneity of production and consumption, (iv) intrinsic motivation as a behavioural driver, (v) emergence of goods, (vi) lack of compensation for the benefits and relational goods' status, (vii) as goods, but not commodities. By doing so, he underscores from a philosophical standpoint his claim that these goods, as an expression of interpersonal interaction, have a value in their own right; however, he does not rule out their coupling with economic goods:

> This does not mean that an authentic relational good cannot be produced in a business relationship, but, if it happens, somehow within an instrumental relationship something new emerges, which is not due either wholly or primarily to instrumentality. (ibid., p. 177)

In the language of the relational economics developed here, relational goods are the unit of difference between economic and moral coding and, as such, represent a third and new type of transaction produced by the melding of previously separate decision logics. They are goods, but not commodities. They have a value, but no price. Their emergence generates both non-material and material costs and exclusively intangible benefits. In the system 'economy' they are coupled with economic goods or commodities. One example of a relational good is the atmosphere of a football match, which, though it may have previously been intentionally fostered and intensified by fan clubs and other spectator activities, is nevertheless ultimately the result of the spontaneous interactions of all spectators present in the stadium. When compared with the feeling of watching the match alone, it becomes clear that, in addition to the sporting event itself, for which the price of admission must be paid—and which is, therefore, a commodity—the experience of watching it as a form of collective activity is a collective good that must be added to the match's benefit or value as a discrete commodity. Another example: a rock concert, which initially consists in the band's performance: a commodity that spectators must pay for in order to see. But there is also the fans' performance, which is a relational good. It has a value—which is produced by the fans' interaction and without which the actual value of the concert as a commodity cannot be accurately gauged—but no price. As a good, as an emerging result, the relation is not identical with the specific interaction of people in itself and can be enjoyed in its own right.

Further examples of relational goods include volunteer work and civic engagement, the atmosphere of a weekly farmers market and other group activities, provided they are coupled with the commodity character of goods (cf. Becchetti, Pelloni, & Rossetti, 2008; Blessi, Grossi, Sacco, Pieretti, & Ferilli 2014; Bruni & Stanca, 2008 and for the connection to happiness research, cf. Becchetti, Trovato, & Londono Bedoya, 2011; Frey, Benesch, & Stutzer, 2007).

I have discussed the coupling of economic commodities with local collective or individual goods in terms of the allocation of recognition, esteem and status to individual and collective actors, who, through their adherence to societal norms and principles, make the cost-optimal completion of economic transactions possible to begin with. This adherence reflects a behavioural assumption that is implicitly included in formal contracts. In this regard, I have distinguished between type-I relations (personal relations, production, products, a capital manager's relations with a firm), type-II relations (dealings with customers, partners, competitors in market relations) and type-III relations (interactions between the economy and society based on the example of external effects) (cf. Wieland, 1996, p. 214 ff.). The allocation of individual or collective moral preferences to economic transactions takes on the form of moral goods, which become inseparably coupled with economic goods and are attributed to the cooperation partners together with them. In this way, they influence a given team's cost and performance level through the status—for example, regarding trustworthiness and reputation—ascribed to the transaction partners. Moral goods are relational goods, which Arrow (1974) has described as follows:

> [...] they have real, practical, economic value; they increase the efficiency of the system, enable you to produce more goods or more of whatever values you hold in high esteem. But they are not commodities for which trade on the open market is technically possible or even meaningful. (ibid., p. 23)

Relational goods are scarce, generate costs, have a value but no price and are, on their own, not marketable. Though they are not reflected in organisations' cost-accounting systems, their impact can certainly be felt in their revenues. For the purposes of the current discussion, the key point is that their allocation represents a fundamental responsibility for firms and other organisations, whose business chiefly rests on incomplete and informal—which is to say, relational—contracts, as doing so can boost the efficiency and effectiveness of said contracts (cf. Wieland, 1996). Two further aspects of relational goods are particularly relevant: firstly, the temporary and specific process of coupling other decision logics with economic transactions, which transforms their characteristics; and secondly, the recognition that this process of relationalising different logics in a single transaction is itself an event in a value-creation process and as such, a form of emergent value creation. The required governance structure is a relation of relations and is itself a relational good. Or, as Nussbaum (2001) has observed: the social relation is itself a relational good (cf. Nussbaum, 2001, Chapter 12).

References

Alchian, A. A., & Demsetz, H. (1972). Production, information costs, and economic organization. *American Economic Review, 62*(5), 777–795.

Arrow, J. K. (1974). *The limits of organization*. New York, NY: Norton.

Artz, K. W., & Brush, T. H. (2000). Asset specificity, uncertainty and relational norms: An examination of coordination costs in collaborative strategic alliances. *Journal of Economic Behavior & Organization, 41*(4), 337–362.

Baker, G., Gibbons, R., & Murphy, K. J. (2002). Relational contracts and the theory of the firm. *The Quarterly Journal of Economics, 117*(1), 39–84.

Baker, S., & Choi, A. (2015). Contract's role in relational contract. *Virginia Law Review, 101*, 559–607.

Becchetti, L., Pelloni, A., & Rossetti, F. (2008). Relational goods, sociability, and happiness. *Kyklos, 61*(3), 343–363.

Becchetti, L., Trovato, G., & Londono Bedoya, D. A. (2011). Income, relational goods and happiness. *Applied Economics, 43*(3), 273–290.

Blackburn, S. (2005). *The Oxford dictionary of philosophy*. Oxford, UK: Oxford University Press.

Blessi, G. T., Grossi, E., Sacco, P. L., Pieretti, G., & Ferilli, G. (2014). Cultural participation, relational goods and individual subjective well-being: Some empirical evidence. *Review of Economics & Finance, 4*, 33–46.

Bruni, L. (2013). Relational goods: A new tool for an old issue. *ECOS Estudos Contemporâneos Da Subjetividade, 3*(2), 173–178.

Bruni, L., & Stanca, L. (2008). Watching alone: Relational goods, television and happiness. *Journal of Economic Behavior & Organization, 65*(3–4), 506–528.

Coleman, J. S. (1988). Social capital in the creation of human capital. *American Journal of Sociology, 94*, S95–S120.

Coleman, J. S. (1990). *Foundations of social theory*. Cambridge, MA: Harvard University Press.

Donati, P. (2010). *Birth and development of the relational theory of society: A journey looking for a deep 'relational sociology'*. Retrieved January 22, 2020, from https://www.relationalstudies.net/uploads/2/3/1/5/2315313/donati_birth_and_development_of_the_relational_theory_of_society.pdf.

Durkheim, E. (2013). *Durkheim: The division of labour in society* (S. Lukes, Ed.). Hampshire, UK: Palgrave Macmillan.

Eisenberg, M. A. (2000). Why there is no law of relational contracts. *Northwestern University Law Review, 94*(3), 805–821.

Foss, N. J., & Weber, L. (2016). Moving opportunism to the back seat: Bounded rationality, costly conflict, and hierarchical forms. *Academy of Management Review, 41*(1), 61–79.

Frey, B. S., Benesch, C., & Stutzer, A. (2007). Does watching TV make us happy? *Journal of Economic Psychology, 28*(3), 283–313.

Gibbons, R., & Henderson, R. (2013). What do managers do? Exploring persistent performance differences among seemingly similar enterprises. In R. Gibbons & J. Roberts (Eds.), *The handbook of organizational economics* (pp. 680–731). Princeton, NJ: Princeton University Press.
Gibbons, R., & Roberts, J. (Eds.). (2013). *The handbook of organizational economics*. Princeton, NJ: Princeton University Press.
Gottlieb, G. (1983). Relationism: Legal theory for a relational society. *The University of Chicago Law Review, 50*(2), 567–612.
Gui, B. (2005). From transactions to encounters: The joint generation of relational goods and conventional values. In B. Gui & R. Sudgen (Eds.), *Economics and social interaction: Accounting for interpersonal relations* (pp. 23–51). Cambridge, UK: Cambridge University Press.
Macaulay, S. (1963). Non-contractual relations in business: A preliminary study. *American Sociological Review, 28*(1), 55–67.
Macneil, I. R. (1974). The many futures of contracts. *Southern California Law Review, 47,* 691–816.
Macneil, I. R. (1978). Contracts adjustment of long-term economic relations under classical, neoclassical, and relational contract law. *Northwestern University Law Review, 72,* 854–905.
Macneil, I. R. (1979). *The new social contract: An inquiry into modern contractual relations*. New Haven/London: Yale University Press.
Macneil, I. R. (1980). *The new social contract*. New Haven, CT: Yale University Press.
Macneil, I. R. (1981). Economic analysis of contractual relations: Its shortfalls and the need for a "rich classificatory apparatus". *Northwestern University Law Review, 75,* 1018–1063.
Macneil, I. R. (1983). Values in contract: Internal and external. *Northwestern University Law Review, 78,* 340–418.
Macneil, I. R. (1985). Relational contract: What we do and do not know. *Wisconsin Law Review, 4,* 483–526.
Macneil, I. R. (2000). Contracting worlds and essential contract theory. *Social & Legal Studies, 9*(3), 431–438.
Malcomson, J. M. (2013). Relational incentive contracts. In R. Gibbons & J. Roberts (Eds.), *The handbook of organizational economics* (pp. 1014–1065). Princeton, NJ: Princeton University Press.
Nussbaum, M. C. (2001). *The fragility of goodness: Luck and ethics in Greek tragedy and philosophy*. Cambridge, UK: Cambridge University Press.
Paulin, M., Perrien, J., & Ferguson, R. (1997). Relational contract norms and the effectiveness of commercial banking relationships. *International Journal of Service Industry Management, 8*(5), 435–452.
Poppo, L., Zhou, K. Z., & Zenger, T. R. (2008). Examining the conditional limits of relational governance: Specialized assets, performance ambiguity, and long-standing ties. *Journal of Management Studies, 45*(7), 1195–1216.
Ritter, J., Gründer, K., & Gabriel, G. (Eds.). (1998). *Historisches Wörterbuch der Philosophie*. Basel: Schwabe Verlag.
Tomasello, M. (2016). *A natural history of human morality*. Cambridge, MA: Harvard University Press.
Uhlaner, C. J. (1989). "Relational goods" and participation: Incorporating sociability into a theory of rational action. *Public Choice, 62*(3), 253–285.
Wieland, J. (1996). *Ökonomische Organisation, Allokation und Status*. Tübingen: Mohr Siebeck.
Wieland, J. (1999). *Die Ethik der Governance*. Marburg: Metropolis.
Wieland, J. (Ed.). (2010). *Behavioural Business Ethics—Psychologie, Neuroökonomik und Governanceethik*. Marburg: Metropolis.
Wieland, J. (2011). Wertemanagement. In M. S. Aßländer (Ed.), *Handbuch Wirtschaftsethik* (pp. 245–252). Stuttgart: Metzler-Verlag.
Williamson, O. E. (1973). Markets and hierarchies. *American Economic Review, 63*(2), 316–325.
Williamson, O. E. (1979). Transaction-cost economics: The governance of contractual relations. *The Journal of Law & Economics, 22*(2), 233–261.

Williamson, O. E. (2005). The economics of governance. *The American Economic Review, 95*(2), 1–18.

Part II
Governance and Polycontextuality

Chapter 4
Governance and Societal Normativity

4.1 Relational Economics and Functional Equivalence

Transactions, regardless of whether they are exchange transactions, relational transactions or relational goods, are social interactions that call for a governance structure tailored to their specific needs. Relational governance is an under-researched field and chiefly a concern of strategic management theory (cf. Claro, Hagelaar & Omta 2003; Ferguson, Paulin & Bergeron 2005; Poppo & Zenger 2002). In this context, relational governance is understood as an informal governance structure, as an implicit contract based on shared norms and, as such, on mutual trust, on interpersonal relationships and on the actors' respective reputations. These reputations ensure, so it is assumed, efficient and effective contractual behaviour and are transaction-cost-optimal, because they are self-enforced.

Implicit contracts are not only substitutes for formal contracts; considering the contingency of future events and the actors' potential opportunism, especially with regard to inter-organisational contractual relations, they also complement, interact and combine with formal contracts (cf. Poppo & Zenger 2002, p. 708 f). The successful combination of formal and informal contracts in relational governance has a significant influence on a given organisation's performance (cf. the detailed study by Cao & Lumineau 2015). That being said, from the perspective presented here, social norms and relational governance are not self-enforced; rather, they are enforced by means of other punitive mechanisms like social criticism and loss of status or reputation. The self-enforcement of relational governance is, at best, possible in the context of Kant's ethics of virtue; yet even here, it would appear to be an example of what Whitehead has dubbed 'the fallacy of misplaced concreteness'. The true difference between formal and informal institutions is not whether or not they are enforced by third parties like courts; rather, it lies in the mechanisms of their enforcement.

Relational governance entails the suitable proportioning of multiple forms of governance and governance mechanisms with regard to a specific transaction. It ensures the continuity of cooperative relations; the process of relationalisation itself is what provides value creation. Accordingly, relational contracts are functional equivalents

J. Wieland, *Relational Economics*, Relational Economics and Organization Governance,
https://doi.org/10.1007/978-3-030-45112-7_4

of formal contracts and of hierarchy in a setting characterised by uncertainty, which is to say, by circumstances that are not fundamental, but selective and temporary. In relational economics, the dominant complementarity of formal and informal governance identified by Cao and Lumineau (2015) is reflected in the function

$$RT = f\{I, O, SII, SFI\}$$

in which I stands for individual, O for organisation, SII for societal informal institutions and SFI for societal formal institutions. The parameters of this relation are functional equivalents for one another and can be (i) complements to or (ii) substitutes for one another, can (iii) interact or (iv) combine (cf. Ellickson, 1991 and the articles in the Journal of Institutional and Theoretical Economics 1994, 150 (1)).

In the case of substitution, one structure replaces the other; in that of complementarity, each compensates for its counterpart's weaknesses. In interaction, changes to one element also affect its respective counterpart, whereas, in the case of combination, the respective strengths are pooled.

Functional equivalence is only possible when the parameters I, SII and O, SFI are mutually accessible. In this regard, Cao and Lumineau (2015) point out that formal contracts have not only a monitoring and enforcing function, but also a coordinating function. Working under this assumption, the following applies:

"When contracts also support coordination, they may not signal a lack of trust but a commitment to the relationship" and "could be valuable in facilitating mutual understanding and improving trust" (Ibid., p. 30). As such, it is not the individual parameters of the governance function that are selective, but their relation. "We discerned that contracts do not reduce opportunism directly but reduce it indirectly by increasing trust and relational norms" (Ibid., p. 32).

This can perhaps best be demonstrated in the interactions between formal compliance systems (I, O) and the integrity of a given organisation's leadership culture (I, SII). Compliance systems that are solely driven by legal logic are ineffective when it comes to preventing fraudulent or malicious behaviour; similarly, in practice, the limitations of exclusively relying on individual moral role models and communication rapidly become evident. It is the relationalisation of both aspects that can prove effective. In order to achieve this goal, interfaces must be made available; these can include employees being both permitted and encouraged, in a formally regulated manner, to interpret an organisation's standards of conduct—at the local level and restricted to certain specific situations—using their individual moral judgment. The regulations do not offer formal solutions or procedures for every possible grey zone; at the same time, not every manager has the moral capacity to make appropriate decisions. Consequently, the recursive combination of the two logics is sound, sensible and provides the basis, for example, of the US Sentencing Guidelines and the World Bank Integrity Standards (cf. Wieland, Steinmeyer & Grüninger 2014). It is the combination of the parameters I (leadership integrity) and O (the compliance system) with informal SIIs (societal informal institutions/the corporate culture) and formal SFIs (societal formal institutions/organisational liability, due diligence specifications) that yields effectiveness. Further, it is the creation of polycontexturalism

	I	O	SII	SFI
Substitutive	x			x
Complementary		x	x	
Interactive	x			x
Combinational		x	x	

Fig. 4.1 Matrix of functional governance equivalencies

(law, economy, ethics) and polylingualism (punishments, incentives, character) that ensures the integrity of economic transactions. The theoretical and practical options for differentiating between functional equivalences with regard to governance of economic transactions are displayed in Fig. 4.1.

As the matrix clearly shows: one can switch from a criminal law approach (SFI) to appealing to individual virtue (I), or compensate for the weaknesses of formal compliance management (O) through the corporate culture (SII). Or one could also consider the interplay of the crowding out of individual virtue (I) by legal compliance (SFI); lastly, combining compliance management (O) and the corporate culture (SII) can open new avenues. In all of these variants, the crux is the relation of parameters, which in turn represent relations themselves. This is the essence of relational governance.

Moreover, Artz and Brush (2000) have confirmed the validity of this type of interplay for other types of economic transaction. In a study involving 393 Original Equipment Manufacturers (OEMs), they found that relations with suppliers that were managed by means of relational contracts reduced the transaction costs through the adherence to relational norms and particularly the *ex-post* costs of regularly renegotiating and modifying the contracts. The costs of the relational behavioural norm 'flexibility' were less than the potential costs involved in enforcing formal contracts (cf. Ibid., p. 335 f.). It follows that:

Management in terms of relationalising governance structures is critical; consequently, in the following, this aspect will be examined in more detail using the examples of stakeholder management and of leading organisations and their interactions with a transcultural setting.

For the time being, it suffices to bear in mind that exchange transactions are paradigmatically and exclusively focused on maximising one's own benefits in a contractual relation, whereas relational transactions instead focus on successful joint planning and problem-solving, for example through mutual trust (cf. Claro et al. 2003,

p. 704). Accordingly, Ferguson et al. (2005) have drawn the distinction between contractual governance as a weak-tie approach and relational governance as a strong-tie approach; together, they represent a transaction-based continuum (exchange transaction/relational transaction), which a given firm must be capable of simultaneously activating (cf. Ibid., p. 217 ff). In this regard, the strong-tie approach is all about activating relational governance norms like flexibility, solidarity and a fair exchange of information to boost the economic performance of cooperative relations. The ability to adapt to unforeseen events (flexibility) depends on a preference for solving problems together (solidarity) and a willingness to share private information (information sharing) (cf. Poppo & Zenger 2002, p. 715). Accordingly, Ferguson et al. (2005) are not unjustified in their summarising statement that "shared norms and values are the hallmark of relational exchange" (Ibid., p. 221). Here, trust, moral values and norms are incorporated in an economic transaction, but cannot be generated by an economic rationale alone.

> The mechanisms through which relational governance attenuates exchange hazards are both economic and sociological in nature. (Poppo & Zenger 2002, p. 710; cf. in similar vein Claro et al. 2003, p. 704)

It is the continuity of transaction that fulfils a socialising function in economic contractual relations. However, this recognition does not clarify why norms have not only restricting but also and especially liberating effects on transactions. These enabling effects ensure not only a specific transaction's integrity, but also its productivity and the dynamics of its evolution by combining and recombining decision logics that can couple with, relationalise and, in the process, continue said transaction. Or, to put it another way: relational economics is not only concerned with safeguards against opportunism or economising on transaction cost but also and especially with maximising the relational rent produced by the cooperation of economic and societal actors. We'll revisit this point later in the book. Beforehand, our focus should be on further clarifying the links between relational transactions, societal forms and governance processes.

4.2 Relations and Events

Governance, viewed as a form of relation and a process of relationalisation, focuses on individuals, organisations and markets from a form perspective and on rationally balancing interests, managing costs and remaining competitive from a process standpoint.

The relational transaction is the basic unit of relational economics (here the connection between this definition and Whitehead's process philosophy, which is characterised by the primacy of relation and the concept of the relational constitution of everything in existence, is self-evident. Cf. Lachmann, 1990, p. 45 ff.). Relations always refer to *an other* and in the case of the economy, to the multivalent resources required to complete a transaction. Although each of these resources is—on its own—limited, both its nature and function are changed when it becomes coupled with a transaction; each now becomes a resource of relation. In this way and only in this way, does it attain its specific productivity. Accordingly, relations are themselves productive assets, because they both generate and process the unity of diversity and the specificity of difference with regard to the resources needed for a transaction. Resources are therefore limited events, yet inherently dynamic, or, to put it in Whitehead's terms: they are always in a process of becoming. Ethical principles, for example, are limited resources in economic, social or technical transactions, in which and through which they become related to other events, which in turn determine the principles' respective effects or consequences. Grasping these interactive connections was and remains at the core of the research agenda for governance ethics (cf. Wieland, 1999 and the series *Studien zur Governanceethik* (Studies on Governance Ethics) (12 volumes, 1999–2017). Metropolis: Marburg).

A relation classifies the events in or resources for a transaction in certain proportions, in suitable relations to one another, which, in an Aristotelian sense (Aristotle, NE 1132 b-31-34; NE 1194 a-16-18.), represent the forms of the events that hold the process together. For example, the market is one form used to view economic exchanges in proportion to one another; organisations and persons are further forms. Their interaction is the form of the relation of relations. Persons, organisations and the market are the three fundamental forms of relation in relational economics. What they all have in common, again in Aristotelian terms, is that they foster social *cohesion*. Given this shared basis, they can combine, interact, complement or replace one another; in short: they can serve as functional equivalents. However, after having interacted, the specificity of the elements, as well as the form and process of their relationalisation, are no longer the same. And this aspect redefines the quality of the function(s) for which they are equivalents (cf. Coleman, 1988, p. 97).

4.3 Structural Couplings and Social Theory

The societal diversity of the resources necessary to complete a given transaction implies the relationality of actual, limited events. A governance structure is what transforms potential relations into actual ones. At a given point in time during the interaction process, the governance of the relation of resources is operatively closed, but communicatively open. This ensures the completion of a precisely specified transaction; at the same time, however, the transaction remains constantly open for signals or judgments from its surroundings. According to Luhmann, relations are structural couplings of events with regard to a transaction and these couplings' connectivity is both limited (fragmentation) and ephemeral (temporalisation). Accordingly, Consumer Culture Theory (CCT) does not explain purchase decisions (T) solely as a function of price, but as the recursive combination of consumers' and producers' individual experiences and convictions (I) with institutionalised social practices (ISP). The purely economic explanation of a purchase decision is linked to its social setting, as a result of which the focus is no longer exclusively on a consumer's price-dictated purchase act, but also on collaborative value creation (cf. Arnould & Thompson 2005, p. 874 f.; Grönroos & Voima, 2013).

Macneil (1974) referred to this aspect as the necessary integration of a relational transaction in the social matrix (cf. p. 711), which is to say, in the diversity of social systems. Anyone interested in pursuing this type of integration is well advised to indicate his or her social theory references, as they would appear to determine how the relationship between Business and Society is understood. Lee E. Preston (1975) contended that the two should, given the equivalence and the combination of their respective goals, be viewed as a multi-purposed (cf. ibid., p. 447) relation, yet never elaborated on the notion. The goal of this chapter is to contribute further ideas to this highly relevant discussion.

The fact that organisational economists tend to shun this discussion and if they participate at all, are generally content to cite social embeddedness or the importance of power (vertical relation), shared values and trust (horizontal relation), is understandable from their established methodology, but not without its consequences: without an explicit social theory, developing a relational economics isn't feasible. If we accept this state of affairs and view it as a challenge, the question that immediately presents itself is how to integrate society into economic theory.

Macneil explicitly states—and I feel this is one of his greatest contributions—his preferences with regard to social theory. The legal scholar draws on the sociological system theory put forward by Talcott Parsons and Neil J. Smelser (here especially Parsons, 1951; Parsons & Smelser 1956), which has garnered him the criticism of a colleague who preferred Niklas Luhmann's system theory (cf. Teubner, 2000). For the purposes of our discussion, the indeed substantial differences between Parsons' actor-structure and system-environment orientation and Luhmann's system functionalism can be ignored. Instead, it should be stressed that in both approaches, language—or to be more precise: communication, as a meaning-producing act between actors (as portrayed in Parsons, 1951) or as interconnecting, binary-coded operations, according to Luhmann (1987)—produces abstract structures, systems, in short, societal relations, either between actors (Parsons) or between the elements of a system (Luhmann). Consequently, the approach developed in this book equally reflects the system theory perspectives championed by Parsons and Luhmann.

As such, in the following, systems, organisations and institutions will be understood as intelligible sets of event relations, generated as forms of thought by social communication and equipped with normative power, which is to say, a behavioural orientation, in a given society. Actions, transactions and events are ascribed to these forms of thought; as previously mentioned, they always have both an experiential and an expectational component (cf. Koselleck, 1979, p. 349 ff.) and represent in this twofold sense human experience and human efforts to create order by drawing on said experience. This process of generating social order can be performed, shaped and sanctioned by the state (through the law), society (through tradition) or the individual (through preferences) (cf. Ellickson, 1991). As such, when in the following we speak of an economic system, organisation or actor with regard to a communicative and normative behavioural orientation, we will substantially employ economic theory-building in its various manifestations, to the extent that it considers these paradigmatic aspects. After all, the theoretical discourse on economics has from the outset consisted in investigating forms of thought.

4.4 Codes, Differences and Behavioural Assumptions

The governance form of the discrete exchange, of exchange transactions involving economic goods and services, is the market, which monolingually encodes all events in the language of price and using the binary codification 'payment—non-payment'. Polyvalent, relational transactions in contrast necessarily call for the comparative integration of multiple forms of governance for the consummation and assessment of economic transactions. Organisations like firms, states and networks are forms of reference for the analysis and design of relational transactions. In this regard, firms, as organisations within the economy, employ the guiding difference '*earnings—costs*', since their only interest lies in securing their continued existence as cooperative forms of productive resources. Although the difference must consistently remain positive for a certain amount of time, that is, must reflect a gain in continuity, this is not—as I have pointed out repeatedly—the decision-making criterion for each individual transaction. For these transactions, all that matters is that they are assessed on the basis of the *earnings* on the external market—or more broadly, in the organisation's environment—and of the *costs* for the organisation. In his essay *The Society of Organizations*, Peter F. Drucker (1993) summarised this aptly:

"Inside a business, there are only costs. The term 'profit center' [...] is a misnomer." (Ibid., p. 49). He then goes on to explain that: "there is no such thing as 'profit'. There are only costs: cost of the past [...] and costs of an uncertain future" (Ibid., p. 72).

Person systems, which is to say, individuals as natural persons or as the agents within an organisation, defined by their roles, form market and organisational systems and use them in order to pursue their own economic interests. In this context, with regard to natural persons the behavioural assumption, in keeping with economic theory, of their limited ability to rationally pursue their individual interests or personal advantage shall apply. In addition to bounded rationality, we will assume that these economic actors, like all human beings, possess certain pro-social skills. These refer to the ability to empathise and inclusive rationality, which allow us to put ourselves in someone else's 'shoes' and to integrate his or her interests into our own rational calculations. In turn, pro-social skills are vital to the evolution of human communities and the formation, promotion and reinforcement of moral preferences, which in turn produce those moral values, performance-, communication- and cooperation-related values of a transaction society that represent important elements of relational transactions and contracts (cf. Tomasello, 2016 and the discussion in Journal of Consciousness Studies, 2000, *1*(1–2)). As we saw in the previous chapter, it is impossible to arrive at an adequate grasp of relational contracts without the assumption of pro-social actor preferences. This assumption will also be one of the theoretical preconditions for our discussion, later in the book, on stakeholder management, transculturalism and leadership. Pro-social behaviour as "shared intentionality" (cf. Tomasello, 2009, 2019) expands the scope of feasible opportunities for cooperation and as such, for private and societal economic value creation with lower transaction costs. In a word: the assumption that pro-social skills can be activated via adaptive governance structures is a cornerstone of Relational Economics.

In addition, crucial factors in the role of an individual as an agent of an organisation include the pursuit of the latter's self-interests and the agent's non-opportunistic compliance with his or her role in keeping with the organisation's guiding difference, which is to say, the agent's behaviour in relation to the role that the organisation expects him or her to fulfil. Expectations concerning organisational roles are what connect the organisation and the individual, who is simultaneously confronted with the various role-related expectations of society. This aspect is a source of potential conflicts of interest, which are in turn an immanent component of the governance of economic transactions, because and to the extent that they influence transaction performance. Accordingly, let us assume that individuals and agents have a preference for conforming with societal and organisational rules, provided the incentives in the transaction setting encourage them to do so, or at least do not prevent them from doing so. In this sense, compliant behaviour is a continuous learning process for both parties the organisation and the agent.

Changed role-related expectations are an expression of changed organisational modes and interact with these modes. Accordingly, if a given company demands integrity and compliance from its agents, these demands must be accompanied by organisational and recursively interlinked guidelines and procedures, such as a Compliance Management System. Managing role-related expectations is a basic function of organisations, one that is simultaneously predicated upon and fosters individual and organisational learning (Cf. Wieland et al. 2014). The following Fig. 4.2 systematically integrates these distinctions in the discussion up to this point.

4.5 Relational Governance and Parameters

Whereas the analysis of the transaction and contract addresses the interaction process between events as Exchange Transactions and Relational Transactions, the governance category focuses on the form of this process as the relationalisation of the actual events involved in a transaction. In terms of its form, governance represents, as previously mentioned, a relational structure, a proportioning of resources, which has a function in terms of the processes at work in a transaction.

Generally speaking, we can say the following: in the context of Relational Economics, for a specific economic transaction (RT) the chief effective parameters of a governance form consist in the interests, perceptions, rationales and convictions of individuals as persons or agents (I) and their resulting actions and behaviour (I);

Transaction	Exchange Transaction	Relational Transaction	
Governance	Market	Organisation	Person
Process	Binary Coding: Payment – Non-payment ⟺	Guiding Difference: Earnings – Costs ⟺	Individual: Interests Bounded Rationality Pro-social Skills Agent: Organisational Interests Compliant Behaviour Ability to Learn
Communication	Monolingual	Polylingual	Polylingual
Time Metric	t_1	t_0-t_1-t_n	t_0-t_1-t_n

Fig. 4.2 Governance forms in relational economics

organisations and the mechanisms of coordination and cooperation that they provide (O); societal informal institutions like values, norms and—particularly relevant here—communicative codes and functional decision logics (SII); as well as societal formal institutions like the law, contracts and codified rules and regulations (SFI). To better understand this effectiveness, here, societal institutions (SI) are divided into informal (SII) and formal variants (SFI). Consequently, the formal representation of relational governance

$$\mathrm{RT} = \mathrm{f(I, O, SII, SFI)}$$

tells us that, with regard to the effective and efficient completion of a specific relational transaction (RT) involving multiple decision logics (economics, the law, ethics and so on), the parameters I, O, SII, SFI are essential, both individually and collectively as a governance form. Here we are dealing with a polyvalent governance form, the parameters of which are themselves polyvalent governance forms. With regard to the latter, in the parameter SII the space for the polycontexturalism and polylingualism of the governance structure and its parameters is marked; this space, in turn, endogenises the relevant decision logics and language games in the analysis of the transaction. Governance is a relation of relations, though neither in the form of an addition nor some form of a balanced mix; rather, as a form it represents the unity of diversity with regard to the actual events and parameters involved in a relational transaction. Consequently, it is more than and a different event than, the sum or combination of its individual parts. Parameters are the concrete forms of the events in a specific transaction and are governance forms in their own right.

In contrast, the conventional economy of discrete market transactions is statically structured and pursues an equilibrium at a certain point in time (t_1). This equilibrium is not only assumed to be market-clearing at the lowest price, but also to achieve maximum private and societal value creation. History and development, dynamics and the cooperation process in which economic transactions and value creation take place are completely ignored. Moreover, in neoclassical theory, the interaction between different governance forms is merely considered to be the adaptation of individuals and organisations to efficiently running markets.

Conversely, relational governance, as a fundamental concept of Relational Economics, focuses on the ceaseless relationalisation of events into a governance structure, which, as a form of the unity of diversity with regard to differing logics, determines the efficiency and effectiveness of their function.

The processes involved in relationalising the parameters and events in a governance form are initially characterised by their *recursivity*: the outcomes of a given process affect the events and their relations to one another. Equally important: the assumption of *simultaneity* in terms of describing the processes in a governance form; their parameters exist and function simultaneously and principally speaking, are also equally valid. With regard to the effectiveness and efficiency of a governance structure, its parameters and their effectiveness can be combined, compensate for one another, interact, or be substituted as functional equivalents, but cannot be eliminated as parameters. After all, the third relational aspect of a given process—its *productivity*—is also crucial. All events in and parameters of a governance form have constraining or enabling effects on one another; they mutually block or foster their productivity and development in individual and organisational learning processes. These two functions also include a double relation of exclusion and amplification, an essential hallmark of the economics of the relations of economic transactions.

The *recursivity, simultaneity* and *productivity* of a governance form are essential determinants for the private and societal value creation that can be achieved through economic transactions. In Relational Economics, value creation can be seen in the size of the cooperation rent that can be achieved on the market, in the positive balance of an organisation's revenues and costs and in the creation of material and non-material value for all organisations and persons involved in the cooperation process as stakeholders (Shared Value Creation).

As such, in terms of analysing governance forms, Relational Economics concentrates on individual analysis and on the relationalisation of and trade-offs between the respective parameters of a relational transaction. As a result, the form and process of relational governance become intertwined. In this regard, Relational Economics focuses on the individual and organisational behavioural patterns and behavioural norms of Relational Contract Theory, discussed in the previous chapter (in brief: integrity, reciprocity, continuity, implementing consensus-based decisions, flexibility, creation of power, propriety of means and adhering to supracontractual norms) and is particularly concerned with

(i) the comparative analysis of specific governance forms for the productivity and uncertainty of relational transactions,

(ii) the cooperation rent for a specific transaction that can be achieved by mobilising and utilising individual and collective resources, as well as
(iii) the adaptive efficiency of the process and form of the governance of parameters in terms of said parameters' relationalisation.

In Relational Economics, the unity of diversity manifests in successful cooperative transactions, in which specific productive assets are used to generate a relational rent.

References

Aristotle. (2011). Nicomachean Ethics. In R. C. Bartlett & S. D. Collins (Eds.). Chicago, London: The University of Chicago Press.

Arnould, E. J., & Thompson, C. J. (2005). Consumer culture theory (CCT): Twenty years of research. *Journal of Consumer Research, 31*(4), 868–882.

Artz, K. W., & Brush, T. H. (2000). Asset specificity, uncertainty and relational norms: An examination of coordination costs in collaborative strategic alliances. *Journal of Economic Behavior & Organization, 41*(4), 337–362.

Cao, Z., & Lumineau, F. (2015). Revisiting the Interplay between contractual and relational governance: A qualitative and meta-analytic investigation. *Journal of Operations Management, 33–34,* 15–42.

Claro, D. P., Hagelaar, G., & Omta, O. (2003). The determinants of relational governance and performance. *Industrial Marketing Management, 32*(8), 703–716.

Coleman, J. S. (1988). Social capital in the creation of human capital. *American Journal of Sociology, 94,* S95–S120.

Drucker, P. F. (1993). *Post-capitalist society*. London, UK: Butterworth-Heinemann.

Ellickson, R. C. (1991). *Order without Law. How neighbors settle disputes*. Cambridge, MA: Harvard University Press.

Ferguson, R. J., Paulin, M., & Bergeron, J. (2005). Contractual governance, relational governance, and the performance of interfirm service exchanges: The influence of boundary-spanner closeness. *Journal of the Academy of Marketing Science, 33*(2), 217–234.

Grönroos, C., & Voima, P. (2013). Critical service logic: Making sense of value creation and co-creation. *Journal of the Academy of Marketing Science, 41*(2), 133–150.

Koselleck, R. (1979). Vergangene Zukunft: Zur Semantik geschichtlicher Zeiten. Frankfurt a. M.: Suhrkamp.

Lachmann, R. (1990). Ethik und Identität: Versuch einer Perspektive auf die Gegenwartsethik ausgehend von A. N. Whitehead. Düsseldorf: Heinrich Heine Universität.

Luhmann, N. (1987). Soziale Systeme: Grundriß einer allgemeinen Theorie. Frankfurt a. M.: Suhrkamp.

Macneil, I. R. (1974). The many futures of contracts. *Southern California Law Review, 47,* 691–816.

Parsons, T. (1951). *The social system*. Glencoe, Ill.: Free Press.

Parsons, T., & Smelser, N. J. (1956). *Economy and society: A study in the integration of economic and social theory*. Glencoe, Ill.: Free Press.

Poppo, L., & Zenger, T. (2002). Do formal contracts and relational governance function as substitutes or complements? *Strategic Management Journal, 23*(8), 707–725.

Preston, L. E. (1975). Corporation and society: The search for a paradigm. *Journal of Economic Literature, 13*(2), 434–453.

Teubner, G. (2000). Contracting worlds: The many autonomies of private law. *Social & Legal Studies, 9*(3), 399–417.

Tomasello, M. (2009). *Why we cooperate*. Cambridge, MA: Boston Review Books.

Tomasello, M. (2016). *A natural history of human morality*. Cambridge, MA: Harvard University Press.

Tomasello, M. (2019). *Becoming human. A theory of ontogeny*. Cambridge, MA: Harvard University Press.

Wieland, J. (1999). *Die Ethik der Governance*. Marburg: Metropolis.

Wieland, J., Steinmeyer, R., & Grüninger, S. (Eds.). (2014). *Handbuch compliance-management: Konzeptionelle Grundlagen, praktische Erfolgsfaktoren, globale Herausforderungen*. Berlin: Erich Schmidt.

Chapter 5
Polylingualism and Coding

5.1 Binary Codes and Guiding Differences

Societies, systems or sectors are, as discussed in the previous chapter, by no means separate spheres that can be entered and then left again. Rather, they are modes of normative communication, the events of which actions, decisions, attitudes and so on are classified using binary decision logics. Accordingly, in layman's terms, one could say that someone working in business (or in administration and so on) makes his or her decisions on the basis of an economic (or political and so on) logic, or one could state the economisation of the life-world (or the moralisation of the economy). The specificity of these decision logics is the result of a societal discourse in which various disciplines and emerging but increasingly acknowledged practices play central roles. They hold normative power and provide behavioural orientation. But that also means that these decision logics and their interrelations are historically contingent. Society is an abstract form, a construct, in which the process of socialisation (as put forward by Max Weber) is one carried out by actors and their respective resources and in their mutual transactions. Society exists only fragmentarily and temporarily, in the occurrence and passing of events and coupled with transactions, the consummation of which is simultaneously the consummation of society. On the basis of this premise, it can be said that economies are always the consummation of society and that socialisation is the consummation of economic transactions. To the best of my knowledge, the ancient Greek philosophers were the first to clearly recognise and describe this state of affairs. Building on Plato's Republic,[1] Aristotle explained the formation of human societies by drawing on the division of labour and exchanges within the polis, in the form of an arithmetic-proportional relationalisation of actors and their economic and moral resources: "In this way, there will always be exchange, and if there is exchange, then there will be community" (Aristotle, NE 1133b15). For Aristotle, community represents the simultaneous equilibrium of economic Quantities of Value on the one hand and moral exchange justice and distributive justice

[1] See 369b ff.

J. Wieland, *Relational Economics*, Relational Economics and Organization Governance,
https://doi.org/10.1007/978-3-030-45112-7_5

on the other (cf. Aristotle, Magna Moralia 1194a, where he argues in a less formal style). Marcel Mauss for gift exchange, Adam Smith and Karl Marx for the capitalist economy and Max Weber and Georg Simmel for modern society—they and many others have made the process of socialization through economic transactions, viewed positively or critically, the object of their study (I have discussed this aspect on many other occasions. Here, the following reference should suffice: Cf. Wieland, 1996, 2012, 2017). Relational Economics builds on this discussion and is, in this sense, a political economy, an economy of societal value creation.

Consequently, Relational Economics does not view the connection between economy and society as a process of embedding, integrating or reintegrating the economy in a hierarchically superordinate life-world. It views the idea of using ethics, politics, culture or religion, in fact, of using any superior system in the society to directly control the economy and firms with considerable scepticism—not because it would be impossible to do so, but because, in its view, doing so would entail prohibitive losses of societal welfare. Markets and organisations are not to be understood as closed containers that have to be coordinated with other closed containers on the basis of their respective hierarchical value to society; rather, they are functions and organisations of society. Markets and organisations are fundamental institutions and organisations of society, with which and within which they perform their economic transactions. They collectively produce different, but equally valid forms of the socialization of economic actors, the relationalisation of which is, as we have seen, contingent on the history of the human race. The forms and underlying premises of the relation between the *oikonomia* in the Greek poli, the medieval household economy and feudal state and modern firms and society could hardly be more different, yet they all share the conviction that the economic organisation of a society is always a process in which both economy and society are consummated simultaneously.

In this sense, our discussion is also linked to the criticism put forward by Granovetter (1985), in which he claims that classical and neoclassical economics have an "undersocialized conception of human action" (Ibid., p. 483) and ignore the fact that economic exchanges are "embedded in concrete, ongoing systems of social relations" (Ibid., p. 487) or, more precisely, in "networks of interpersonal relations" (Ibid., p. 504). Though his criticism is accurate, it limits the scope of investigation to the level of personal networks. Relational Economics generalises the argumentation by replacing exchange with transaction as the basic unit of analysis, especially by including institutions and organisations, as well as their respective modes of communication and decision-making in the scope of investigation. At the same time, Relational Economics agrees to some extent with Granovetter's observation that anonymous market relations are "virtually nonexistent" (cf. Granovetter, 1985, p. 495), though he himself overlooks the fact that modern economics is systematically and solely interested in investigating the exchange of Quantities of Value, while it gladly ignores the fact that doing so presupposes a normative order. In the resulting subject-object (exchange actor—commodities) relation, the actor becomes an object too and, as *homo economicus*, one that can be economised.

The problem of integrating economy and society operationalises Relational Economics as a form and process of mutual relationalisation between Exchange Transactions and Relational Transactions that involve the transition from market transactions to organisational transactions and vice versa. Accordingly, the whole of the society in which economic operations could be embedded, is, at least from this theoretical perspective, not observable from an Archimedean (religious or ideological) stance, which would pave the way for holistic descriptions and a stable, normatively controlled integration as part of the whole. Free and open societies are realised in the appearance, disappearance and continued existence of events and as such, also in their relational transactions. It is thus their polyvalence that transports the society in the economy and the economy in the society. This process of mutual embedding, which represents the constitutive polycontextuality of economic transactions, is operationalised with the aid of the previously mentioned polycontexturality and polylingualism, which we will discuss in the following.

Polycontextuality and polycontexturality characterise transactions that take place in a multifaceted environment of operatively closed, communicatively open and functionally autonomous systems. For economic transactions, these include not only the market but also and especially the law, politics, the civil society, ethics, religion and science. Accordingly, various polylingual decision logics of different systems are applied to relational economic transactions, in the form of binary codes: "payment–non-payment" for the market, "power–no power" for politics, "legal–illegal" for the law, "the common good–private interests" for the civil society, "right–wrong" for ethics, "transcendence–immanence" for religion and "true–false" for science. Different types of organisation specialise in these modes of communication via a guiding difference, such as "earnings–costs" for firms, "govern–oppose" for political parties, "guilty–not guilty" for courts of law, "engagement–non-engagement" for NGOs, "conformity–non-conformity" for forms of moral agency like families, "belief–non-belief" for religious communities and "academic–not academic" for universities.

Figure 5.1 on the following page shows this selection of systems and organisations (polycontextuality), together with their modes of communication and decision logics (polylingualism, polycontexturality), which can be applied to economic transactions (cf. Luhmann, 1987, 2000 and for civil society, Putnam, 1993).

5.2 Functional Difference and Programming

As previously stated, these various systems aren't closed containers; they are communicatively open and therefore available to one another. They are functional equivalents that can be substituted for or combined with local transactions; further, they can interact with and/or complement one another, but cannot be eliminated. For the transactions they engage in, individual and collective actors alike can and must remain open for and select from multiple contexts and their corresponding decision

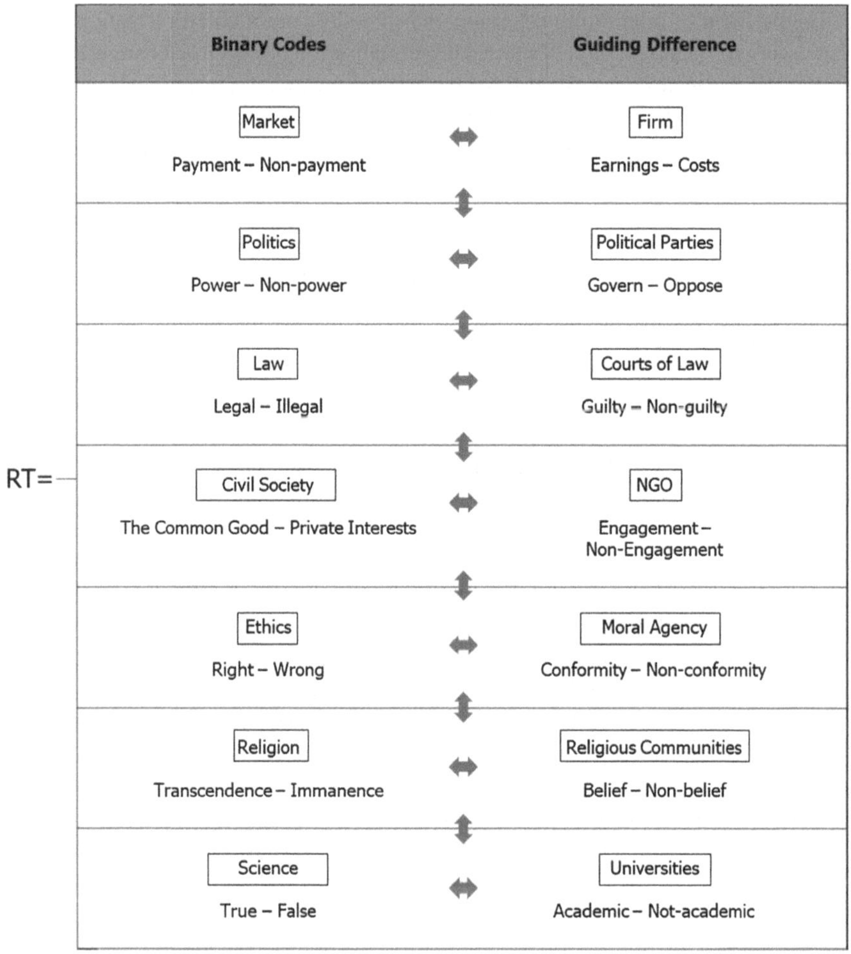

Fig. 5.1 Polycontextural and polylingual codings

logics. From an economic standpoint, there can be cost-related or value-creation-related arguments for or against doing so. As such, what we're dealing with here is a "multitude of irreducible distinctions" [own translation] (Baecker, 2017, p. 25), which firms must implement for their transactions by means of suitable agendas, guidelines and procedures.

The requisite programming (cf. Luhmann, 1986) for the economy and firms is a two-stage process. In the first stage, the management functions in which the requirements for societal normativity can be translated must be specified. In this way, integrity, compliance, social standards or ecological sustainability are transformed into risk management, human resources management, quality management or innovation management, the purpose of which is to make societal normativity into something that can be processed by firms and other organisations in the first place. In the second stage, those operations in which normative expectations are integrated into the organisation's transactions must be specified. This is achieved in the form of guidelines and procedural instructions provided by the respective management functions, for example, codes of conduct, policy and procedures for supplier management, or corporate social responsibility agendas. This process should by no means be misconstrued as the pragmatic integration of societal normativity into a firm's efforts to generate revenues; rather, it represents the unity of diversity that combines different decision logics to create a wholly new one. Morality, to name just one example, is now an event that constitutes a difference with accompanying consequences. Of course, a given firm is concerned about what its compliance management programme costs, even though, assuming the programme is based on legal, professional or societal standards, said firm can't simply discard the programme due to high costs. And the situation is similar for social standards, human rights and sustainability. The task consists in interlinking economic competitiveness (earnings, costs, orders) and societal normativity (law, ethical standards) in such a way as to create a new business model (the consequence of the unity of diversity). In other words, business ethics is not business plus ethics, but rather a new entity of its own, a new relational transaction in which the previous transactions continue to exist, but are modified by new events that become coupled with them. Supplier management systems that are complemented by guidelines on complying with social standards and human rights are still supplier management systems, but no longer the same ones and no longer have the same consequences for a given organisation's costs and revenues. In precisely this way, transactions can be simultaneously preserved and transformed; change is what makes continuity possible. The differentiation of modes of communication and decision logics is maintained and integrated into the polyvalence of corporate transactions (regarding the programming of system logics, cf. Luhmann, 1986, pp. 75–100).

Two further examples may help to make this point a bit clearer: a firm sells its products or services to a customer. These Exchange Transactions receive an additional context when the country in which the customer resides doesn't have a particularly impressive ranking on the corruption index released by an NGO: an event that emerges and, initially at the communicative level, becomes coupled with what were, up to this point, purely economic transactions. The transactions now receive further contexts and decision logics, namely those of the law (legal–illegal, guilty–not guilty) and of civil society (the common good–private interests, engagement–non-engagement). The firm's adaptation to these codings takes place in connection with risk management, which now applies to the transactions and produces certain effects in terms of the guiding difference "earnings–costs". The firm programs the event by introducing a compliance management system, which is initially merely designed to satisfy the legal requirements for due diligence so as to avoid liability claims (guilty–not guilty). Let's assume that, because of the firm's and its senior management's culture, the compliance system proves to be ineffective: legal compliance is nominally acknowledged, but not actually practised. Here, too, critical communications from the civil society and the law can create suitable normative expectations. In addition, a political debate emerges concerning the need to introduce a new type of corporate criminal law, the goal being to more effectively force firms to act responsibly. In response, the firm in question, as a legal form for economic processes, feels it has no choice but to expand its compliance system to include the aspect of integrity. Accordingly, it modifies its agendas, guidelines and procedures to include the ethical coding, becoming a source of moral agency in the process. At the same time, the firm seeks to share its own principles on and approaches to combating corruption with the political community and civil society, so as to politically and ethically contribute to the formation of suitable legal regulations. In other words, on a temporary and fragmentary basis, it becomes an actor in the world of politics and civil society, without becoming an organisation in political or civil society (Scherer & Palazzo, 2007, explain this point by implying that political engagement can transform a firm into an actor in the political system). The firm does not adopt the civil society's binary coding (the common good–private interests); rather, it temporarily and fragmentarily employs the guiding difference "engagement–non-engagement" used by civil society organisations. Thanks to its own guiding difference (earnings–costs), it remains focused on the market (payment–non-payment) and economic transactions and continues to be part of the economy. That doesn't mean it can use arguments based on the costs of compliance, or declining earnings due to maintaining integrity in highly competitive markets, to justify ignoring legal requirements. But the firm's guiding difference "earnings–costs" does offer it insights into the consequences of implementing an integrity and compliance management system. Its challenge consists in programming the changed contexts and logics that now apply to its transactions in a way that allows it to continue to conduct its former Exchange Transactions on the market, now in the form of Relational Transactions. Alternatively, the firm can opt to withdraw from the market in question, to no longer conduct business there and start looking for new, less risky markets where it can offer its goods and services. Changes of this sort take place constantly at firms and are a driving force for their economic performance.

A second, diametrically opposed example: the provision of charitable services on the part of religious organisations, in this case, Christian churches. Their charitable mission can be traced back to the message of brotherly love in the Bible. As such, it is purely religiously codified as a testament of faith, in pursuit of transcendence and manifests in individual acts of charity. In the course of history, various monastic religious communities that provide such services on a professional basis have formed. Through professionalisation, the religious coding, which was originally individual in nature, was expanded to include an organisational context that views the message of brotherly love as an organised testament of faith that is supported by donations and which is intended to produce certain effects in the church (theological relevance of poverty and humility) and in society (social obligations of the rich) alike. In this way, the immanence of these transactions is underscored. Today's Christian charitable organisations see their transactions as being linked to certain legal, economic, political and ethical contexts, in which the original Christian coding, the aspect of transcendence, is at risk of being lost. Consequently, in many cases, they no longer view themselves (as the monasteries did) as religious organisations, but as civil society organisations. This raises the existential question as to whether or not they have long since transformed into purely economic organisations or political appendages (for a discussion of this point, cf. Richter, 2016). For the purposes of our discussion, the key point is that in the course of an extremely long historical process these transactions, which were once purely religious in nature, accrued additional logics and that, as a result, not only has the classification of religious and charitable organisations changed in modern discourses (from religion to civil society) but in modern societies, their transactions are being carried out by professional and profit-oriented organisations, which provide them as market services in the same or better quality. As such, at least from the initial religious standpoint, these organisations' continued survival is in doubt.

For firms in the economy and in fact for all organisations in society, the task is to translate societal communication into agendas and procedures that are compatible with their guiding difference "earnings–costs". In the process, law, morality, science, sustainability and so on are translated into value management, risk management, compliance management, social innovation management, or sustainability management, so as to understand which practical measures need to be initiated and managed and to gauge their likely contributions to the earnings/costs balance. The requisite communication can be viewed as lobbying (relation: economy—politics—law) or as a multi-stakeholder dialogue (relation: economy—politics—civil society—science), with very different consequences for the relational dimension of the transactions and corresponding economic rationales. The latter are not limited to considerations on earnings. Unlike the market, in the long term no firm can ignore the fact that, as an organisation of society and a nexus of Relational Transactions, it is constitutively oriented on generating a cooperation rent and allocating it to all stakeholders involved (shared value).

These two examples will suffice for the time being; in the following section, we will discuss a number of more general conclusions.

5.3 Characteristics of Exchange and Relational Transactions

1. When they make "payments–non-payments", churches, universities, NGOs, political parties, courts of law and so on operate in relation to the system "market"; similarly, firms, when they take part in social innovation, the fulfilment of social responsibilities and so on in the form of multi-stakeholder dialogues, operate in relation to politics, civil society and science, although any patents involved and potential human rights violations could also be evaluated using the system "law". But just as these churches, universities, NGOs, political parties and courts of law do not become economic organisations, nor do firms become political

organisations. On a temporary basis and in pursuit of certain outcomes for specific transactions, they may be economic, political, legal and ethical actors, but in terms of their organisational guiding difference, they remain coupled with the system "market". Let us recall: for Relational Economics, Relational Transactions with their polyvalent modes of communication and decision logics are the basic unit of epistemic interest, not the status of belonging to a specific system or social context. Relational Economics is transaction-based, not space-of-action-based.

2. Organisations and their members are constitutively polylingual societal actors who possess the ability to reconstruct the decision logics of other systems and incorporate them in their own decision-making rationales, while preserving their intrinsic value. Their specialising classification to functional systems is achieved by their respective guiding differences, which are themselves an operationalisation of the system's binary coding and yield certain improvements in effectiveness and efficiency. The advantages of specialisation are what make it possible to generate and allocate a relational rent. On this basis, firms and their senior managements are economic actors with specialisation expertise and can and must participate in designing and concluding ethical, political, legal and scientific transactions. The key point of reference for Relational Economics is the organisation, not the system "market".
3. The situation is analogous for the other organisations mentioned. In terms of the organisational level of ethical communication, in modern societies various forms of agency for moral socialisation, such as families, schools and religious communities, but today also firms, have formed, none of which can claim to fulfil a fundamentally special function for the morality of a given society. Relational Transactions take place within and between organisations, which is why this interaction is of particular interest for Relational Economics.
4. The classification of transactions using exclusive binary codings and evaluative, inclusive guiding differences is not something "carved in stone"; rather, it depends on the distinct transactions and the specification of various factors: their productivity, uncertainty, resource specificity and cooperation rent, as well as the adaptability of their governance. On the market, transactions are assessed by means of prices. In organisations, they are incorporated into leadership and management processes via programmes, guidelines and procedures; for this purpose, they must by converted into a communicative form that is compatible with the respective guiding difference. If this does not occur, the result is confusion, which can lead to a reorientation of the organisation. Although polycontexturality is a characteristic of the environment, say, for firms, it is also a goal that must be pursued in the context of leading and managing organisations.
5. The relation between Exchange Transactions with an exclusive economic coding and one guiding difference and Relational Transactions with multiple codings and guiding differences is a dynamic continuum on an axis that can be shifted in either direction. Their purest forms, which empirically speaking are quite hard to come by, represent the two poles. Figure 5.2 provides a comparative list of the respective characteristics of pure Exchange Transactions and pure Relational

	Exchange Transaction (ET)	Relational Transaction (RT)
Basic unit	**Exchange**	**Transaction event**
Actors	Dyadic Maximisation of Earnings	Multiple Maximisation of the Cooperation Rent
Process assumptions	Competition Static equilibrium Predictability Optimal or complete information Unlimited rationality	Co-opetition Oscillating equilibrium Unavoidable uncertainty Incomplete information Bounded rationality
Media	Market Commodity or service Price Monolingual communication Classical or neoclassical contract	Organisation Resources Cost Polylingual communication Relational or societal contract

Fig. 5.2 Characteristics of exchange and relational transactions

Transactions that we have developed so far and which, with regard to transactions, can be specifically combined and recombined.

In terms of the basic unit of analysis, we initially draw a distinction between exchanges on the one hand and transactions as events on the other. Exchanges involve two actors who are solely seeking to maximise their own advantages and are therefore only of interest as an incarnation of the economic function, that is, as *homo economicus*. Transactions involve more than two actors, who, in addition to pursuing their own interests, also have a collective interest in generating a cooperation rent. Accordingly, their identities as persons, such as their moral convictions, play a decisive part. The theoretical framework is provided, on the one hand, by the assumption that competition, static equilibrium, predictability, optimal or complete information and unlimited rationality apply, but on the other by the assumption that the simultaneity of cooperation and competition (co-opetition) (cf. Brandenburger & Nalebuff, 2011; Walley, 2007), oscillating equilibrium, unavoidable uncertainty, incomplete information and limited rationality also apply. Lastly, Exchange Transactions and Relational Transactions differ in terms of the media in which and through which they take place. For the former, these include the market, a commodity or service, prices as a monolingual form of communication and the classical or neoclassical contract; for the latter, they include the organisation, resources, costs, polylingualism and the relational or societal contract.

Figure 5.2 also shows that all economic transactions have a societal character, the complexity and relevance of which grow with the transition from Exchange Transactions to Relational Transactions. Even the purely economic exchange assumes the existence of a legal order as an externality, which it confirms in its own consummation. In contrast, the Relational Transaction explicitly recognises this relation, which it depicts as simultaneous, mutually influential events. It is an explicit attractor for various societal logics, like the economy, law, ethics and so on. They are no longer an externality but an endogenous element of economic transactions. In more abstract terms, this continuous process can also be portrayed as the fundamental transformation from purely economic Exchange Transactions (ET) to polyvalent Relational Transactions (RT):

$$ET_e$$

$$\text{to}$$

$$RT_{e,i,m\,\ldots n}$$

Moreover, this transformation dictates that the connection between Exchange Transactions and Relational Transactions can only be achieved by structurally coupling the market assessment and organisational assessment of a given transaction and must be created in organisations, here, primarily in firms. This relationalisation shapes the firm's guiding difference for a given economic transaction via the earnings from market operations; and shapes societal welfare via the achievable size of the cooperation rent.

1. Relational Economics concerns itself with transactions within and as relations; in this regard, the form of relation and the process of relationalisation are themselves value-creating. Accordingly, every organisation—such as a firm—is constitutively viewed as a contractually regulated relational nexus of stakeholder interests with regard to the completion of economic transactions, that is to say, as a relation of multiple material and intangible stakeholder resources. Firms are societal organisations that can and must gauge how their existence (value creation, legality, legitimacy) and their transactions (revenues, compliance, responsibility) are viewed by others, which they do by observing communication on the market, between other organisations and between individual members of society. Here the polycontextuality, polycontexturality and polylingualism of organisations, which is to say, of firms, come into play; traits that allow us to operationalise the societal link in Relational Economics.
2. Relations interconnect different events (actors, logics and so on). In response, a new form emerges that encompasses the events of previously existing forms, which it views in interaction with new events. This produces new forms of organisation, as it represents a new combination of logics, which has to be expressed in the organisational process in order to produce an effect. Compliance offices are not identical to previously existing legal departments; sustainability boards

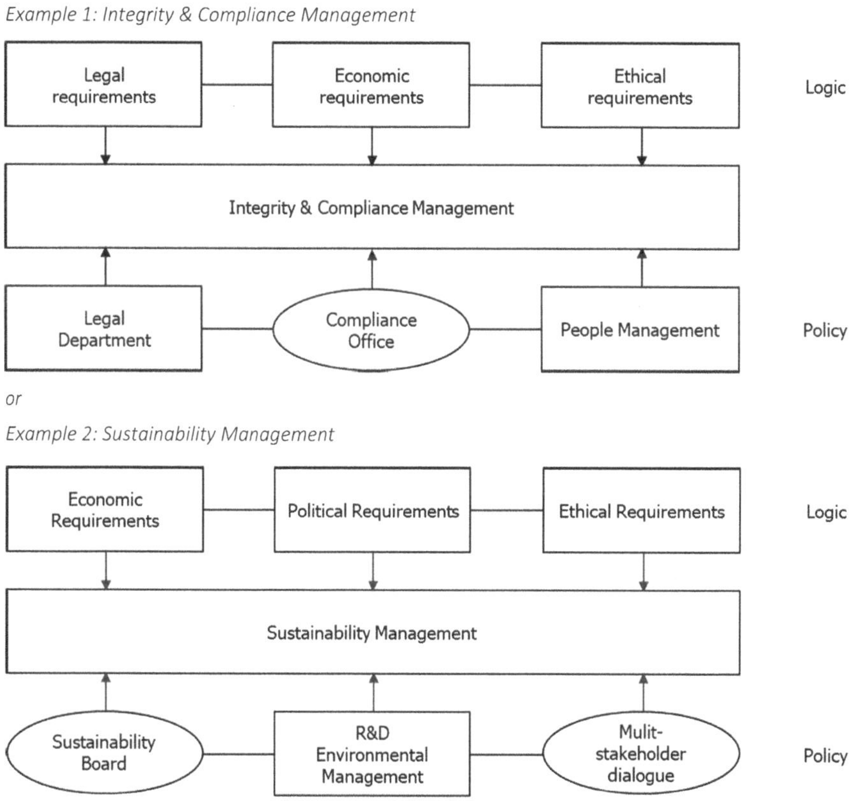

Fig. 5.3 Connecting relational logics and programming

now have very little to do with environmental management and global transcultural management is not the same as traditional diversity management. Here, a re-relationalisation of the events in a given transaction finds expression in new organisational forms, which in turn describe a new, dynamic equilibrium of relational transactions. Formally speaking, for the examples used here, the process looks as in Fig. 5.3 (here the new organizational forms are presented in the ovals).

As previously and repeatedly mentioned, each of these new organisational forms is not merely a selective or additive mix of available structures; rather, it is a means of processing the unity of diversity in multiple logics for a new type of Relational Transactions.

References

Aristotle. (1915). Magna Moralia. In W. D. Ross (Ed.), *The works of Aristotle*. Oxford: Clarendon Press.

Aristotle. (2011). *Nicomachean ethics*. In R. C. Bartlett & S. D. Collins, (Eds.). Chicago, London: The University of Chicago Press.

Baecker, D. (2017). Von der Kunst, die Wirklichkeit unmöglich zu machen. *Zu Heiner Müller. Merkur: Deutsche Zeitschrift für europäisches Denken, 71*(813), 16–28.

Brandenburger, A. M., & Nalebuff, B. J. (2011). *Co-opetition*. New York, NY: Crown Business.

Granovetter, M. S. (1985). Economic action and social structure: The problem of embeddedness. *The American Journal of Sociology, 91*(3), 481–510.

Luhmann, N. (1986). *Ökologische Kommunikation: Kann die moderne Gesellschaft sich auf ökologische Gefährdungen einstellen?*. Berlin: Springer.

Luhmann, N. (1987). *Soziale Systeme: Grundriß einer allgemeinen Theorie*. Frankfurt a. M.: Suhrkamp.

Luhmann, N. (2000). *Die Politik der Gesellschaft*. Frankfurt a. M.: Suhrkamp.

Plato. (1941). *The Republic of Plato*. In F. M. Cornford, (Ed.). New York, London: Oxford University Press.

Putnam, R. D. (1993). *Making democracy work: Civic traditions in modern Italy*. Princeton, NJ: Princeton University Press.

Richter, S. (2016). *Zivilgesellschaft – Überlegungen zu einem interdisziplinären Konzept. Docupedia-Zeitgeschichte*. Potsdam: Zentrum für zeithistorische Forschung.

Scherer, A. G., & Palazzo, G. (2007). Toward a political conception of corporate responsibility: Business and society seen from a Habermasian perspective. *Academy of Management Review, 32*(4), 1096–1120.

Walley, K. (2007). Coopetition: An introduction to the subject and an agenda for research. *International Studies of Management & Organization, 37*(2), 11–31.

Wieland, J. (1996). *Ökonomische Organisation, Allokation und Status*. Tübingen: Mohr Siebeck.

Wieland, J. (2012). *Die Entdeckung der Ökonomie*. Marburg: Metropolis.

Wieland, J. (2017). Unternehmung und Gesellschaft – Notizen –. In FUGO—Forschungsgruppe Unternehmen und gesellschaftliche Organisation (Ed.), *Unternehmen der Gesellschaft. Interdisziplinäre Beiträge zu einer kritischen Theorie des Unternehmens* (pp. 313–336). Marburg: Metropolis.

Part III
The Firm and Polycontextual Management

Chapter 6
Stakeholder Resources and Stakeholder Interests

6.1 Theory of the Firm and Society

The research agenda being developed here for a Relational Economics is a political economy that is traditionally concerned with the causes and conditions of simultaneously achieving private and societal value creation. Adam Smith's (1776) *invisible hand* guiding *the market as a modern system of commerce* (cf. Smith, 1776/1981, WN I, vii. 12) is one such simultaneous allocation mechanism that celebrated its heyday in the eighteenth century. Less than two centuries later, *the Modern Corporation* (Berle & Means, 1932/1991), the firm,—"that collective capitalism we call the 'corporate system'" (ibid., 1932/1991, p. xx) –, represents the central form of allocation in the relational economy. Accordingly, it is always also a societal event, a bundle of stakeholder interests, the existence of which "cannot be justified except on the ground that the community is better off—and not unless most members of the community share it" (ibid., p. xxxv). Firms are the backbone of all modern societies and have "passed far beyond the realm of private enterprise—they have become more nearly social institutions" (ibid., p. 46). My thoughts in the following section are based on the same conviction.

In this regard two questions, each with a long history but most often considered separately, are combined: the question 'What is the nature of the firm?' and the question as to the relation between 'Business and Society', both of which are now to be understood as a relation of relations, of economic and societal events. The fact that today's mainstream economics is unable to adopt this perspective is due to its research agenda. In his highly readable essay *Corporation and Society: The Search for a Paradigm*, Preston (1975) points out that the discussion on the relation between business and society is not concerned with irrelevant details, but with the form and content of economic value creation itself. Further, he argues that modern economic theory's disinterest with regard to this area of research is a categorical problem:

> [...] the corporation-society relationship requires rigorous and comprehensive conceptions of *both* the corporation *and* society; and these conceptions must be articulated in comparable, or at least translatable, terms. (Ibid., p. 446)

J. Wieland, *Relational Economics*, Relational Economics and Organization Governance,
https://doi.org/10.1007/978-3-030-45112-7_6

For Relational Economics it is the category of *Relational Transactions* that allows us to analyse, understand and shape not only the nature of the firm but also its ties to society and vice versa, in connection with private and societal value creation. As previously discussed, society translates Relational Economics as the polycontextuality of governance processes for economic transactions.

6.2 Stakeholder Resources and Interests

In his seminal work *The Functions of the Executive*, Barnard (1938) provides a system theoretical understanding of the firm as an organisation of cooperating activities:

> I define an organization as a *system* of *cooperative activities* of two or more persons—something intangible and impersonal, largely a matter of relationships. (Ibid., p. 75)

The firm as an organisation is an abstract form, a system that is independent of its actors' interests, in short: an *entity in its own right*. It is the form and process of relations between activities and actors, the mode of existence of relations. Coase (1937) has pointed out that the transition to transactions in the context of economic analysis cannot be achieved without a theory of systemic relationships: "a firm, therefore, consists of the system of relationships" (Ibid., p. 393).

In the following discussion, I will argue that the firm is a governance structure for the relationalisation of stakeholder resources and interests, which the firm, in turn, requires for the completion of its transactions and for its continued existence. Although I have extensively developed and explained the theoretical framework underlying this definition elsewhere (cf. Wieland, 1996, 2014), in light of its crucial role in understanding the relation between firm and society, I would like to at least briefly summarise it here—starting with the view of the firm as a relation of stakeholder resources and interests (Fig. 6.1).

The essential idea is that the firm is an organisational form for cooperatively doing business, the goal of which is to efficiently and effectively enable and consummate transactions in teams and networks. The firm as an organisation is (again) an *entity in its own right*, it exists independently of its stakeholders and its only purpose is to ensure its own (theoretically infinite) existence as a form of collective action. It is precisely this continuity that makes organisational value creation possible and effective. To support this—the enablement and consummation of transactions and continuity of cooperation—stakeholders invest their tangible or intangible resources, which they ultimately retain control over and in return for which they expect to reap returns on investment. They are production factors that contribute to the firm's value creation. For example, an Original Equipment Manufacturer (OEM) working with a given firm contributes its innovation potential and in return expects to see its own business grow. In similar vein, a joint venture partner contributes capital and market access; it expects to receive returns on its investment and access to modern technologies.

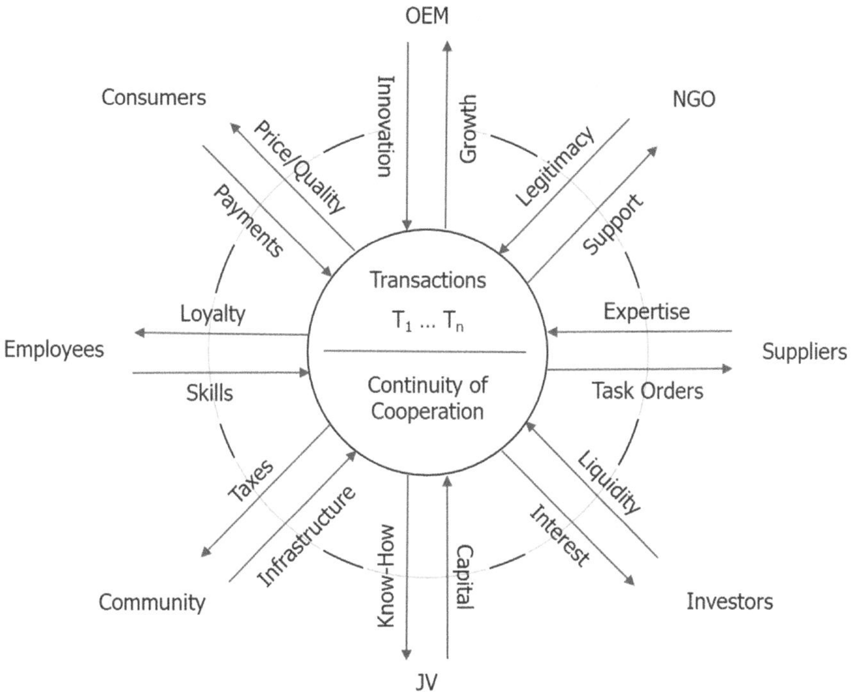

Fig. 6.1 The firm as a relation of stakeholder resources and interests

In the context of Relational Economics, the firm is not to be understood as an input-output function (cf. Varian, 2009) or contractually organised form of team production (cf. Alchian & Demsetz, 1972) that is designed to maximise private profits (cf. Trivedi, 2003) or shareholder value (cf. Jensen & Meckling, 1976); and not because these interpretations are absurd or have no basis in economic practice, but because they do not allow us to capture the essence of the firm as a relation of tangible and intangible resources and interests, its nature as an organisation. In brief, the theory of the firm as a form of governance for stakeholder relations and as a process of relationalising stakeholder resources is based on the following assumptions:

- Every stakeholder invests specific resources in a firm, which are required for the completion of a transaction and/or the theoretically infinite continuation of the firm's existence.
- These resources can be of a tangible or intangible, economic or societal nature and the stakeholders ultimately retain control over them. The degree of their specificity for a transaction or for the organisation's continuing existence determines their contribution to private or societal value creation within and through the firm.
- As compensation for the productions factors it invests, every stakeholder expects to receive a material or non-material income, the size of which depends on its respective contribution to joint, cooperative value creation. Accordingly, the

shared goal of the firm and its stakeholders is to generate individual factor incomes and a collective cooperation rent.

- The factor incomes are based on the resources/production factors invested by the stakeholders. The cooperation rent is a type of income without any specific and additional individual performance. It is the product of the cooperation of all stakeholders as a supernormal profit for the firm, in other words, in collective form and is allocated to the organisation and all relevant stakeholders in tangible or intangible form.
- The combination of factor incomes and cooperation rent is what motivates a given resource owner to join a specific collaborative project or, more generally, a specific firm.
- The governance of the firm as a nexus of stakeholder relations for the purpose of shared value creation is a two-stage process, which consists in identifying the relevant stakeholder resources and prioritising them on the basis of the firm's transactions and its continuation.
- The stakeholder nexus is based on formal and informal contracts, each of which can, in keeping with Macneil's distinction, be classical, neoclassical or relational, but which collectively form a relation. The firm is a form of the relation of relations and the processes or events it uses in order to complete specific transactions can be based on various types of contracts.
- The integration of societal stakeholders into the firm is based on a social contract between the firm and society, which, from the firm's standpoint, is a transaction-specific event that cannot be codified in or enforced by a formal contract, which is to say, it is a relational contract.
- The firm as an autonomous and independent form of governance for multiple types of contracts is the principal of all stakeholders; the firm's leadership and management are its agents and are chiefly responsible for shaping social relations, which is to say, for selecting, coordinating and promoting cooperation between the requisite stakeholder resources and interests. If other independent organisations stakeholders in a firm, we speak of a 'principal-principal' relationship.
- Only those who invest relevant resources in a firm's form and processes and who, in this way, contribute to its sustainability and cooperation rent, can be stakeholders.

Presented in a somewhat different form (Fig. 6.2) shows the firm as a relation of stakeholder relations. Though we'll discuss the cooperation rent in more detail in a subsequent chapter, it is mentioned here in the interest of completeness.

So, to summarise, we have established that the theoretical architecture of the firm as a network of stakeholder interests and resources—the interactions of which determine an organisation's productivity and with it, said organisation's position and strength in competitive markets—implies that each of these resources can be assigned to a factor income and/or cooperation rent.

The discussion on factor incomes has a long tradition in economic theory. In this view, resources are necessary input factors for the provision of goods or services. In a highly competitive market, they are, at least according to the standard theory, remunerated on the basis of their marginal productivity. This presents us with a

Governance	Stakeholder	Resources	Factor incomes -pecuniary-	Cooperation rent -tangible/intangible-
Relational contract	Private property owners	– Capital – Leadership/ Management	– Profits – Income	– Goodwill – Reputation
	Investors	– Capital – Commitment – Trust	– Return on investment – Minimising risk	– Effective compliance – Integrity – Value-Management
	Employees	– Skills – Character – Loyalty	– Income – Mandatory social benefits – Voluntary social benefits	– Job security – Advancement opportunities
	Leadership/ Management	– Followership – Coordination – Personality	– Salary – Sharing in success – Decision-making power	– Power – Benefit – Status – Prestige
	OEMs	– Innovation	– Growth	– Market power
	Joint Ventures	– Capital – Market access	– Profits – Know-How	– Know-How
Neoclassical contract	Suppliers	– Expertise – Reliability	– Orders – Turnover	– Expanding their competencies – Reputation – Long-term cooperation
	Customers	– Payment	– Price/Quality – Brand	– Loyalty
	Creditors	– Liquidity – Risk capital	– Interest	– Reliable repayments
Classical contract	Short-term investors	– Financing – Efficiency	– Return on investment	
	One-time buyers	– Payment	– Price-Performance	
Relational Social contract	Communities	– Infrastructure	– Taxes	– Prosperity – Attractive locations
	NGOs	– Knowledge – Legitimacy	– Expertise – Financial support	– Reputation – Influence

Fig. 6.2 The firm as a relation of stakeholders

challenge: the traditional theory of factor incomes, with its three production factors *capital* (interest, profits), *labour* (wages) and *land* (leasing fees, rent), does not suffice to explain the economy of relational transactions. Instead of this theory, we should focus on describing the characteristics of the factor incomes and cooperation rent for stakeholders like suppliers, customers and organisations in civil society and on grasping the nature of their relationalisation. (I would like to thank Marco Möhrer for our fruitful discussion on the following distinctions).

Some time ago, Andreas Heck and I made an initial attempt to address this problem and proposed viewing the diversity of the organisation-specific or transaction-specific stakeholders' incomes as the result of polycontextural contractual agreements (cf. Wieland & Heck, 2013, p. 53 ff.). Accordingly, in keeping with the discussion up to this point, in Fig. 6.2 I distinguish between relational, neoclassical, classical and social contracts. Contracts can provide stakeholders with both pecuniary and non-pecuniary benefits. Factor incomes like profits, wages, interest, rent and other monetary forms of income are pecuniary benefits. In contrast, cooperation rents can be both pecuniary and non-pecuniary in nature. They are forms of income that are disbursed by an organisation and go beyond individually contractible compensation. For example, a firm's voluntarily provided social benefits are pecuniary types of cooperation rent, while integrity, opportunities for advancement, prestige, knowledge, predictability and attractive locations can be non-material types. However, this only refers to the stakeholder perspective; from the organisation's standpoint, things look somewhat different. Here the distribution of non-material rents is based on cooperation with regard to the organisation's specific transactions or programmes; these, in turn, entail costs that must be covered by earnings. Examples include the non-cash benefits offered by a firm, say, in the form of internal continuing training opportunities or other voluntary CSR measures that increase the stakeholder's total income. In this regard, the non-negotiable guiding difference for all economic organisations, namely 'earnings—costs', is particularly relevant and here we also see the twofold challenge of strategically conceptualising firms' societal or political engagement as a 'shared value creation' strategy and of operationalising that strategy by monitoring the balance between costs and earnings. This will be discussed in more detail later in the book.

These considerations can also be applied to organisations in civil society. For example, NGOs can classify donations, consulting fees and compensation for monitoring sustainability standards as pecuniary factor incomes, while their reputation and public influence are non-pecuniary. Here, too, we see the potential connections and interactions between factor incomes and cooperation rents. Further, this not only applies at the level of the organisation. A leading member of an NGO who acquires a specific type of expertise as a non-pecuniary rent can subsequently take advantage of it in business or politics, where they can capitalise on it as a pecuniary factor income at standard market prices. And the list of examples can be continued, say, with direct price subventions for consumers from the rent produced by a network, the continuous flow of orders for suppliers and higher taxes for municipalities.

In other words: factor incomes are always pecuniary. They manifest as costs for firms and as returns on investment for the corresponding stakeholders. Cooperation rents can be both pecuniary and non-pecuniary, are accrued by organisations and must be distributed by them, which incurs costs. The two forms are connected by a direct relation of interaction or transfer. The concrete form of this relation is determined by the types of contract involved and their polycontexturality.

The central point with regard to this (here only generally outlined) theoretical framework is that, unlike conventional stakeholder theory, here stakeholders not only have legally or morally justified entitlements with regard to the firm but are also entitled to a return on investment (factor income and cooperation rent) as compensation for investing their tangible and intangible resources.

This economic conception for the legitimation of stakeholder networks stands in contrast to their political interpretation as power relations. A paradigmatic advocate of this stance is Rowley (1997), who views the firm as a network of stakeholders, but who only sees in these circumstances a certain challenge for the firm: namely to either resist stakeholder pressure or to yield to stakeholder demands (cf. Rowley, 1997, p. 893). Relational Economics views the matter differently. As demonstrated in Fig. 6.1., stakeholders are stakeholders both with regard to the continuation of the organisation and with regard to the governance of its specific transactions, in the course of whose consummation the firm is constituted and reproduced. Moreover, there are not only relations between stakeholders and the organisational form, but also between stakeholders; as such, they form a network. In this regard, it is important to differentiate between the various relations of the firm as a nexus of stakeholder relations: stakeholder—organisation, stakeholder—transaction, stakeholder—stakeholder and resource—resource. Accordingly, stakeholder management does not involve a unilateral and discrete exchange between two parties; rather, it involves the interactions in an intra-, inter- and extra-firm (societal) network of actors, resources and events, on the basis of multiple contracts.

Consequently, the twenty-first century firm has been characterised as a network that shapes expertise and abilities for the purposes of corporate value creation (cf. Alvarez, Barney & Anderson, 2013; Alvarez & Busenitz, 2001 and, for social entrepreneurs, Ehrenberger, 2017). The following quote from Powell (2001) summarises the point aptly:

> In sum, firms are coming to resemble a network of treaties because these multistranded relationships encourage learning from a broad array of collaborators and promote experimentation with new methods, while at the same time reducing the cost of expensive commitments. (Ibid., p. 61)

What exactly drives this type of network and what its chief traits are, form the heart of an ongoing sociological (cf. for an overview DiMaggio, 2001), digital (cf. for an overview Greenstein, Goldfarb & Tucker, 2013; Goldfarb, Greenstein & Tucker, 2015) and organisational economics (for an overview Ménard, 2013) discussion. One thing is for certain: networks are formed because they allow access to and the use of resources and abilities that the firm does not/cannot own. These especially include relevant know-how, the use of complementary resources, learning in networks for the joint development of new products and reducing transaction costs (Cf. Capaldo, 2007, p. 587, Czakon, 2009 and Dyer & Singh, 1998).

In addition, it is generally agreed that networks or hybrids represent alternative forms of governance to the market and hierarchy—*make, buy or ally* (cf. Child, Faulkner & Tallman, 2005); those are the options. The contractual basis of networks refers to economic transactions that contain significant non-contractibilities (cf. Ménard, 2013, p. 1076), which is to say, they are of a relational nature and cannot be formally enforced by, say, a court of law. Consequently, the governance of non-contractible events in interactive relations must allow (i) open communication, especially with regard to sharing information and expertise, (ii) trust, (iii) the acceptance of the parties' mutual dependence and (iv) regional and global cooperation (ibid.). These are the four dimensions of relational governance that deviate from the traditional dimensions of transaction cost theory (asset specificity, uncertainty, frequency), while not contradicting them. Networks can deal with uncertainty on a transaction-specific basis and are predominantly formed in order to ensure access to expertise, markets and other resources. They differ from firms in terms of their specific rules for allocating decision-making and supervisory rights and in terms of the partners' autonomy. Based on the stakeholder perspective developed here, they also include civil society, political and state actors, who also invest resources in the network for a specific transaction on either a short-term or long-term basis and who in return demand a high degree of autonomy and transparency.

In brief, what we can say here is that economic networks are forms of governance for trans-sectoral, private and societal value creation and that the interactions within them are fundamentally shaped by demands for and the provision of, both a factor income (return on the resources invested) and a cooperation rent (earnings from jointly used resources).

From an economic standpoint, the following aspects are typical of the firm as a stakeholder network:

(i) All stakeholders retain ownership of their resources, which they only provide access to on a temporary and limited basis.
(ii) Every stakeholder, as a result of its ownership rights, continues to retain its own private information. In other words, the sharing of expertise and information cannot be fully contractually regulated; rather, it depends on an incentive-sensitive motivational and governance structure.
(iii) Every stakeholder, as an actor, may represent not just one individual decision logic, but multiple decision logics. In other words, it remains unclear which language game a given actor uses to interpret an event or a decision on the part of the firm. The actor may choose an economic interpretation, or they may not; they may just as well choose a moral interpretation, producing other behaviours and actions in the process.
(iv) Actor behaviour is non-contractible. Non-contractible behavioural dispositions refer to the fact that, in stakeholder networks, the ways in which resource owners are dealt with and managed are predominantly intended to induce suitable forms of behaviour. This has already been shown in the analysis of Macneil's works and should be explored in more detail in connection with relational leadership.

6.3 Governance and Global Value Chains

The network-forming process continues apace around the globe and in the last two decades has led to the creation of Global Value Chains (GVCs) and Global Production Networks (GPNs) (for a discussion on GVCs cf. Gereffi & Fernandez-Stark, 2011, 2016; Gereffi, Humphrey & Sturgeon, 2005; Gereffi, 2018; on GPNs cf. Henderson, Dicken, Hess, Coe & Yeung, 2002, Coe et al., 2004; Coe, Dicken, & Hess, 2008, Coe & Hess, 2013, Fichter & Sydow, 2002). The governance of this global value creation calls for a mixture of market, hierarchy, relation and—depending on the perspective—further means of control and is linking firms, employees, customers,

NGOs and so on, all around the world. In these 'global factories', the specific form of governance is what determines the distribution of profits and the economic rent (cf. Buckley & Strange, 2015). Networks are predicated upon the ability of all partners to combine the economic logic of value creation with the legal logic of the (in many cases unclear) regulatory framework and the ethical logic of social standards, human rights, health risks, sustainability and inclusivity. "Early use of GVC methodology focused principally on economic and competitiveness issues, while recently social and environmental dimensions have been incorporated." (Gereffi & Fernandez-Stark, 2011, p. 4; see also p. 29 and p. 32).

Figure 6.3 "Governance of GVCs" serves to illustrate this discussion and distinguishes between value creation in the context of market relations and vertical integration in the context of the standard make or buy decisions; intra-firm relations on the basis of global investments in joint ventures or mergers & acquisitions (FDI); and inter-firm relations in the context of allying strategies. Societal organisations concerned with political, legal, social and ethical events in the GVCs are allocated to these three categories.

GVCs are networks consisting of firms, business areas and societal actors and which, according to estimates from UNCTAD (2013) and OECD (2018), are now responsible for roughly 70–80% of international trade. Further, according to estimates from the ILO (cf. Kizu, Kühn & Vieglahn, 2016), in 2013 roughly 453 million people in 40 countries worked for a GVC. Accordingly, a firm's revenues are no longer simply the product of its market transactions, but also its interactions with other organisations. As such, the term 'global trade' is misleading as long as it only reflects market transfers to end customers.

> The traditional view of international trade is that each country produces finished products that are then exported to consumers in another country. This type of trade, however, represents only 30% of total trade in goods and services. Today, 70% of international trade involves a variety of transactions where services, raw materials, parts and components are exchanged in global value chains (GVCs) across countries, before being incorporated into final products that are shipped to consumers all over the world. (OECD, 2018)

In reality, international trade encompasses the global and cooperative development, production and distribution of goods and services, based on the division of labour. As a result, according to UNCTAD, an estimated 28% of global commerce (cf. UNCTAD, 2013, p. 136, see also Gereffi, 2018, p. 431) is reported twice, simply because suitable statistics for this form of value creation either don't exist or are not yet uniformly used (on the methodological difficulties cf. Bernard, Jensen, Redding & Schott, 2010, Bonturi & Fukasaku, 1993 and, for commerce within Europe, Fernandes, 2014). Further, not only are the numbers on global intra-firm trade and intermediate goods unreliable; the same is true for the dynamics of this trend: though GVCs were a key driver of global growth from 1995 to 2008, the numbers declined from 2012 to 2015. The reasons for this change remain unclear. Potential explanations include increasingly protectionist trade policies, digitalisation and the economic 'upgrading' of the newly industrialised countries, which was so successful that cross-border division of labour and fragmentation of production has declined (cf. Degain,

Meng & Wang, 2017). In any case, it is clear that Global Value Chains and therefore the firm have become a key factor in the global economy and a main driver of prosperity and growth.

Early in the twentieth century, Alfred Marshall pointed out the theoretical challenges of the systematic connections between trade and industrial organisation:

> A country's foreign trade is something more than a number of dealings between individuals at home and abroad; it is the outcome of the relations in which the industries that belong to her, that are a part of her life, and embody much of her character, stand to the industries of other countries. (Marshall, 1919/2006, p. 4)

The globalisation and fragmentation of industrial production and distribution networks and the attendant problems concerning macroeconomic classification have only more distinctly highlighted something that was recognisable as a theoretical problem from the outset. Trade (whether national or international), as a distinct exchange, is a dissatisfactory epistemological assumption of economic theory-building, because it ignores the fact that trade is always also "the outcome of the relations" of industrial organisation. This was also the basis for Marshall's interest in questions concerning the formation of economic industries and clusters (for the current discussion cf. De Marchi, Di Maria, Gereffi, 2018).

The emerging global production and value creation networks have a significant influence on the economic and societal evolution of industrialised and newly industrialised countries alike. Accordingly, for Relational Economics they are not only of interest from a purely economic standpoint but also as networks of economic, political and civil society organisations (for this discussion cf. the information on GPNs e.g., Capaldo, 2007, p. 587; Czakon, 2009 and Dyer & Singh, 1998).

Figure 6.3 "Governance of GVCs" in the following is intended to portray the complex relations within these value chains and production networks. Whereas the column "Market – Hierarchy" mainly has to do with supplier management so as to reduce costs, boost efficiency and establish power on the market, GVCs focus on increasing value creation in every stage and at every node in the network. This, in turn, provides opportunities for newly industrialised countries to upgrade (cf. Gereffi & Fernandez-Stark, 2011 and 2016) their own share of global value creation, which is also one of the reasons for the resurgence of the debate on protectionism in political circles (for the mechanism based on the example of US-Chinese relations cf. Dollar, 2017).

To make this a bit clearer, let's return to our previous example, T-shirt production: a given firm maintains a business relation with a supplier, which, over time, develops into an OEM and complete service provider in a global value creation network. NGOs have now established a relation (criticism regarding human rights violations) with the supplier or OEM (stakeholder—stakeholder) regarding a specific transaction (the manufacture and sale of T-shirts) and—on this basis—also regarding the transactions of the firm and its continuation in the context of a management system for social standards and human rights (Human Rights Compliance).

In turn, political organisations, unions and potentially courts of law become coupled with the transaction, which also creates new relations between them (on the

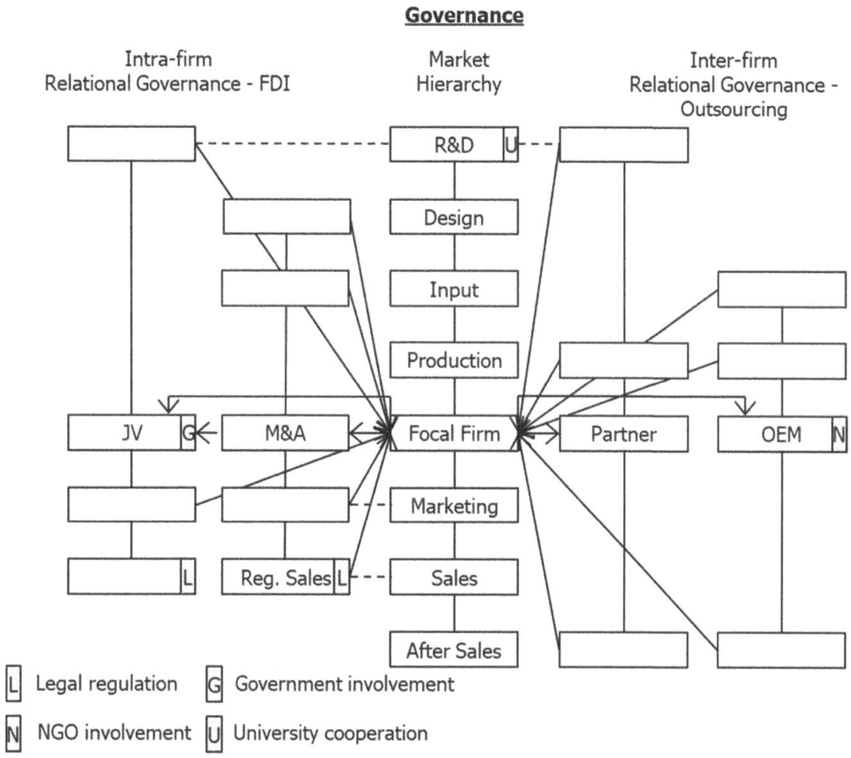

Fig. 6.3 Governance of GVCs

role of civil society in GVCs cf. Teegen, Doh & Vachani, 2004). The dynamics of the events and their relationalisation are what make an Exchange Transaction into a Relational Transaction and accordingly into a polycontextual challenge for a firm's leadership and management. Not only because the outcome of this relationalisation is unknown and unpredictable, but also because the successful governance of the network's recursive nature is the problem. Now, however, the firm's societal relation is no longer an exogenous (regulatory) event, but rather an endogenous component of a transaction. In the consummation of said transaction, the firm and society are simultaneously reproduced. It is readily apparent that the conventional economic view cannot capture this network and its consequences for a firm's transactions and continuing existence—and therefore for its economic success—because these aspects are categorically ignored by the exchange-based paradigm. Yet the bilateral exchanges between a firm and its suppliers can tell us very little, especially with regard to the most important connections. This example serves to demonstrate the previously formulated thesis that, in the twenty-first century, the aspect of relations between the firm and society is directly relevant to explaining economic value creation.

6.4 Identifying and Prioritising Stakeholders

Every stakeholder theory of the firm as a regional or global relational network of resources and actors faces two main challenges: on the one hand, identifying and prioritising those stakeholders who are relevant for a transaction or organisation; on the other, dealing with the trade-offs regarding their contributions to value creation, including allocations to the investing stakeholders. I have discussed this point elsewhere, referring to it as the contractual, resource, cooperation or investment relevance of stakeholder relations (see also Wieland, 2014, p. 115 ff., p. 131 ff.); as such, I'll only mention it briefly here. The main point is that identifying and prioritising the stakeholders involved in a transaction or organisation represents the essential third element, which limits the theoretically infinite trade-offs between events and relations and therefore opens the door for scientifically analysing and practically shaping them. In Part I of this book, limiting our scope to specific economic transactions and linking them to polyvalent relational transactions, were identified as the first two elements for avoiding holistic over complexity and paving the way for economic analysis. For purely market-based relations, we can consider these questions to have been satisfactorily answered. Stakeholder management is the fundamental method for specifically defining the necessary limitation of the trade-offs in relational relations and unlocking their potential in the value creation process.

In terms of identifying stakeholders, it is self-evident that, first of all, only those persons or groups who possess resources that are essential to a firm's or network of firms' economic performance, or to the consummation of its transactions, can be stakeholders. The organisation-specific and transaction-specific resources contribute to the cooperation rent that the firm can achieve. These contributions may be of a financial (reducing costs, boosting demand for products), non-financial (reputation, risk screening), functional (specific expertise or skills) or structural nature (transcultural competence, moral principles).

In terms of prioritising stakeholders, one main factor to consider is the degree of specificity regarding the organisational or transaction investment they make, as it is coupled with a given stakeholder's contribution to value creation. A second aspect is how long they invest a resource, whether their commitment is short-term (NGOs, investors, customers making one-time purchases) or long-term (family capital, funds, employees). Third and lastly, their willingness and ability to cooperate should be taken into account, as it determines a stakeholder's reliability, ability to overcome conflicts and sense of responsibility.

In Part IV, I will discuss the second issue, the trade-offs regarding the generation and subsequent allocation of factor incomes and the cooperation rent, in detail. For the time being, allow me to say the following: the specificity of the investment that, in theory, all stakeholders make and which can potentially make each a residual claimant and residual risk-taker, is a pivotal aspect (cf. Blair & Stout, 1999). All stakeholders are contractual partners, even if the form of contract and specific risks and investments vary. The temporary but ongoing relationalisation of stakeholder relations is achieved via governance mechanisms like incentive systems, financial and non-financial reporting, monitoring stakeholder performance, conflict resolution mechanisms and stakeholder representation in organisational structures. It also includes procedures for allocating the cooperation rent and the tasks of leading and managing the firm. The leaders and management are, as previously mentioned, agents of the principal *firm* as an *entity in its own right* and should be understood as mediators for stakeholder relations. This aspect will be discussed in-depth in the following section, chiefly by exploring the relation between economy and society.

References

Alchian, A. A., & Demsetz, H. (1972). Production, information costs, and economic organization. *The American Economic Review, 62*(5), 777–795.

Alvarez, S. A., Barney, J. B., & Anderson, P. (2013). Forming and exploiting opportunities: The implications of discovery and creation processes for entrepreneurial and organizational research. *Organization Science, 24*(1), 301–317.

Alvarez, S. A., & Busenitz, L. W. (2001). The entrepreneurship of resource based theory. *Journal of Management, 27*(6), 755–775.

Barnard, C. I. (1938). *The functions of the executive*. Cambridge, MA: Harvard University Press.

Bernard, A. B., Jensen, J. B., Redding, S. J. & Schott, P. K. (2010). Intra-firm trade and product contractibility (Long Version) (No. w15881). Cambridge, MA: National Bureau of Economic Research.

Blair, M. M., & Stout, L. A. (1999). A team production theory of corporate law. *Virginia Law Review, 85*(2), 248–328.

Bonturi, M., & Fukasaku, K. (1993). Globalisation and intra-firm trade: An empirical note. *OECD Economic Studies, 20*(Spring), 145–159.

Buckley, P. J., & Strange, R. (2015). The governance of the global factory: Location and control of world economic activity. *Academy of Management Perspectives, 29*(2), 237–249.

Capaldo, A. (2007). Network structure and innovation: The leveraging of a dual network as a distinctive relational capability. *Strategic Management Journal, 28*(6), 585–608.

Child, J., Faulkner, D., & Tallman, S. (2005). *Cooperative strategy: Managing alliances, networks, and joint ventures*. Oxford, UK: Oxford University Press.

Coase, R. H. (1937). The nature of the firm. *Economica, 4*(16), 386–405.

Coe, N. M., Hess, M., Yeung, H. W. C., Dicken, P., & Henderson, J. (2004). «Globalizing» regional development: A global production networks perspective. *Transactions of the Institute of British Geographers, 29*(4), 468–484.

Coe, N. M., Dicken, P., & Hess, M. (2008). Global production networks: Realizing the potential. *Journal of Economic Geography, 8*(3), 271–295.

Coe, N. M., & Hess, M. (2013). Global production networks, labour and development. *Geoforum, 44*, 4–9.

Czakon, W. (2009). Relational capability of organizations—Theoretical advances. *Journal of Economics and Management/University of Economics in Katowice, 5*, 47–65.

Degain, C., Meng, B., & Wang, Z. (2017). Recent trends in global trade and global value chains. In International Bank for Reconstruction and Development/The World Bank (Ed.), Global value chain development report 2017: Measuring and analyzing the impact of GVCs on economic development (pp. 37–68). Washington: World Bank.

De Marchi, V., Di Maria, E., & Gereffi, G. (Eds.). (2018). *Local clusters in global value chains. Linking actors and territories through manufacturing and innovation*. New York: Routledge.

DiMaggio, P. J. (Ed.). (2001). *The twenty-first-century firm: Changing economic organization in international perspective*. Princeton, NJ: Princeton University Press.

Dollar, D. (2017). Global value chains shed new light on trade. Washington DC.: Brookings Institute. https://www.brookings.edu/blog/order-fromchaos/2017/07/10/global-value-chains-shed-new-light-on-trade/.

Dyer, J. H., & Singh, H. (1998). The relational view: Cooperative strategy and sources of interorganizational competitive advantage. *Academy of Management Review, 23*(4), 660–679.

Ehrenberger, M. (2017). *Corporate Social Entrepreneurship—Prozess und Form ökonomischer Organisation zur Kreation sozialunternehmerischer Opportunitäten*. Marburg: Metropolis.

Fernandes, I. D. (2014). Intrafirm Trade: Ansätze zu einer Analyse mithilfe des EuroGroups-Registers. In Statistisches Bundesamt (Ed.), *WISTA—Wirtschaft und Statistik, November Ausgabe* (pp. 648–656). Wiesbaden: Statistisches Bundesamt.

Fichter, M., & Sydow, J. (2002). Using networks towards global labor standards? Organizing social responsibilityin global production chains. *Industrielle Beziehungen: Zeitschrift für Arbeit, Organisation und Management, 9*(4), 357–380.

Gereffi, G., Humphrey, J., & Sturgeon, T. (2005). The governance of global value chains. *Review of International Political Economy, 12*(1), 78–104.

Gereffi, G. & Fernandez-Stark, K. (2011). Global value chain analysis: A Primer. Durham, NC: Center on Globalization, Governance and Competitiveness (CGGC) Duke University.

Gereffi, G. & Fernandez-Stark, K. (2016). *Global value chain analysis: A primer* (2nd ed.). Durham, NC: Center on Globalization, Governance and Competitiveness (CGGC) Duke University.

Gereffi, G. (2018). *Global value chains and development: Redefining the contours of 21st century capitalism*. Cambridge, UK: Cambridge University Press.

Goldfarb, A., Greenstein, S., & Tucker, C. (Eds.). (2015). *Economic analysis of the digital economy*. Chicago, IL: University of Chicago Press.

Greenstein, S., Goldfarb, A., & Tucker, C. (Eds.). (2013). *The economics of digitization*. Northampton, MA: Edward Elgar.

Henderson, J., Dicken, P., Hess, M., Coe, N. M., & Yeung, H. W. C. (2002). Global production networks and the analysis of economic development. *Review of International Political Economy, 9*(3), 436–464.

Jensen, M. C., & Meckling, W. H. (1976). Theory of the firm: Managerial behavior, agency costs and ownership structure. *Journal of Financial Economics, 3*(4), 305–360.

Kizu, T., Kühn, S. & Vieglahn, C. (2016). *Linking jobs in global supply chains to demand*. ILO Research Paper No. 16. Geneva: ILO.

Marshall, A. (2006). *Industry and trade*. New York: Cosimo Classics.

Ménard, C. (2013). Hybrid modes of organization. In R. Gibbons & J. Roberts (Eds.), *The handbook of organizational economics* (pp. 1066–1108). Princeton, NJ: Princeton University Press.

OECD. (2018). Trade policy brief: Trade policy implicaitons of global value chains. Retrieved January 27, 2020, from https://www.oecd.org/trade/topics/global-value-chains-and-trade/.

Powell, W. W. (2001). The capitalist firm in the twenty-first century: Emerging patterns in western enterprise. In P. J. DiMaggio (Ed.), *The twenty-first-century firm: Changing economic organization in international perspective* (pp. 33–68). Princeton, NJ: Princeton University Press.

Preston, L. E. (1975). Corporation and society: The search for a paradigm. *Journal of Economic Literature, 13*(2), 434–453.

Rowley, T. J. (1997). Moving beyond dyadic ties: A network theory of stakeholder influences. *Academy of Management Review, 22*(4), 887–910.

Smith, A. (1776). An inquiry into the nature and causes of the wealth of nations. Carmel, IN: Liberty Fund.

Teegen, H., Doh, J. P., & Vachani, S. (2004). The importance on nongovernmental organizations (NGOs) in global governance and value creation: An international business research agenda. *Journal of International Business Studies, 35*(6), 463–483.

Trivedi, M. (2003). *Managerial economics: Theory and applications*. New York, NY: Tata Mcgraw Hill.

UNCTAD. (2013). *Global value chains and development: Investment and value added trade in the global economy*. Genf: United Nations.

Varian, H. R. (2009). *Intermediate microeconomics: A modern approach*. New York, NY: Norton & Company.
Wieland, J. (1996). *Ökonomische organisation, allokation und status*. Tübingen: Mohr Siebeck.
Wieland, J. (2014). *Governance ethics: Global value creation, economic organization and normativity* (Vol. 48). Cham: Springer.
Wieland, J., & Heck, A. E. (2013). *Shared value durch stakeholder governance*. Marburg: Metropolis.

Chapter 7
Normativity and Polycontextual Governance

7.1 Polycontextual Cooperation and Normativity

For roughly the past two decades and in connection with the emergence of Global Value Chains, the relation between firms in the economy on the one hand and society on the other has been discussed under the paradigmatic concept of Corporate Social Responsibility (CSR). Reformulated in the terminology of Relational Economics, CSR is a polycontextual project. Areas like the economy, politics and civil society are involved and must cooperate in order to promote the governance of societal responsibility (for example, adhering to social standards and respecting human rights in global value creation chains, sustainable production processes and products and introducing disruptive innovations). However, from a Relational Economics standpoint, the goal of this cooperation is not merely to cope with societal challenges, but also private and societal value creation, that is, the generation of shared value for all economic and societal stakeholders involved. As such, there are good reasons for a firm to create governance structures for the management of multi-sectoral transactions. In the context of Relational Economics, CSR focuses on transactions, which *sui generis* have a normative, legal, political, moral and sundry other dimensions. Compliance, inclusion, sustainability, integrity, fairness and justice are just a few of the values that specify the value creation chains of firms in connection with CSR.

In the following section, I will discuss the prerequisites for and consequences of the transition from the firm's societal responsibility to polycontextual governance, as well as managing the normativity of relational transactions. In an initial approach to the topic, CSR is, in a more traditional economic language, viewed as an attempt to internalise the negative external effects of economic value creation in transactions, but based on the efforts of private organisations and societal discourse. However, this requires firms to systematically manage normativity, or in other words, to manage the moral side of their business. In the following, I will seek to develop a suitable model for this purpose. In turn, this model for the management of polycontextual cooperation leads to a discussion of critical aspects of governance and the essential conditions for managing normativity and polylingualism.

J. Wieland, *Relational Economics*, Relational Economics and Organization Governance,
https://doi.org/10.1007/978-3-030-45112-7_7

7.2 Corporate Responsibility and Externalities

In the current public debate, responsible behaviour on the part of the firm is being explored and/or demanded in various areas. Working for the benefit of the firm's home region; adhering to social standards on the production of goods and services at both the global and national level; mitigating or solving social problems; managing urbanisation, energy and water provision; respecting human rights at the national and international level; and ensuring the integrity and legality of corporate activities around the globe via compliance management—this is just a small sampling of the topics addressed in CSR, which are to a large extent informed by the United Nations' Sustainable Development Goals (SDGs) (for an overview cf. Bhattacharya, 2011; Freeman & Hasnaoui, 2011; UN Global Compact, 2015).

The responsibility expected from firms is based on political, legal or social events in the context of economic transactions for global value creation, the *impacts* of which are attributed to the firm as a component and consequence of its strategy and business operations. As a rule, firms respond to societal demands for their engagement on the basis of traditional ties to a certain region; by means of established leadership policies based on social partnership; or, in the case of global relations, by adhering to international standards, which are most often the outcomes of multi-stakeholder dialogues or other decision-making platforms (cf. Wieland, 2014, especially Chaps. 5, 6 and 8). From both a legal and political standpoint, CSR standards codify events that are voluntary but not arbitrary (cf. BMAS, 2010, 2018). They are not arbitrary because standards, as Lawrence Busch (2011) has claimed, are recipes for reality:

> Standards are means by which we construct realities. [...] they are part of the technical, political, social, economic and ethical infrastructure that constitutes human societies. (Ibid., p. 13)

Standards of conduct and technical standards seek to create order through differentiation and, in this way, provide a basis for coordinating social cooperation. From this perspective, the growing efforts to standardise the societal responsibility of economic organisations holds few surprises, as it is precisely the lack of regulation in global political and economic cooperation that drives it.

> It is the contractual governance of myriad quasi- or pseudostates that complement or supersede much of the governance of the state, that produce a wide range of complex, often difficult to perceive recipes for realities. [...] the new pseudostates – whether firms or voluntary organizations – usually lack judicial functions. (Ibid., p. 237)

I have argued elsewhere that these standards should be understood as national or global public goods (cf. Wieland, 2014, Chap. 5) that can only be efficiently developed and effectively implemented through the cooperation of public (governments, supranational institutions) and private (firms, civil society) organisations. They are the product of trans-sectoral governance (for an overview cf. Elster, 1997; Held, 1995; Palazzo & Scherer, 2006; Scherer & Palazzo, 2007, 2011) and, as such, are themselves intermediate global public goods (cf. Kaul, Grunberg & Stern, 1999, p. 13 f). By identifying this relation, the firm is transformed from the mere object of external, political or moral regulations, to a co-producer of these societal standards in civil society.

Consequently, from an economic perspective, there are sound reasons for viewing the services expected from firms in these standards as public goods—as, for example, Kitzmueller and Shimshack (2012) have argued in their informative article *Economic Perspectives on Corporate Social Responsibility*. The services demanded in the name of societal responsibility, they claim, are an expression of the global market system's negative external effects, which the system cannot internalise using prices. This leads to a *market failure*, which neither the market itself (through, for example, creating scarcity and adjusting prices) nor national states (through, for example, regulation or taxation) are capable of remedying. In other words: the internalisation of societal responsibility in Exchange Transactions cannot succeed because a firm's societal responsibility is a genuine Relational Transaction.

Accordingly, economic organisations represent a third party, situated between the market and state, which society expects to internalise these externalities (for a suggestion on the internalisation of external effects via strategic management cf. especially Kitzmueller & Shimshack, 2012; Porter & Kramer, 2011; Wieland, 2017). It expects them to do so and assumes they are capable of doing so because firms are who initiate, organise and profit from the national and global value creation networks in which social standards and human rights are violated and in which non-sustainable production systems are employed. This view stems from two sources. Firstly, a given firm's value creation chains are based on private, formal contracts between the business partners and both parties have a hand in shaping their content. In this way, classical and neoclassical contracts become relational contracts. Secondly, a firm, as a nexus of stakeholder relations, enters into an informal, societal contract with NGOs and other representatives of societal interests and in the process agrees to comply with social and other standards. As a result, the firm is also a stakeholder of the society and, as a corporate citizen, is expected to help solve societal problems, just as all other citizens are. This aspect, too, is expressed in the now completely relational character of the contractual relation. As such, the negative external effects discussed here are not merely the externalities of some *vaguely global economy*; rather, they must be more precisely localised as the externalities of private, formal contracts and internalising them necessitates changing the type of contract used (relational contracts). Additional decision logics become coupled with the once purely economic transaction, fundamentally changing its character and governance. This can also be seen in the fact that firms cannot transform *public bads* into *public goods* through organisational internalisation alone.

> The standard argument states that the provision of public goods should be based on public preferences or social objectives. (Kitzmueller & Shimshack, 2012, p. 54)

But firms, when viewed from a purely economic vantage point as private organisations with a private interest in making profits, cannot be systematically seen as representatives of public preferences and societal goals; at best, they can help to implement them. In the classical view, the state stands for these qualities. Consequently, from an economic perspective, CSR can only be effective if the state either entirely fails to provide, or fails to provide in sufficient quantity, the public goods defined under CSR. And in today's globalised world, this is increasingly becoming the case in many areas. Consequently, when firms wish to address their societal responsibilities in a system-immanent manner (in other words, not via charity or philanthropy), they can't simply devise a market strategy for an Exchange Transaction. Instead, they must develop a policy that is tailored to their nature as societal organisations in the economy, as a form of governing relational transactions. In other words: they have to bear in mind their own relational goals, namely organising private and societal value creation. The internalisation of negative external effects or, put another way, the endogenisation of societal normative communication, must be translated using internal codes and programmes before it can produce decisions and effects in a given firm. The public discourse on the societal impact of the firm transforms into internal and external communication about private and societal value creation (SVC). Precisely this point forms the basis of the discussion regarding the *business case* for creating shared value (CSV) in CSR, which has continued for the past several years and which, in its current form, cannot be resolved (cf. for example Barnett, 2007; Carroll & Shabana, 2010; Margolis & Walsh, 2003; Orlitzky, 2011; Orlitzky, Schmidt & Rynes, 2003; Perrini, Russo, Tencati & Vurro, 2011; Porter & Kramer, 2011). The discussion essentially oscillates between the view that there are economic or political incentives for firms to act responsibly and the concern that, as a result, firms could exploit CSR's moral and emancipatory potential for their own economic purposes, destroying it in the process.

Both points of view can be taken into account if we accept the premise that internalising negative external effects by orienting the firm on the collective generation of value for private and public actors alike can succeed if the transactions involved in the internalisation are not viewed as market-driven Exchange Transactions but as Relational Transactions. At the level of corporate codes and agendas, strategies and operations, the firm's CSR engagement then becomes chiefly oriented on *entrepreneurial opportunities*, such as chances to create new markets, products and services through innovation. However, this creation of shared value by innovatively capitalising on opportunities can only succeed if the definitions of what shared value and innovative solutions actually mean are clarified in a process of dialogue between economy and society, within and between various societal sectors and if these definitions are ultimately accepted by all stakeholders. This is one of the main goals on the agendas of multi-sectoral CSR forums, which can be established within companies and in civil society alike (cf. Jhunjhunwala, 2014; Lee, 2011; Lock & Seele, 2016; Sachs, Groth & Schmitt, 2010; Spitzeck & Chapman, 2012; Spitzeck & Hansen, 2010; Spitzeck, Hansen & Grayson, 2011; Wieland 2014). The discussion of these aspects will continue in the following section.

7.3 Shared Value Creation (SVC) and Polycontextual Governance

The discussion up to this point has shown that the emergence of the CSR movement, which began more than 20 years ago, was hardly random or the product of political whims. Rather, it reflects a fundamental phenomenon in societies, which is de-centrally reproduced by organisations and their transactions. Drucker (1992/2006) helped to reinforce this view by noting that: "The issue of social responsibility is also inherent in the society of organizations" (2006, p. 145). A firm, as an organisation within society, "has full responsibility for its impact on community and society" (Ibid., p. 146). Though CSR may experience its fair share of highs and lows, it is not a cyclical event; rather, it is a constitutive event in modern societies.

Corporate Social Responsibility, Sustainable Development Goals and Business and Human Rights are logical responses to the formation of global value creation chains or networks and the massive institutional and organisational shifts that they entail and which, in their polyvalence, have forced the once purely economic transactions to assume a new, relational form. In this regard, two aspects require more detailed exploration, namely the aforementioned legitimation of CSR through societal preferences and the integration of private and societal interests.

Let's begin with the question of legitimation (cf., Wieland & Fischer, 2020 in press). It goes without saying that firms are, on the one hand, private organisations that pursue private interests. In other words, they neither pursue public interests, nor can their own interests be reconciled with public interests. However, I believe it also goes without saying that firms are simultaneously organisations within the society they consummate their economic transactions with. This view reflects the distinction between Exchange Transactions and Relational Transactions. In the eyes of economists, the function of the firm is to address the problem of scarcity with regard to goods and resources by means of successful market operations and in this way to promote private and public welfare. And it is precisely here that the Stakeholder Theory of the Firm (cf. Freeman, 1984, Freeman, Harrison, Wicks, Parmar, & de Colle, 2010, 2004) comes into play. In the variant put forward by R. Edward Freeman, the goal of stakeholder management is organisational value creation for all primary and—in another sense—derivative stakeholders involved. In addition to the property owners and short- and long-term investors, these generally include the creditors, employees, suppliers, consumers and ultimately the society, divided between the civil society and the state. Consequently, firms may be private organisations but are also from the outset organisations within a society, which sanctions and supports their economic interests. In their historical analysis of the rise of firms, Micklethwait and Wooldridge (2005) aptly observe that:

> To keep on doing business, the modern company still needs a franchise from society, and the terms of that franchise still matter enormously. (Ibid., p. 178)

Accordingly, in their transactions, firms must bear in mind that they are enfranchised by society, which holds the power to limit or revoke their *licence to exist and to grow*, in short: to regulate them.

As a nexus of stakeholder relations, every firm constantly and permanently oscillates between its ties to the market and ties to society. Any attempt to alter this state of affairs by cutting the ties to society and the *Shareholder Value Theory* was and remains one such attempt is systematically doomed to fail. In other words: for firms, securing societal legitimation is the rule, not the exception. As such, with regard to our current discussion, the legitimation of corporate solutions——economic and technical alike—to moral and political issues becomes coupled with deliberative discourse (cf. Palazzo & Scherer, 2006; Wieland, 2014, Chap. 6) methods as socially acceptable forms of multi-stakeholder dialogue for the creation of CSR standards.

This, in turn, leads us to the formation and realisation of societal interests and expectations. These discourses and other forms of the stakeholder dialogue are where it can be clarified which goods, services, procedures and actions society expects from the firm. Accordingly, from the firm's standpoint, CSR is a potential source of legitimation for its past, present or future market and organisational innovations, though this can only be achieved in a fair dialogue with society, which is to say, with the accepted representatives of legitimate societal interests. Therefore, with regard to the articulated societal preferences, new markets for goods and services arise, along with corresponding management methods, which the firm is responsible for organising. To describe this strategy, Porter and Kramer (2011) have suggested the term Creating Shared Value (CSV). Though their suggestion has been met with criticism (cf. Crane, Palazzo, Spence & Matten, 2014), in my view both the criticism and Porter and Kramer's idea itself miss the mark because they fail to realise that CSV cannot exclusively, nor even primarily, be a purely economically driven corporate marketing strategy. It is always also a societal innovation and production strategy that requires societal legitimation in order to function economically (for the aspect of the open innovation strategy cf. Chesbrough & Appleyard, 2007 and for that of social innovation strategies cf. Mulgan, 2006). This calls for a management strategy that views the firm's goals as consisting in economic value creation for all stakeholders participating in the process, who have invested their resources and competencies and expect to see a return on their investment. The ultimate goal of shared value production is therefore not the strategic management of previously established market activities, but the normativity (cf. Wieland, 2017, 2018) of societally legitimated future markets, which are characterised by their unpredictability. Managing normativity is a form of risk management and can only succeed if a given firm is truly capable of accurately interpreting society's preferences, both for the present and for the foreseeable future and of translating said preferences into products, services and management methods that are desired and legitimated by society—in short: into business models, policies and programmes. As previously mentioned, only then do societal events in connection with a transaction become quantifiable as costs or earnings for an organisation, allowing them to be linked to the market system through pricing. Polylingualism, which is to say, the ability to understand and integrate the various language games used in society by managing all organisations within it, including firms, is a requisite competency that must be anchored in the firm's structures and staff. In addition to polylingualism, a firm requires trans-contextual competency: the ability to create

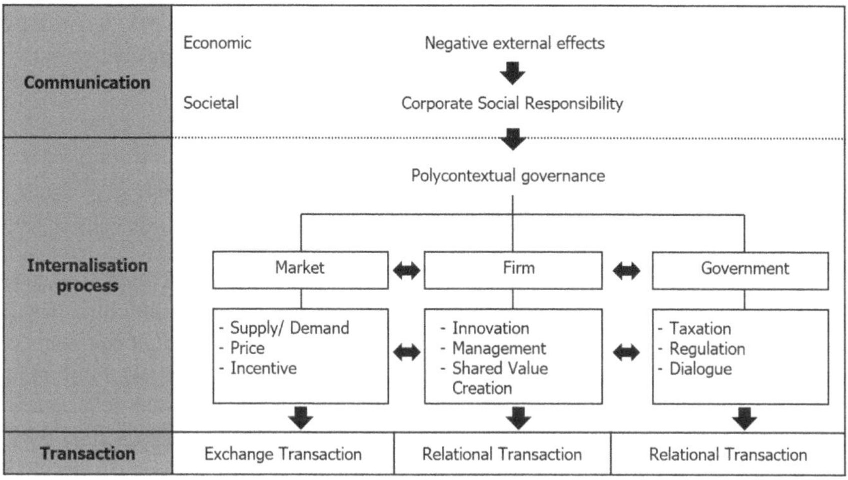

Fig. 7.1 Corporate social responsibility and polycontextual governance

governance structures for relational (because they involve various societally embedded interests and resources) transactions, which require adaptive structures in order to efficiently and effectively cope with the diversity of contexts. In other words, the goal is to identify, mobilise and integrate all of the resources and competencies to be found in various corners of society for the consummation of a specific transaction and which are vital to efficient and effective shared value creation (SVC).

Figure 7.1 depicts the connections between CSR, SVC and polycontextual governance discussed above.

If systems consist of communication, then the societal discourse must first of all succeed in translating the negative external effects of economic transactions (human rights violations, failing to comply with social standards, lack of sustainability) into a variety of language games, which are compatible with multiple systems. The term Corporate Social Responsibility (CSR) permits this structural coupling, as it holds economic, organisational, legal and societal connotations that allow the subject matter involved to be cooperatively addressed. Events are portrayed as negative external effects because they cannot be quantified or reflected in the pricing language used by the market. Accordingly, each must be transformed into a polycontextually compatible term, which in turn shapes the course of development for the process of internalising externalities. Either awareness for corporate responsibility can be successfully generated on the market, for example, through demand from consumers with moral preferences and the readiness to pay; or the political community can introduce suitable regulations, which may be based on dialogues with interested stakeholders. For their part, firms can seek to respond by rolling out innovative products or policies with a societal welfare component. In reality, what we often see is a combination of these three internalisation strategies, which yields optimal efficiency and effectiveness. The form of internalisation and how it is communicated then determine the character of the transaction in question, which, as can be seen in Fig. 3.1 "Continuity of Exchange – Relation – Exchange" in Chap. 3, continually oscillates between two poles: discrete exchange and relational transaction.

7.4 Trans-sectoral Governance and Civil Society

The discussion on the internalisation of externalities on the part of the market or state is a standard topic in economic theory-building (cf. Buchanan & Stubblebine, 1962; Coase, 1960; Pigou, 1920). More recently, it is also referred to as *global commons* in connection with global externalities like climate change or preserving the rainforests (cf. Kaul et al., 1999). Here my goal is to contribute to polycontextual governance, achieved by firms' strategic management of normativity, which is an important component of the general theory of Relational Economics. After all, one of the most fundamental characteristics of CSR and firms' implementation of CSR is that it is based on the successful interplay of the functional logics and normativity of various areas of society: of the market, civil society and political and state organisations.

Beginning with the Public Private Partnership discussion in the 1980s, various terms have been coined for the question of polycontextural governance, depending on the respective profession or research approach: for public management, the terms *intergovernmental management*, *intersectoral management* (cf. Berry & Brower, 2005) and *cross-sector collaborations* (cf. Bryson, Crosby & Stone, 2006) have been proposed. From the institutional economics standpoint, the term *intersectoral alliances* (cf. Buttkereit, 2009) has been put forward. Development theorists speak of *intersectoral cooperation* (cf. Kalegaonkar & Brown, 2000) or *intersectoral partnering* (cf. Waddell & Brown, 1997) and management theorists discuss *strategic alliances* (cf. Austin, 2000) or *collaborative value creation* (cf. Austin & Seitanidi, 2012a, 2012b), while *cross-sector partnership* is the preferred term in the organisational sciences (cf. Selsky & Parker, 2005). In business ethics, the topic is addressed under the heading *multi-organizational cross-sector social partnerships* (cf. Clarke & Fuller, 2010). In turn, leadership theories focus on the individual skills and traits required for trans-sectoral or inter-sectoral leadership and use the term *triple-strength leadership* (cf. Lovegrove & Thomas, 2013).

The various and sundry definitions proposed for inter- and trans-sectoral governance are correspondingly diverse. Here is just a small sampling:

> Intersectoral cooperation consists of bringing actors from the state, market and civil society sectors together to achieve mutual understanding on an issue and negotiate and implement mutually agreeable plans for tackling the issue once it is identified. (Kalegaonkar & Brown, 2000, p. 2)

Cross-sector partnerships "are defined as cross-sector projects formed explicitly to address social issues and causes that actively engage the partners on an ongoing basis." (Selsky & Parker, 2005, p. 850)

> Intersectoral alliances are coalitions of two or more organizations from at least two different social sectors; they share their resources and a joint governance structure and are – at least partly – set up to produce a good or service for a third party. (Buttkereit, 2009, p. 11)

Given the fact that, in this discussion, precisely what is meant by 'intersectoral' or even 'sectoral' doesn't appear to have been fully clarified, I prefer to use the terms polycontextuality and polycontexturality. When the quotations above mention *actors*, then *projects* and then *organizations*, they refer to very different decision-making and behavioural systems. Though the distinction between market, state and civil society is generally recognised, the question as to how systematic and complete this sectoral differentiation is remains open.

At the level of a given society's systems, which in my view is the level addressed by this sectoral differentiation, one question that arises is the classification of science, law or religion. These three spheres' decision logics often play a central part in the discussion on CSR or global commons. Assigning them all to civil society is conceivable, but involves considerable difficulties.

For example, in Europe's intellectual history, civil society is seen as the counterpart to the state. Accordingly, the economy is part of civil society (cf. Richter, 2016). The distinction between economy, state and civil society is predicated upon a functional differentiation in modern societies. If, as a result, civil society essentially becomes a catch-all category (for everything that is neither state nor economy) (cf. Luhmann, 2008, Chap. 1), the term becomes so heterogeneous that it offers precious little information for specific transactions, campaigns or projects (for the critique cf. Richter, 2016). In turn, the proposal to view civil society as a specific type of societal behaviour (cf. ibid.; for the discussion also. Adloff, Birsl & Schwertmann, 2005; Sprengel, 2007) seeks to redress this heterogeneity by only focusing on the actions and campaigns of NGOs. However, if only NGOs (like environmental protection organisations or labour unions) belong to civil society, then the systems science, law and religion, together with their respective actors, cannot be classified using the schema, at least not systematically (for a fundamental critique on the concept of civil society cf. Luhmann, 1998, Chap. 4). There are also certain arguments for viewing NGOs as actors in the political or economic system, for example, when they see themselves as the opposition to government policy or as lobbies against firms in connection with specific issues. Though they would still be civil society organisations, given their basic nature, they would also temporarily be political or economic actors, a theoretical circumstance that we have previously discussed with regard to organisations in the economy.

Accordingly, for the purposes of Relational Economics, civil society is not appealing as a separate sphere or specific type of action, but as a specific coding for social transactions, as a transaction-based contextural decision logic. This shift in the basic unit of civil society events to Relational Transactions codifies their activities using the system difference 'the common good—private interests' and the organisational guiding difference 'engagement—non-engagement'. In this theoretical architecture, civil society refers to the community of free citizens who work for the common good. Independence (free citizens) and the process of self-activation (engagement) on the part of the actors are fundamental criteria for transactions oriented on the common good. The common good is embedded in the Constitutional Act of the Federal Republic of Germany as an unspecified legal term and its concrete, local meaning is defined on a case-by-case basis by courts of law. Consequently, other basic rights—like the right to private property or, more generally, to pursue private interests—may be curtailed in favour of the common good. The local concretisation of this codification takes place in and through societal discourses, standards and procedures, which include the discussion on CSR and firms' obligation to shared value creation (SVC)—which can be seen as the operationalising translation of moral or legal demands for pursuing the common good.

Adopting this view allows us to understand why firms, in their societal engagement with regard to specific transactions, can be actors in civil society, without consequently having to be classified as civil society organisations. The same is true for the previously mentioned religiously codified and voluntary-based charitable organisations, which naturally have to bear in mind the economic code used by the market (payment—non-payment) and the formula for economic success used by all organisations (earnings—costs) as relevant language games for their operations, but which do not become economic organisations in the process. Every organisation engages in economic activities, but not every organisation is an economic organisation (cf. Weber, 1921/2002 and, for a discussion of medical organisations, Bär, 2011, p. 24 ff). With regard to the discussion on civil society as a sphere of action or type of action, the change of perspective to polycontextual and polycontextural relational transactions and a specific decision-making code proposed here not only has the advantage of resolving a prolonged and to date fruitless discussion but also shifts the focus to the specific resources that civil society provides for the consummation of societal transactions. Civil society appears, fades and exists in the continuous completion of these transactions. Viewed in this light, it is no longer a hanger-on of the political system, nor is it a sector or sphere of our life-world that must be protected from economic rationalisation. Rather, it is a specific form of societal value creation that can only be productive when economic, political, moral or religious aspects of a successful life are relationalised within it. Civil society processes a productive and value-creating decision-making logic of modern societies, one that will grow in importance in the context of global value creation chains. Though we won't pursue it further at this point, this discussion warrants further clarification and empirical analysis.

7.5 Efficiency and Effectiveness of Cooperation

We'll now turn to leadership and management in connection with polycontextual transactions and their governance. As a form and process of cooperation between various actors and events, leadership's efficiency and effectiveness are predominantly based on (i) the individual and collective actors' willingness to cooperate, (ii) their ability to cooperate and (iii) their mutual expectations regarding a cooperation rent.

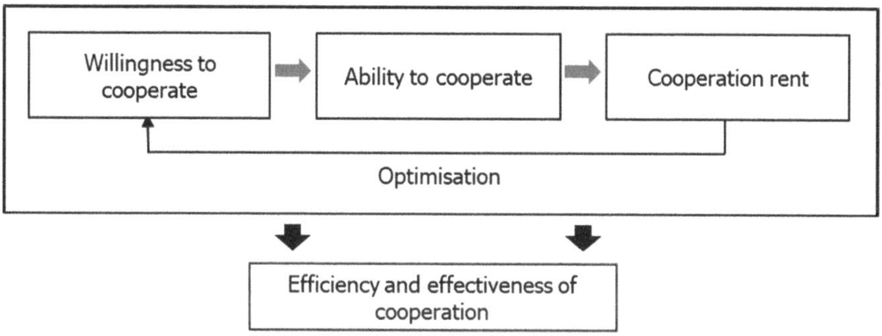

Fig. 7.2 Form and process of cooperation

I have examined this aspect in detail elsewhere (cf. Wieland, 1996, 1998 and 2014, Chaps. 3 and 7) and will return to it in the following chapter.

For the time being, the introduction of this categorical distinction is merely intended to lend structure to the previous discussion on inter-sectoral and trans-sectoral leadership and, accordingly, on management with regard to Relational Economics. The systematic connections between these three factors are reflected in Fig. 7.2.

Regarding (i) the *willingness to cooperate*: Selsky and Parker (2005, p. 853 ff) underscore the importance of the willingness and ability to jointly identify shared problems and of establishing trust, as prerequisites for inter-sectoral cooperation and as constitutive elements of a *partnership logic*. For Clarke and Fuller (2010, p. 88 ff) the acceptance and existence of a *deliberative discourse culture* are an expression of the willingness to cooperate. In turn, Austin and Seitanidi (2012a, p. 732) maintain that the existence and pursuit of mutually dependent interests are what leads to the willingness to cooperate. The prerequisite is that the actors involved possess the following qualities that can be activated:

> [S]kills like listening intensely, questioning perceptively, building trust, integrating of multiple perspectives, negotiating power and resource differences, identifying common ground, and creating shared visions. (Waddell & Brown, 1997, p. 2)

This also includes individuals' and organisations' willingness and ability to engage in cooperation and to abandon sectoralism as their mental model in favour of joint benefits (cf. Buttkereit, 2009, p. 132), communal sharing and equity matching (cf. Bridoux & Stoelhorst, 2016; for a cognitive sciences discussion of these aspects cf. the relational model theory from Fiske, 1991, 1992, 2004).

Regarding (ii) the *ability to cooperate*: Trans-sectoral management cannot run smoothly without organisational governance structures for stakeholder management and *organisational learning* (cf. Selsky & Parker, 2005, p. 850 ff). At the individual level, *leadership characteristics* (cf. Lovegrove & Thomas, 2013, p. 49 ff) like clear communication, a shared mission and values and relationship management skills (cf. Selsky & Parker, 2005, p. 855 ff) are essential. The ability to engage in *collaborative strategies* (cf. Clarke & Fuller, 2010, p. 85 f) also depends on the type and degree of complementarity and the use of inter-sectoral resources (cf. Austin & Seitanidi, 2012a, p. 729 f). Austin and Seitanidi have stressed the importance of the *fit of partnership* (cf. Austin & Seitanidi, 2012b, p. 932 ff) in all of its manifestations. From a games theory standpoint, monitoring and punishments for shirking (cf. Buttkereit, 2009, p. 95) are central elements of successful cooperation. To return to the level of individual leadership, the ability to balance competing and conflicting motives, to 'put yourself in someone else's shoes', contextual intelligence, the ability to devise a shared intellectual challenge and to form an integrative network, are indispensable aspects of the ability to cooperate (cf. Lovegrove & Thomas, 2013, p. 49 ff).

Regarding (iii) the *cooperation rent*: The cooperation rent refers to the delta above an average factor income that a given actor can achieve through the cooperative use of his/her resources, in relation to a situation in which he/she uses this factor on an individual basis, or to an alternative collaborative project. Accordingly, though the rent is the result of collective action, it must be distributed in a stakeholder-specific manner and can, as previously argued, encompass both material and intangible forms of income.

For firms, this rent from polycontextual governance can manifest in an intangible form, such as reputation, community building and recognition, or in their being seen as companies of choice; or in a tangible form, such as improved and more efficient and effective management for societal and political risks (cf. Austin & Seitanidi, 2012b, p. 964). Whereas Porter and Kramer (2011) focus on the creation of shared value (CSV), other authors stress the value of *enhanced credibility*, improved *innovativeness* and increased *brand recognition* for firms' products (cf. Austin & Seitanidi, 2012b., p. 946 f).

For NGOs, a cooperation rent in the form of increased visibility, an improved relational network, accumulation of market intelligence and opportunities for learning (cf. Austin & Seitanidi, 2012b, p. 945 f) can be achieved.

At the level of state and political organisations, in the extant literature the cooperation rent is often viewed in terms of *overcoming creative limitations*, preserving their own *capacity to act* and in frugally *managing limited resources* (cf. for example Austin, 2000, p. 13 ff).

A brief review of the literature reveals that the success factors for trans-sectoral cooperation share certain similarities with those for *relational contracting*, discussed above. If we then take these academic investigations of inter- or cross-sectoral cooperation and summarise their most important aspects for Relational Economics, we arrive at the following tentative definition: polycontextual governance is a specific form of cooperation management for individual and organisational, tangible and intangible resources and abilities. Its goal is to generate a rent from sharing resources for all stakeholders involved—in intra-firm, inter-firm or extra-firm networks—by efficiently and effectively completing multi-sectoral transactions. Its performance depends to a great extent on the polylingual and polycontextural capabilities of the actors, in the sense of their willingness and ability to accurately recognise and reconstruct the interests of all relevant stakeholders and to integrate those interests into a shared perspective.

Armed with this definition, we can now return to the problem briefly outlined at the beginning of the chapter, namely, how to approach CSR as the polycontextual governance of relational transactions.

7.6 Trans-sectorality and Stakeholder Management

Whether or not the aspects of internalising external effects and fulfilling societal responsibility through inter-sectoral networks are successful, the discussion concludes, depends on whether and to what extent, firms succeed in identifying, mobilising and integrating all of the private and societal resources and competencies required for efficient and effective transactions. This mainly involves the introduction of microstructures for a partnership-building process that is characterised by uncertainties with regard to the outcomes of the opportunities it creates (for the co-creation of innovative opportunities and capitalising on them, the driving force is also social entrepreneurship. cf. Ehrenberger, 2017).

In this regard, the governance of a given organisation's or network's stakeholder relations offers a fundamental perspective on and structure for, polycontextual management. In contrast to conventional methods for stakeholder analysis (cf. also Mitchell, Agle & Wood, 1997), from this perspective it's not simply about the question of which stakeholders are entitled to certain claims towards the organisation or network and on the basis of which interests. Rather, the operationalizing questions in trans-sectoral stakeholder management are:

(i) for what problem or project, which is to say, for what transaction (T) it is needed,
(ii) what individual or collective stakeholders are involved (identification),
(iii) on the basis of what private or societal contractual relations (prioritisation),
(iv) who contributes or could contribute what resources and competencies to the inter-sectoral network (prioritisation),
(v) what form of factor incomes and cooperation rent the respective stakeholders expect to receive (value creation) and
(vi) what share of the value generated the respective stakeholders expect to receive (allocation of the cooperation rent).

These six aspects allow us to operationalize stakeholder management as the governance of relational transactions. In order to process these aspects in a systematic and integrative manner, in the following I will develop a mechanism for analysing stakeholder governance, which involves five steps (Fig. 7.3).

(A) **Identify the transaction.**

Selsky and Parker, drawing on Waddell (2005), have rightly noted that, in the context of *cross-sector partnerships*, "organizations and interest groups are seen as stakeholders of issues, not of organizations" (Selsky & Parker, 2005, p. 852). This difference to conventional stakeholder theory is noteworthy. In the theoretical context,

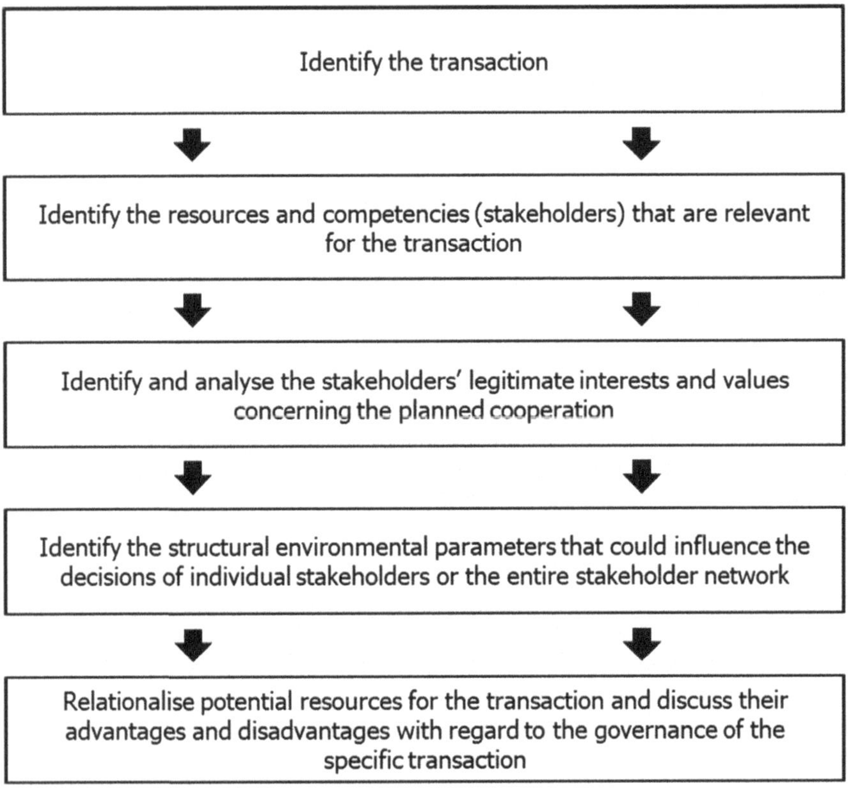

Fig. 7.3 The stakeholder governance process

I have developed in this book, the focus on concrete problems that must be solved represents the next logical step, following on the premise that firms and organisations are networks of stakeholder interests and invested stakeholder resources, the latter of which are necessary for the completion of a specifically defined transaction. This first, descriptive step in the development of a polycontextual governance mechanism is particularly important because the description of the characteristics of and challenges involved in a relational transaction shapes all subsequent steps. As such, it should be as accurate as possible and above all, describe the correct task.

(B) **Identify the resources and competencies (stakeholders) that are relevant for the transaction.**

Polycontextual management involves stakeholders from the market, the political community, civil society and other systems in society. Firms and professional associations, for example, belong to the market, while governments, administrations and parties belong to the functional system 'politics'. Civil action groups and consumer groups are examples of stakeholders from civil society, while independent experts are a typical example from the system of the sciences. Here, too, it is essential to identify and integrate those actors who possess, for example, relevant economic, political, moral or professional resources and are prepared to invest them in the network.

(C) **Identify and analyse the stakeholders' legitimate interests and values concerning the planned cooperation.**

Trans-sectoral collaboration is systematically based on a combination of identical, complementary and conflicting interests and values. Buttkereit (2009) has used tools from game theory to show that the resultant social dilemmas can be overcome and how to do so, namely by means of incentives; a hierarchy that can transform the rules of the game; "unilateral and mutual self commitment" (Ibid., p. 41); and by establishing trust. In this regard, the legitimacy of the interests depends on the type of contractual relation: private or social; and classical, neoclassical or relational contracting (cf. Wieland, 2014, p. 114). In terms of the values, it's not only about the moral component; rather, it's about combining and balancing performance values (such as user expectations or technical skills), communication values (like openness and transparency), cooperation values (like respect and commitment) and moral values (like integrity and honesty). I have discussed these relations in the context of a values management system at length elsewhere (cf. Wieland, 2005, 2014; Wieland & Heck, 2013, Chap. 10); as such, I won't discuss them in greater detail here.

(D) **Identify the structural environmental parameters that could influence the decisions of individual stakeholders or the entire stakeholder network.**

The analysis of the structural parameters of Relational Transactions (RT=I, O, SFI, SII) should employ the same methods for all problems and questions considered; only in this way can it yield mutually comparable results. Typical parameters include (i) decision-making stress (for example, due to political or media pressure), (ii) intrapersonal values conflicts (conflicting values arising from the individual actors' role-based expectations), (iii) inter-organisational values conflicts (such as ideals held by the collective actors involved, which they refuse to abandon and are non-negotiable), (iv) intercultural values conflicts (like differences in the moral doctrines of different cultures), (v) information deficits (for example, regarding the scope and consequences of an assigned task), (vi) communication deficits (resulting, for example, from the type of communication between the network partners), (vii) responsibility diffusion (for example, who is responsible for creating and solving a given problem and on what grounds) and (viii) rules deficits (resulting, for example, from the lack of private or state regulation, or from its unenforceability).

(E) **Relationalise potential resources for the transaction and discuss their advantages and disadvantages with regard to the governance of the specific transaction.**

In this regard, it should be kept in mind that, for certain problems, there are often a number of potential solutions. However, typical resources and decision logics for trans-contextural problems and solutions include economic, legal, moral and technical approaches and combinations thereof. There are technical and legal solutions for moral problems, just as there are moral solutions for economic problems. Here the key is to identify the problem-solving advantages and disadvantages of each decision logic, to discuss them and to subsequently convey them as a complete package. Therefore this fifth step also includes a problem-solving procedure, for example, by combining deliberative elements with more hierarchical ones.

In summary, we can say that steps (B) and (C) focus on identifying and prioritising the stakeholders involved and consequently, also reflect the motivational parameters within the network. In contrast, step (D) focuses on the structural parameters of Relational Transactions, while the successful interplay of individual motivation and organisational structure (in step E)) is what chiefly determines whether or not alliances thrive.

References

Adloff, F., Birsl, U., & Schwertmann, P. (Eds.). (2005). *Wirtschaft und Zivilgesellschaft*. Wiesbaden: VS Verlag für Sozialwissenschaften.

Austin, J. E. (2000). Strategic collaboration between nonprofits and businesses. *Nonprofit and Voluntary Sector Quarterly, 29*(1), 69–97.

Austin, J. E., & Seitanidi, M. M. (2012a). Collaborative value creation: a review of partnering between nonprofits and businesses: Part I: Value creation spectrum and collaboration stages. *Non-Profit and Voluntary Sector Quarterly, 41*(5), 726–758.

Austin, J. E., & Seitanidi, M. M. (2012b). Collaborative value creation: a review of partnering between nonprofits and businesses: Part II: Partnership processes and outcomes. *Non Profit and Voluntary Sector Quarterly, 41*(6), 929–968.

Barnett, M. L. (2007). Stakeholder influence capacity and the variability of financial returns to corporate social responsibility. *Academy of Management Review, 32*(3), 794–816.

Berry, F. S., & Brower, R. S. (2005). Intergovernmental and intersectoral management: Weaving networking, contracting out, and management roles into third party government. *Public Performance and Management Review, 29*(1), 7–17.

Bär, S. (2011). *Das Krankenhaus zwischen ökonomischer und medizinischer Vernunft*. Wiesbaden: VS Verlag für Sozialwissenschaften.

Bhattacharya, C. B. (2011). *Leveraging corporate responsibility: The stakeholder route to maximizing business and social value*. Cambridge, UK: Cambridge University Press.

BMAS. (2010). *Empfehlungsbericht des Nationalen CSR-Forums an die Bundesregierung*. Bonn: Bundesministerium für Arbeit und Soziales.

Bridoux, F., & Stoelhorst, J. W. (2016). Stakeholder relationships and social welfare: A behavioral theory of contributions to joint value creation. *Academy of Management Review, 41*(2), 229–251.

Bryson, J. M., Crosby, B. C., & Stone, M. M. (2006). The design and implementation of cross-sector collaborations: Propositions from the literature. *Public Administration Review, 66*(s1), 44–55.

Buchanan, J. M., & Stubblebine, W. C. (1962). Externality. *Economia, 29*(116), 371–384.

Busch, L. (2011). *Standards: Recipes for reality*. Cambridge, MA: MIT Press.

Buttkereit, S. (2009). *Intersectoral alliances: An institutional economics perspective*. Berlin: Wissenschaftlicher Verlag Berlin.

Carroll, A. B., & Shabana, K. M. (2010). The business case for corporate social responsibility: A review of concepts, research and practice. *International Journal of Management Reviews, 12*(1), 85–105.

Chesbrough, H. W., & Appleyard, M. M. (2007). Open Innovation and strategy. *California Management Review, 50*(1), 57–76.

Clarke, A., & Fuller, M. (2010). Collaborative strategic management: Strategy formulation and implementation by multi-organizational cross-sector social partnerships. *Journal of Business Ethics, 94*(1), 85–101.
Coase, R. H. (1960). The problem of social cost. *Journal of Law and Economics, 3*(1), 1–44.
Crane, A., Palazzo, G., Spence, L. J., & Matten, D. (2014). Contesting the value of «Creating Shared Value». *California Management Review, 56*(2), 130–153.
Drucker, P. F. (1992). *Managing for the future: The 1990s and beyond*. New York, NY: Truman Talley Books.
Drucker, P. F. (2006). *Classic Drucker: Essential wisdom of Peter Drucker from the pages of Harvard business review*. Cambridge, MA: Harvard Business Review Press.
Ehrenberger, M. (2017). *Corporate Social Entrepreneurship—Prozess und Form ökonomischer Organisation zur Kreation sozialunternehmerischer Opportunitäten*. Marburg: Metropolis.
Elster, J. (1997). The market and the forum: Three varieties of political theory. In J. Bohman & W. Rehg (Eds.), *Deliberative democracy: Essays on reason and politics* (pp. 3–33). Cambridge, MA: MIT Press.
Fiske, A. P. (1991). *Structures of social life: The four elementary forms of human relations: Communal sharing, authority ranking, equality matching, market pricing*. New York, NY: Free Press.
Fiske, A. P. (1992). The four elementary forms of sociality: Framework for a unified theory of social relations. *Psychological Review, 99*(4), 689–723.
Fiske, A. P. (2004). Relational models theory 2.0; In N. Haslam (Ed.), Relational models theory: A contemporary overview (pp. 3–25). Mahwah, NJ: Psychology Press.
Freeman, R. E. (1984). *Strategic management: A stakeholder approach*. Cambridge, UK: Cambridge University Press.
Freeman, R. E., Wicks, A. C., & Parmar, B. (2004). Stakeholder theory and «The Corporate Objective Revisited». *Organization Science, 15*(3), 364–369.
Freeman, R. E., Harrison, J. S., Wicks, A. C., Parmar, B. L., & de Colle, S. (2010). Stakeholder theory: The state of the art. *The Academy of Management Annals, 4*(1), 103–445.
Freeman, I., & Hasnaoui, A. (2011). The meaning of corporate social responsibility: The vision of four nations. *Journal of Business Ethics, 100*(3), 419–443.
Held, D. (1995). *Democracy and the global order. From the modern state to cosmopolitan governance*. Cambridge, UK: Polity Press.
Jhunjhunwala, S. (2014). Intertwining CSR with strategy—The way ahead. Corporate governance. *The International Journal of Business in Society, 14*(2), 211–219.
Kalegaonkar, A., & Brown, D. (2000). Intersectoral cooperation: Lessons for practice. *IDR Reports, 16*(2), 1–25.
Kaul, I., Grunberg, I., & Stern, M. A. (Eds.). (1999). *Global public goods*. Oxford, UK: Oxford University Press.
Kitzmueller, M., & Shimshack, J. (2012). Economic perspectives on corporate social responsibility. *Journal of Economic Literature, 50*(1), 51–84.
Lee, L. (2011). Business-community partnerships: Understanding the nature of partnership. *Corporate Governance: The International Journal of Business in Society, 11*(1), 29–40.
Lock, I., & Seele, P. (2016). CSR governance and departmental organization: A typology of best practices. *Corporate Governance: The International Journal of Business in Society, 16*(1), 211–230.
Lovegrove, N., & Thomas, M. (2013). Triple-strength leadership. *Harvard Business Review, 91*(9), 46–56.
Luhmann, N. (1998). Die Gesellschaft der Gesellschaft. (Vol. 2). Frankfurt a. M.: Suhrkamp.
Luhmann, N. (2008). Die Politik der Gesellschaft. Frankfurt a. M.: Suhrkamp.
Margolis, J. D., & Walsh, J. P. (2003). Misery loves companies: Rethinking social initiatives by business. *Administrative Science Quarterly, 48*(2), 268–305.
Micklethwait, J., & Wooldridge, J. (2005). *The company: A short history of a revolutionary idea*. New York, NY: Modern Library.

Mitchell, R. K., Agle, B. R., & Wood, D. J. (1997). Toward a theory of stakeholder identification and salience: Defining the principle of who and what really counts. *Academy of Management Review, 22*(4), 853–886.
Mulgan, G. (2006). The process of social innovation. *Innovations: Technology, Governance, Globalization, 1*(2), 145–162 Nussbaum, M. C. (2001). The fragility of goodness: Luck and ethics in Greek tragedy and philosophy. Cambridge, UK: Cambridge University Press.
Orlitzky, M., Schmidt, F. L., & Rynes, S. L. (2003). Corporate social and financial performance: A meta-analysis. *Organization Studies, 24*(3), 403–441.
Orlitzky, M. (2011). Institutional logics in the study of organizations: The social construction of the relationship between corporate social and financial performance. *Business Ethics Quarterly, 21*(3), 409–444.
Palazzo, G., & Scherer, A. G. (2006). Corporate legitimacy as deliberation: A communicative framework. *Journal of Business Ethics, 66*(1), 71–88.
Perrini, F., Russo, A., Tencati, A., & Vurro, C. (2011). Deconstructing the relationship between corporate social and financial performance. *Journal of Business Ethics, 102*(1), 59–76.
Pigou, A. C. (1920). *The economics of welfare*. Carmel, IN: Liberty Fund.
Porter, M. E., & Kramer, M. R. (2011). Creating shared value. *Harvard Business Review, 89*(1/2), 62–77.
Richter, S. (2016). Zivilgesellschaft—Überlegungen zu einem interdisziplinären Konzept. Docupedia-Zeitgeschichte. Potsdam: Zentrum für zeithistorische Forschung.
Sachs, S., Groth, H. & Schmitt, R. (2010). The«Stakeholder View» approach: An untapped. Opportunity to manage corporate performance and wealth. *Strategic Change, 19*(3–4), 147–162.
Scherer, A. G., & Palazzo, G. (2007). Toward a political conception of corporate responsibility: Business and society seen from a Habermasian perspective. *Academy of Management Review, 32*(4), 1096–1120.
Scherer, A. G., & Palazzo, G. (2011). The new political role of business in a globalized world—A review of a new perspective on CSR and its implications for the firm, governance, and democracy. *Journal of Management Studies, 48*(4), 899–931.
Selsky, J. W., & Parker, B. (2005). Cross-sector partnerships to address social issues: Challenges to theory and practice. *Journal of Management, 31*(6), 849–873.
Spitzeck, H., & Hansen, E. G. (2010). Stakeholder governance: How stakeholders influence corporate decision making. *Corporate Governance: The International Journal of Business in Society, 10*(4), 378–391.
Spitzeck, H., Hansen, E. G., & Grayson, D. (2011). Joint management stakeholder committees: A new path to stakeholder governance? *Corporate Governance: The International Journal of Business in Society, 11*(5), 560–568.
Spitzeck, H., & Chapman, S. (2012). Creating shared value as a differentiation strategy—The example of BASF in Brazil. *Corporate Governance: The International Journal of Business in Society, 12*(4), 499–513.
Sprengel, R. (Ed.). (2007). *Philanthropie und Zivilgesellschaft*. Frankfurt a. M.: Peter Lang.
UN Global Compact. (2015). The SDGs Explained for Business. Visited December 13, 2017. https://www.unglobalcompact.org/sdgs/about.
Waddell, S. (2005). *Societal learning and change*. Sheffield, UK: Greenleaf.
Waddell, S., & Brown, D. L. (1997). Fostering intersectoral partnering: A guide to promotion cooperation among government, business, and civil society actors. *IDR Reports, 13*(3), 1–26.
Weber, M. (1921). Wirtschaft und Gesellschaft [Reprinted: 2002]. (J. Winckelmann, Ed.). Tübingen: Mohr Siebeck.
Wieland, J. (1996). *Ökonomische Organisation, Allokation und Status*. Tübingen: Mohr Siebeck.
Wieland, J. (1998). Kooperationsökonomie. Die Ökonomie der Diversität, Abhängigkeit und Atmosphäre. In G. Wegner & J. Wieland (Eds.), Formelle und informelle Institutionen der Ökonomie. Genese und Evolution (S. 14–43). Marburg: Metropolis.
Wieland, J. (2005). Corporate governance, values management, and standards: A european perspective. *Business and Society, 44*(1), 74–93.

Wieland, J. (2014). *Governance ethics: Global value creation, economic organization and normativity* (Vol. 48). Cham: Springer.

Wieland, J. (2017). Shared value creation—Theoretical concepts, practical challenges. In J. Wieland (Ed.), *Creating shared value—Concepts, experience, criticism* (pp. 9–26). Berlin: Springer.

Wieland, J. (2018). CSR—Shared value creation through Intersectoral Governance. In L. Sacconi & G. Degli Antoni (Eds.), Handbook on the economics of social responsibility: Individuals, corporations and institutions. Cheltenham, UK: Edward Elgar Publishing.

Wieland, J., & Heck, A. E. (2013). *Shared value durch stakeholder governance*. Marburg: Metropolis.

Wieland J., & Fischer, D. (2020 in press). Transaction cost theory and business legitimacy. In J. Rendtorff (Ed.), Handbook of business legitimacy. Springer, Cham.

Chapter 8
Leadership and Transculturalism

8.1 Leadership and Value Creation

Marx used the cooperative character of the production process to identify the task of a firm's leaders, which he defined in economic-deterministic terms: "As a specific function of capital, the leadership function has specific characteristics" [own translation] (MEW 23, p. 350), namely to maximise capital profit, to professionalise coordination and supervision and to supplement the owner of capital with "senior and junior officers", "who are in command during the labour process, on behalf of the capital" [own translation] (Ibid., p. 351). For Marx, the focus is on exercising authority and monitoring rights, achieved through hierarchy and reporting lines. Later the distinction between *ownership and control* would manifest in the principal-agent theory, which seamlessly is in line with Marx' earlier thoughts.

The similarities between the principal-agent theory, Marx's views on leadership and a transactional leadership concept are both readily apparent and remarkable because in the 1930s Berle and Means had already recognised the need for a new perspective on leadership with regard to de-personalised capitalistic societies. The nature of these societies, the two authors claim, is "participation accruing to each share" (1932/2009, p. 142) and is accordingly expected by the employees in this form: "Their demand will be for participation" (Ibid., p. xxxix). Some years later, this insight would form the basis of the transformational leadership concept.

From here, it's not much of an intellectual leap to a more relational take on leadership as a social process (for the distinction between transactional, transformational and relational leadership cf. Wieland, 2017)—namely, a process of value creation, as Barnard (1938) also astutely recognised in the 1930s:

> Leadership does not annul the laws of nature, nor is it a substitute for the elements essential to cooperative effort; but it is the indispensable social essence that gives common meaning to common purpose, that creates the incentive that makes other incentives effective, that infuses the subjective aspect of countless decisions with consistency in a changing environment, that inspires the personal conviction that produces the vital cohesiveness without which cooperation is impossible. (Ibid., p. 283)

J. Wieland, *Relational Economics*, Relational Economics and Organization Governance,
https://doi.org/10.1007/978-3-030-45112-7_8

In this regard, Barnard defines the three building blocks of the social exchange process, which determine the quality of the relation between the actors and accordingly also the effectiveness and direction of action of leadership. These are (i) the creation of shared relations of perception and meaning, (ii) the activation of incentives that are not effective on their own, but only in conjunction with leadership behaviour and (iii) the coherency of decisions in a volatile setting, which can be clearly recognised by all parties involved. Taken together, they create the shared motivation and conviction required for successful cooperation.

8.2 Relational Leadership and Social Exchange

The efficiency and effectiveness of stakeholder governance largely depend on the leadership of a given firm at all levels and on the abilities of its top-tier managers.

As previously mentioned, the management of multi-sectoral transactions in general and of those transactions intended to make firms assume societal responsibility in particular largely focuses on achieving a successful interplay of individual motivation and organisational structure. Motivation stems from the values, integrity and character traits of those persons involved in the transactions, while structure refers to the institutional and organisational mechanisms whose adaptive efficiency and effectiveness promote the stability and continued existence of the cooperative network. In this regard, motivation and structure are not isolated entities; rather, they are mutually referential—a form of recursive coupling in which each of the two 'poles' can become an expression of its counterpart. Philip Selznick (1957) described and analysed this relation as the institutionalisation of the form 'organisation' and its functions:

> In what is perhaps its most significant meaning, 'to institutionalize' is to *infuse with value* beyond the technical requirements of the task at hand. (Ibid., p. 17)

In this context, then, leadership is a decisive quality and here we're not talking about leading a given organisation in the technical sense, but in a transformed manner, tailored to the governance of relational transactions: as Relational Leadership (cf. Uhl-Bien & Ospina, 2012; Uhl-Bien, 2006; Wieland, 2017). The term Relational Leadership also encompasses research programmes that approach leadership as a social relation in their analyses, for example, Complexity Leadership (cf. Uhl-Bien & Arena, 2017), Responsible Leadership (cf. Maak, 2007) and Ethical Leadership (Brown, Treviño & Harrison, 2005). Relational Economics approaches leadership as an event in the process of private and societal value creation or, as Drucker has concisely stated it: "Leadership does matter, of course [...] its essence is performance" (Drucker, 1992, p. 119).

Relational Leadership should not be construed as a trait of, or the charisma of, a given leader; rather, it is the result of a social exchange process between the leaders and the led in an organisational and institutional setting. Accordingly, it can and must seek to influence both motivation and structures in such a way that the services everyone is pursuing can be delivered. Leadership is the result of a "process of organizational design and change" (Uhl-Bien, 2006, p. 661), which embeds motivational skills in dynamic and adaptive structures; in the research community, this is referred to using the term Complexity Leadership (cf. Lichtenstein et al., 2006; Marion & Uhl-Bien, 2001). Here, *leaders* are less important than *leadership*:

> [...] the key difference between relational and entity perspectives is that relational perspectives identify the basic unit of analysis in leadership research as *relationships*, not individuals. (Uhl-Bien, 2006, p. 662)

When the relation of events is the basic unit of analysis, then the social distinction between the leaders and the led, not to mention the organisational distinction between managers and subordinates, is particular and temporary at best. Depending on the specifics of a given transaction, everyone involved can assume any position (cf. Seers & Chopin, 2012, p. 60).

This represents a major contrast to the principal-agent theory, according to which leadership is based on a relationship of power and on a formal contract delineating the exchange of performance and remuneration, together with an accompanying status and authority to give directives (cf. for example Bolton & Dewatripont, 2013, p. 352). This is the paradigm of Exchange Transactions in its purest form. In a world of relational contracts and transactions, of intra-firm, inter-firm and societal networks, not only is this type of leadership no longer feasible; pursuing it would entail prohibitively high transaction costs. Here, leadership is based on the readiness of the led to cooperate of their own free will and the leaders become, for example, arbiters (for conflict resolutions, sanctions), experts (with superior knowledge) and coordinators (who identify and maintain team equilibrium) (cf. Hermalin, 2013, p. 437f.). In this way, leaders can exert an accepted form of influence on the nature of individual and organisational cooperative relations, especially by communicating shared knowledge and purpose. This helps leaders to promote relational identities (cf. Seers & Chopin, 2012, p. 47) in connection with specific transactions (ibid., p. 60) and their forms and to replace a static and societal view of identity with one that is temporalised, flexible and role-based. To the extent, then, that leadership is a dynamic and continuous process of social negotiation focused on the organised consummation of transactions, in the course of said consummation leadership is either voluntarily accepted by those being led, or isn't (ibid., p. 71). "The leader/follower labels are continually recreated during each relational interaction" (Seers & Chopin, 2012, p. 67).

Accordingly, here, too, a specific process environment and corresponding governance structure produce specific requirements concerning their relationalisation. Generally speaking, we can say that organisations characterised by line hierarchies require transactional leadership, while matrix organisations cannot be managed without transformational leadership. Just as relational transactions and governance do not lead to the dissolution of exchange relations on the market or to vertical integration, neither does relational leadership fundamentally signal the end of transactional or transformational models for leading organisations (for a summary of the difference between transactional and transformational leadership cf. Bass, 1990). In essence, what we're talking about is the suitable relationalisation of leadership concepts with regard to the respective transaction. Orienting the leadership theory on the specific features of an individual transaction and on the dynamic process of relationalising events allows the leadership process to be integrated into Relational Economics. In this theoretical design, leadership is a triad consisting of:

(i) an individual and organisational resource for private and societal value creation, which has a substantial effect on the productivity of all material and intangible assets that are invested and cannot be fully controlled by authority,
(ii) a transaction-specific and organisation-specific asset that, by defining goals and by coordinating and initiating learning processes in cooperative projects, serves to mitigate uncertainty and contingency. In this regard, the purpose of establishing a cooperative goal is to ensure the continuity of value creation by introducing adaptive governance structures,
(iii) a governance structure that seeks to achieve a dynamic balance of resources, one that has a major influence on the transaction costs involved in cooperation.

In a nutshell, leadership aims at the creation, activation and combination of intra- and inter-organizational resources. Each of these three leadership aspects produces its own forms of earnings and costs—which we'll take a closer look at in Part IV of this book (cf. Wieland, 2017, p. 241)—, both of which depend in no small part on the skills of the leader; in other words, on the extent to which he or she succeeds in relationalising and, if need be, hierarchically organising the available classification and decision logics—system, organisation, person—for a given transaction. Lovegrove and Thomas (2013) claim that "'tri-sector-leaders' – people who can bridge the chasms of culture, incentive and purpose [...] are best suited to solve the problems of this scale" (Ibid., p. 49) is certainly correct. However, it should be supplemented with the observation that, in communicative terms, trans-sectoral governance has various reference systems at its disposal and their respective relevance for a given economic or societal transaction must be understood and relationalised. As such, polylingualism proves to be the art of (i) recognising the behavioural reasoning and language games used by the other participants in terms of their own logic, (ii) forming your own position on the basis of that insight and then (iii) reformulating that position as the partnership logic (Selsky & Parker, 2005, p. 853) for all cooperation partners.

8.3 Transactional, Transformational and Relational Leadership

We can clearly distinguish between the concepts of transactional, transformational and relational leadership using the distinctions shown in the following matrix: distinctions that are of an analytical nature and serve to visualise the main differences, but which are no means 'either-or' categories; further, they do not represent a progressive model and should be understood as complementary elements. In practice and depending on the type of transaction, all three leadership concepts are selectively or simultaneously used. Accordingly, the differences shown here should be understood as additions to the respective leadership concept (see Fig. 8.1).

With regard to the leadership process, transactional and transformational leadership are tailored to intra-firm relations, whereas the relational perspective focuses more on social exchange processes in networks of all kinds. Accordingly, these approaches produce differing functions. The coordination and monitoring of processes and making necessary decisions are supplemented by motivation, creating purpose and building trust.

In the relational concept, the focus is also on establishing resource equilibrium, initiating learning processes and ensuring the continuity of cooperation. The economic goals of individual or organisational performance, team success and shared value run parallel to the social goals of subordination, trust and inclusion by creating a shared purpose. At the level of the actors, transactional leadership is based on the

Leadership Process	Transactional	Transformational	Relational
Organisation	Firm	Firm	Network
Functions	Coordination Monitoring Decision-making	Motivation Creating purpose Trust	Resource equilibrium Learning processes Continuity
Economic goals	Performance	Team Success	Shared value
Social goals	Subordination	Trust	Inclusion
Actors	Principal/agent	Manager/employee	Stakeholder
Decision logic	Directives Monitoring Incentives	Goal orientation Participation	Dialogue 'swarm'
Legitimation	Ownership of capital	Financial capital Ownership of capital	Social capital Knowledge
Power	Position Status Hierarchy	Acceptance Team skills	Voluntariness Ability to cooperate De-centrality
Contract	Classical Principal/agent	Neoclassical Team	Relational Stewardship
Culture	Leader: Traits	Leadership: Corporate culture Identity Homogeneity	Character Skills Transculturalism
Coding	Monolingual: Economic	Bilingual: Economic/ethical	Polylingual: Multivalent

Fig. 8.1 Leadership concepts: transactional, transformational and relational

principal-agent model, whereas transformational processes are concerned with the relations between managers and their participating employees. Relational leadership calls for the identification and prioritisation of stakeholder processes, as well as their management.

The concepts also differ in terms of their decision logics: providing incentives to deliver better performance against the backdrop of authority and monitoring rights is complemented by target agreements, dialogues and the effects of decentralised swarm intelligence. What is more, the basis of legitimation for the leadership could hardly be more different. Whereas here, capital, financial capital and human capital are the answer, in the relational process, social capital and knowledge play a pivotal role in connection with the question: Who does the leading and why? Accordingly, decision-making power emanates from a hierarchical position, from team skills, or from the ability and willingness to fairly pursue the interests of all stakeholders, which is to say, from stewardship. These aspects are in turn based on classical, neo-classical, or relational contracts, which both require and produce suitable leadership cultures. While, in the conventional case, the emphasis is on leadership skills, in the transformational concept what matters most is leaders' ability to create a homogenous corporate culture characterised by shared values and ethical principles and which offers employees a vision and source of identification: integrity and transcultural skills are key to relational leadership. And lastly, so as not to neglect the aspect of communicative coding, transactional leadership limits its focus to economic and legal language games, whereas transformational leadership adds social and ethical communication to the mix and relational leadership requires polylingualism.

8.4 Cross-Cultural and Transcultural Management

As previously mentioned, the efficiency and effectiveness of relational transactions and the corresponding requirements concerning the behaviour of individual and collective actors, are constitutively bound to (the adherence to and effects of) societal norms, which Macneil has proposed be referred to as supracontract norms (cf. Macneil, 1978, p. 898). In this way, societal expectations with regard to ethical principles and values like justice, freedom, dignity and equality become endogenous events in a relational transaction and thus also in its analysis. Williamson (1975, p. 37 ff., 1993, p. 480) has exogenously classified these events, albeit in a somewhat offhand remark, as belonging to the atmosphere of a given transaction, which, as the *economics of atmosphere*, can influence the transaction costs due to situational and behavioural uncertainty, but which remain systematically outside the focus of transaction cost theory (cf. Wieland, 1996).

Relational Economics generalises norms as cultural events, which couple with transactions, changing the latter's character and process dynamics and which are, as societal informal institutions (SII), also serve as a parameter in the governance form for relational transactions: RT = f (I, O, SII, SFI). This also changes the perspective on how cultural factors affect the economy. Their influence at the level of transaction costs is on the one hand limited to specific transactions because established cultural differences have a massive influence on the selection of suitable cooperation partners (searching and information costs), bargaining and decision-making costs in global interactions and the monitoring and enforcement of contracts (cf. Wernerfelt, 2016). On the other hand and here we can recognise a distinction between the transaction-costs and adaption-costs perspectives, culture is an informal institution tasked with enabling and completing the economic value creation process for cooperative interactions themselves. The emergence of global value creation chains and stakeholder networks, as well as their stability and productivity, are causally dependent on the success of transcultural transactions, which, in our context, means how they are led and managed (cf. Wieland, 2016). In this regard, the differences to intercultural and diversity management (cf. Hofstede, 1991; Trompenaars & Hampden-Turner, 2012) are of paradigmatic importance. Intercultural management is assuming a growing importance in the world of International Trade, characterised by cross-border exchange transactions, whereas transcultural management stems from the relational transactions taking place in global value creation networks. Consequently, for Intercultural and Diversity Management the point of departure lies in the comparison of national cultures, which are assumed to be closed and homogeneous and which, the theory claims, co-determine the respective actors' identities when they interact. From this perspective, the national-cultural differences and the frictions they are expected to produce at the individual behavioural level are the main focus. As such, the task of the leadership and the management consists in familiarising themselves with these differences and their effects on day-to-day business and in seeking practical means of achieving their 'reconciliation' (cf. Trompenaars & Hampden-Turner, 2012). These two key assumptions of Intercultural and Diversity Management—regarding the homogeneity of national cultures and their direct manifestation at the level of individual identity and individual behaviour—have been the subject of critical discussion for some time now (for a summarising discussion from the standpoint of management theory cf. McSweeney, 2015). The point of reference for transcultural management is no longer the identities of national actors, but instead the completion of multicontextual transactions, regardless of whether they are global, national or regional. In a certain sense, the transcultural perspective shifts the classification of difference from the level of the actors' identities to the temporary event-specificity of transactions. In this regard, the actors' different identities are themselves nothing more than events, which, for the purposes of a transaction, have to be relationalised, but do not have to be overcome. In other words, the focus is on suitably proportioning different cultures and viewing them in relation to one another. Moreover, the goal is not to arrive at a compromise that reconciles their differences but to create a new cultural situation of rapprochement in connection with a specific, local transaction.

Hence, the concept of national cultures as closed containers is abandoned in favour of a plurality of cultural actors—individuals, professionals, organisations, regions, nations, global institutions and organisations: the latter are only somewhat open to change, which they themselves achieve through the joint consummation of economic transactions and the learning processes that accompany them. In practical terms, this has less to do with reconciling differences and far more to do with creatively defining new normative similarities and new cooperative communities of practice (CoP) that are chiefly the result of a given transaction's success or failure from a practical standpoint.[1] Whereas global Intercultural and Diversity Management paradigmatically views cooperation as a problem and hindrance, Transcultural Management sees it as a positive opportunity for creating productive communities of practice, which can lead to collaborative value creation and which is also, as a relation of cooperating actors, a source of mutual happiness. In this regard, Nussbaum's (1986/2001) observation that "all human activities [...] are in some way relational" (ibid., p. 343) is an important one. More important, however, is her insight, gained by revisiting ancient Greek thought, that human interactions are not only good because of the respective objective, but also in their own right. This double relation between the actor, to himself or herself and to others or to a cause, is also economically important, because it affects performance: "the mutuality and pleasure of the personal relationship enter deeply into the work itself" (Ibid., p. 363). Without adopting this stance, stakeholder management, leadership and transculturalism are unattainable. And it's precisely here that the modern economy, which only recognises those things as being good that help produce a certain benefit—in Greek thought, the most primitive form of human behaviour, since it can also be found in the animal kingdom—reveals its limitations.

Relational Economics not only concerns itself with the effects of moral values and principles on specific transactions but also with the interaction and the integrative management of performance values, communication values, cooperation values and moral values in this context (cf. Wieland, 2011). This differentiation stems on the one hand from the Aristotelian distinction between ethical and non-ethical virtues, in other words, between justice, honesty and integrity on the one hand and prudence, success, usefulness and competition on the other (cf. the article on virtue in Blackburn, 2005). However, it also stems from the proportionalisation of polyvalent logics, the result of their relationalisation during the completion of transactions.

Accordingly, transcultural management is a continuous learning process geared toward the production of cultural similarities, complementarities and communities, which form organisation-specific and network-specific global common goods (cf. Wieland, 2016). With regard to the governance of global value creation networks, the ability to productively deal with polycontextuality and polylingualism is both a key task and an outcome.

8.5 Diversity and Cultural Learning

Therefore, transcultural management is not so much interested in dealing with cultural differences or ostensibly shared values per se, but instead in establishing accepted relations between specific cultural events (values, principles, traditions,

[1] For the literature of CoP see Wieland (2020 in press) and Wenger et al. (2002).

political and religious convictions and so on) for a local transaction; through relationalisation, said events become new cultural events, each of which can either establish itself as a form or cease to exist once the transaction is complete. The methodological basis for this process is the previously mentioned assumption of certain pro-social abilities, social actors' willingness and ability to practise empathy and inclusive rationalism. The goal here is not to create a new, say, cosmopolitan or global values culture, but to create (bearing in mind Whitehead) a new transaction society, a community of cultural events that are relationalised in the course of a learning process, one that ensures the stability and productivity of a given transaction. This can lead to the establishment of new forms and generalised normativity, but mustn't necessarily do so.

To understand this process a bit better, it is important to bear the following main aspects in mind.

Transcultural leadership and transcultural management do not chiefly assess cultural differences between nations. They are a matter of fact and therefore the starting point of the analysis. Rather, they seek to identify the interplay of cultural forms and processes at various levels, through which the consummation of a transaction is influenced. Further, they do not assume any homogeneity among cultural actors, but instead, assume that cultural events can be particularly effective and that cultural difference's direction of action is not predetermined. The following figure helps to illustrate the following discussion on the three aspects of transcultural process logic (Fig. 8.2).

A given economic transaction is influenced by cultural actors at a variety of levels. These can include national cultures, organisational cultures, the cultures of specific professions (such as engineers, managers, bankers and doctors) and the culturally shaped convictions held by individuals. In economic practice, there is no culture in and of itself, but only in connection with actors and concretised in institutional forms. The transaction is not influenced by the cultural actors per se, or by the totality of culture. None of these actors are culturally homogenous containers; rather, they consist of cultural events. Nations have several differing regional cultures and the differences between the urban and rural settings are also important. Firms as organisations have sectoral, divisional and departmental cultures and the same holds true for professions. And last but not least, there are the culturally shaped convictions held by individuals, which are virtually unparalleled in their diversity.

Here it becomes evident that the basic idea of intercultural or cross-cultural management—namely, that we can draw on a presumably homogenous national culture in order to predict the behaviour of concrete, individual actors—isn't particularly convincing and in practice, is in fact absurd. Instead, only specific elements of a cultural actor (a, b, c … n) are relevant for a specific transaction. Consequently, when considering the risk of corruption in an economic transaction, the trait 'Chinese culture' is not terribly helpful. Even if we focus the term to Confucianism, it is anything but self-explanatory, since the philosophy's hierarchy-based orientation could be seen as being conducive to corruption, though its emphasis on the integrity of individual behaviour points in precisely the opposite direction. As such, attempting to explain the supposedly 'typically Chinese' affinity for corruption using the

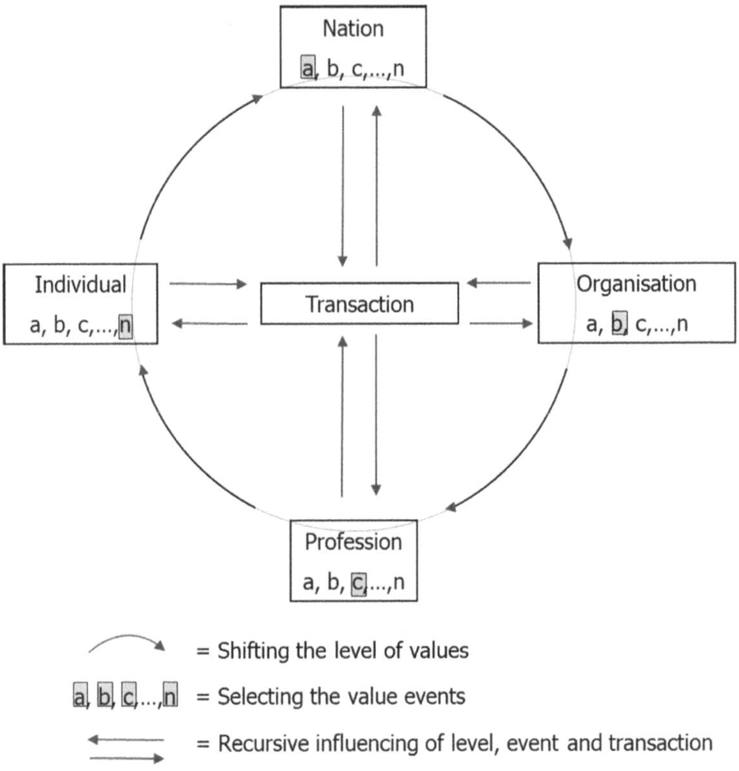

Fig. 8.2 Transcultural process logic

culture's ties to Confucianism proves to be highly problematic (for more on this ultimately unresolvable discussion cf. Wang, 2014). And it is even more questionable what role, if any, these two factors play in the behaviour of a given organisation or individual.

In contrast, the theoretical approach proposed here helps to demonstrate that certain cultural events can have a negative or positive effect on a given transaction. Further, by changing the level of actors or values, it is possible to change the direction of action for culture-based moral concepts. Firms that stress integrity instead of hierarchy will have other and possibly better, options on the Chinese market. Shaping options as a social exchange process is precisely what transcultural leadership is all about. Therefore, acknowledging cultural differences is viewed as a potentially useful point of departure for our considerations, not as a prohibitive problem. It can just as easily be the solution to the problem if local effects are taken into consideration. Here the goal is to relationalise difference in a process of rapprochement, which can produce local or continuous forms. In this regard, the transcultural perspective is a productive element and makes productivity possible, because it expands the pool of shared moral interpretations of economic transactions and with it, the number of opportunities for mutually advantageous global cooperation.

8.6 Leadership in Exchange and Relational Transactions

In closing this chapter, we can draw some fairly fundamental conclusions regarding the role of leadership from a Relational Economics standpoint.

First of all, we should bear in mind that every form of leadership is a relation but not relational. No matter how it is conceptually understood or which notions regarding the appropriate leadership style it may entail, every type of leading involves a relation: between leadership and followership. Consequently, the difference between the countless theoretical proposals on the meaning of leadership and resultant effective leadership styles is not due to their systematical character as a relation, but to the types of transaction, they are intended to promote, which is to say, whether the focus is on exchange transactions or relational transactions. It has to do with the interaction of events (e.g., social norms) that dock with these transactions and are caused by them. In terms of a general definition, we can say the following: the focus of leadership is on the effective and efficient preparation, execution and monitoring of social transactions for the alternating or mutual benefit of the actors involved. In Fig. 8.3, I summarise the main distinctive aspects of exchange and relational transactions and their impact on the nature and function of leadership.

Form of Transaction	Exchange Transaction	Relational Transaction
Base of Transaction	Classical or Neo-classical Contract	Relational Contract
Normative Foundation	Performance	Social Norms
Roles of Actors	Principal/Agent Supervisor/Subordinate	Stakeholder Management Partnership Logic
Governance	Hierarchy	Network
Base of Followership	Demanded	Voluntarily
Decision Making & Implementation	Power Law Direction	Discourse Motivation Conviction
Motivation	Income Performance Equilibrium	Multivalent Values Joint Value Creation Recognition Role/Identity
Leadership Theories	Transactional Leadership	Transformational-, Transcultural-, Ethical-, Collaborative-, Servant-, Authentic-, Complexity Leadership

Fig. 8.3 Leadership in exchange and relational transactions

When we leave behind the level of general definitions and consider a few examples of the numerous competing approaches—such as transactional, transformational, transcultural and ethical leadership, as well as collaborative, servant, authentic and complexity leadership—a number of differences, which are highly relevant through the lens of Relational Economics, become apparent. They are systematically presented in Fig. 8.3.

Leadership as exchange transactions is based on a classic or neoclassic contract that defines the actors' roles and performance. A given actor is either a principal or agent, either a supervisor or subordinate. There is a hierarchy voluntarily accepted by all parties *ex-ante*, which means, in practical terms, that every follower is contractually obligated to comply with the instructions given by their supervisor. Accordingly, decisions are based on the power and right to issue instructions and on the obligation to carry them out. The motivation for adhering to this type of contract is a specific balance between the agreed-upon services that must be rendered on the one hand and the corresponding financial compensation on the other. Transactional leadership theory is the pinnacle of this view of leadership.

Relational transactions are based on relational contracts, which we have already discussed extensively. They refer, no matter whether within a firm or a network of organisations, to social norms and a partnership logic and the attendant need to manage stakeholder relations. In these networks, leadership cannot be contractually enforced; rather, it relies on the parties' voluntary acceptance. The leader's right to lead corresponds to the follower's freedom to follow. Decisions tend to be made more on the basis of discourse, shared motivations or convictions, though these motivations are not exclusively pecuniary. Far more important is the desire to collaboratively create value, as well as the recognition and acceptance that various values, which produce role identities and a sense of belonging, are important for the network. Whereas transformational leadership recognises that employment contracts are not spot contracts, but instead have a long-term orientation on identity and forming a moral bond, transcultural leadership, as we have seen, is based on the interactions in multivalent global value creation networks. In contrast, ethical leadership theories focus on the central and binding role of ethical leadership principles. What these theories share with collaborative, servant, authentic and complexity leadership is an interest in the fundamental role of values, trust and legitimacy—in short, the normative qualities of relational interactions.

In Fig. 8.4, this discussion has been applied to the previously introduced continuity axis between exchange transactions and relational transactions. If we apply the specification of performance and its monetary evaluation, power and monitoring resources to the y-axis; and apply the relative importance of social norms and shared values and degree to which reciprocity and role identities are accepted to the x-axis, it produces the following schema:

Transactional and ethical leadership, at points a_1 and a_4 respectively, are pure ideal forms; though their importance in leadership practice is indisputable, they only rarely and temporarily manifest in this ideal form. Transformational leadership (a_2) underscores opportunities for participation and seeks to promote identification, especially through shared values. The fact that what this involves, in reality, is the

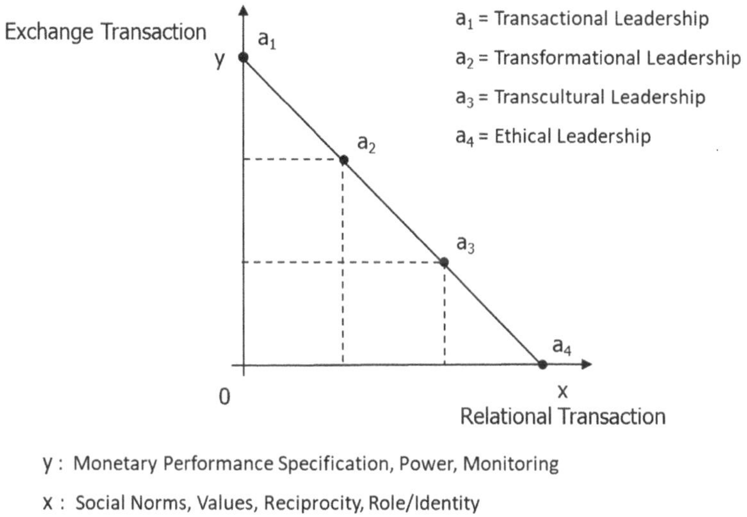

Fig. 8.4 Leadership axis of continuity

values culture defined by the firm is one of the more critical aspects of this theory and is due to its focus, which is limited to the supervisor/subordinate relation. And the last form discussed in this chapter is transcultural leadership, which is a product of the relational economy.

References

Barnard, C. I. (1938). *The functions of the executive*. Cambridge, MA: Harvard University Press.

Bass, B. M. (1990). From transactional to transformational leadership: Learning to share the vision. *Organizational Dynamics, 18*(3), 19–31.

Berle, A. A., & Means, G. (2009). *The modern corporation and private property [Reprint: 1962]*. New Jersey: Transaction Publishers.

Blackburn, S. (2005). *The oxford dictionary of philosophy*. Oxford, UK: Oxford University Press.

Bolton, P., & Dewatripont, M. (2013). Authority in organizations. In R. Gibbons & J. Roberts (Eds.), *Handbook of organizational economics* (pp. 342–372). Princeton, NJ: Princeton University Press.

Brown, M. E., Treviño, L. K., & Harrison, D. A. (2005). Ethical leadership: A social learning perspective for construct development and testing. *Organizational Behavior and Human Decision Processes, 97*(2), 117–134.

Drucker, P. F. (1992). *Managing for the future: The 1990's and beyond*. New York, NY: Truman Talley Books.

Hermalin, B. E. (2013). Leadership and corporate culture. In R. Gibbons & J. Roberts (Eds.), *Handbook of organization economics* (pp. 432–478). Princeton, NJ: Princeton University Press.

Hofstede, G. (1991). *Cultures and organizations: Software of the mind* (2nd ed.). London: McGraw-Hill/Irwin.

Lichtenstein, B. B., Uhl-Bien, M., Marion, R., Seers, A., Orton, J. D. & Schreiber, C. (2006). Complexity leadership theory: An interactive perspective on leading in complex adaptive systems. *Emergence: Complexity and Organization, 8*(4), 2–12.

Lovegrove, N., & Thomas, M. (2013). Triple-strength leadership. *Harvard Business Review, 91*(9), 46–56.

Maak, T. (2007). Responsible leadership, stakeholder engagement, and the emergence of social capital. *Journal of Business Ethics, 74*(4), 329–343.

Macneil, I. R. (1978). Contracts adjustment of long-term economic relations under classical, neoclassical, and relational contract law. *Northwestern University Law Review, 72,* 854–905.

Marion, R., & Uhl-Bien, M. (2001). Leadership in complex organizations. *Leadership Quarterly, 12*(4), 389–418.

Marx, K. (1890). *Das Kapital, Bd. I* [MEW23; 1972]. Berlin: Dietz Verlag.

McSweeney, B. (2015). Hall, hofstede, huntington, trompenaars, GLOBE: Common foundations, common flaws. In Y. Sanchez & C. F. Bruhwiler (Eds.), *Transculturalism and business in the BRIC states: A handbook* (pp. 13–58). Farnham, UK: Gower.

Nussbaum, M. C. (2001). *The fragility of goodness: Luck and ethics in Greek tragedy and philosophy*. Cambridge, UK: Cambridge University Press.

Seers, A., & Chopin, S. (2012). The Social production of leadership. In M. Uhl-Bien & S. Ospina (Eds.), *Advancing relational leadership research: A dialogue among perspectives* (pp. 43–82). Charlotte: IAP.

Selsky, J. W., & Parker, B. (2005). Cross-sector partnerships to address social issues: Challenges to theory and practice. *Journal of Management, 31*(6), 849–873.

Selznick, P. (1957). *Leadership in administration: A sociological interpretation*. Evanston, IL: Harper & Row.

Trompenaars, F., & Hampden-Turner, C. (2012). *Riding the waves of culture: Understanding diversity in global business*. London: Nicholas Brealey Publishing.

Uhl-Bien, M. (2006). Relational leadership theory: Exploring the social processes of leadership and organizing. *Leadership Quarterly, 17*(6), 654–676.

Uhl-Bien, M., & Ospina, S. (2012). *Advancing relational leadership research: A dialogue among perspectives*. Charlotte, NC: IAP.

Uhl-Bien, M., & Arena, M. (2017). Complexity leadership: Enabling people and organizations for adaptability. *Organizational Dynamics, 46*(1), 9–20.

Wang, T. (2014). Is confucianism a source of corruption in chinese society? A new round of Debate in Mainland China. *Dao, 13*(1), 111–121.

Wenger, E., McDermott, R., & Snyder, W. M. (2002). *Cultivating communities of practice*. Boston, MA: Harvard Business School Press.

Wernerfelt, B. (2016). *Adaptation, specialization, and the theory of the firm: Foundations of the resource-based view*. Cambridge, UK: Cambridge University Press.

Wieland, J. (1996). *Ökonomische organisation, allokation und status*. Tübingen: Mohr Siebeck.

Wieland, J. (2011). Wertemanagement. In M. S. Aßländer (Ed.), *Handbuch Wirtschaftsethik* (pp. 245–252). Stuttgart: Metzler-Verlag.

Wieland, J. (2016). Transculturality and economic governance. In J. Wieland & K. M. Leisinger (Eds.), *Transculturality—Leadership, management and governance* (pp. 12–32). Marburg: Metropolis.

Wieland, J. (2017). Relationale Führung und Intersektorale Governance. In M. Lehmann & M. Tyrell (Eds.), *Komplexe Freiheit: Wie ist Demokratie möglich?* (pp. 237–258). Wiesbaden: Springer.

Williamson, O. E. (1975). *Markets and hierarchies, analysis and antitrust implications*. New York, NY: The Free Press.

Williamson, O. E. (1993). Calculativeness, trust, and economic organization. *Journal of Law and Economics, 36*(1, Part 2), 453–486.

Wieland, J. (2020, in press). Transculturalism and innovation in global business networks. A relational approach. In J. Wieland & J. Baumann Montecinos (Eds.), Brazilian perspectives on transcultural leadership. Marburg: Metropolis.

Part IV
Cooperation Rent and Societal Value Creation

Chapter 9
Organisational Cooperation and Rent

9.1 Economic Rents and Property Rights

The fact that Relational Economics concerns itself with the earnings and costs of private and public value creation stemming from the cooperation of individual and collective actors and their resources is one that we have previously discussed a number of times and from various perspectives. With regard to the earnings, a distinction should be made between factor incomes and incomes from the cooperation rent. Simply put, the cooperation rent is the share of an organisation's or firm's value creation produced by the relationalisation of the tangible and intangible resources invested by the stakeholders. Before addressing this aspect in detail, I would like to first clarify the term 'rent', which has a long tradition in economic theory.

In classical economics, especially David Ricardo addressed the distinction between and relations between price, profit and rent. In the context of industrialisation and the emergence of the capitalistic market system, his focus was on the rent that a tenant has to pay to a landowner. In an attempt to explain the nature of the rent and the laws that determine whether it increases or decreases, Ricardo supplied the following definition:

> Rent is that portion of the produce of earth, which is paid to the landlord for the use of the original and indestructible powers of the soil. (Ricardo, 1819/2004, p. 67)

With regard to this definition, first of all, the distinction between property rights and usage rights is relevant. On the one hand, the rent is a form of compensation for the capital (land) supplied by the landowner; on the other, it is a payment on the part of the tenant for the right to use the land. However, whether or not a rent is due and if so, in which amount, do not depend on the property rights or on the usage rights, but on the productivity of the respective piece of land in its natural state in comparison to the next-best piece of land. In the case of two pieces of land with differing natural productivities, the first-class piece of land produces a rent, the amount of which depends exclusively on the initial quality of the two pieces of land, without any need for further assessment.

J. Wieland, *Relational Economics*, Relational Economics and Organization Governance,
https://doi.org/10.1007/978-3-030-45112-7_9

> Whenever I speak of the rent of land, I wish to be understood as speaking of that compensation, which is paid to the owner of land for the use of its original and indestructible powers. (ibid., p. 68 f.)

The rent stems neither from the investments made or work done by the tenant, nor from the property rights of the landowner, but from the soil's natural productivity (cf. Ricardo 1819/2004, p. 70). In the context of (classical) labour theory of value and with regard to the two actors—tenant and landowner—it represents a form of free income not based on an additional performance.

> [...] the amount of that rent will depend on the difference in the quality of these two portions of land. (ibid., p. 70) Or, to put it in the terminology of labour theory of value:

> [...] for rent is always the difference between the produce obtained by the employment of two equal quantities of capital and labour. (ibid., p. 71)

Accordingly, the rent is not an *ex-ante* component of a commodity price; instead, it is derived *ex post* from the market price, which is solely determined by supply and demand.

> It is not from the produce, but from the price at which the produce is sold, that the rent is derived. (ibid., p. 77)

For Ricardo, then, it is only the free natural productivity that determines the existence and size of the rent. The rent of land is a monopoly rent, which can be generated in the market system without the need to provide any additional service and on the basis of the resource owner's property rights and usage rights.

9.2 Rent and Cooperation

Later, it would be Karl Marx who took up this topic—albeit not the term 'rent'—in his investigations of added-value production and discussed its connection to the cooperation of the workers. In the eleventh chapter of the first volume of *Capital* (MEW 23), he argues that cooperation constitutes not only "an increase in the productive power of the individual," but also "the creation of a new power, namely, the collective power of the masses" [own translation] (MEW 23, p. 345). Yet this does not stem from the productivity of the individual worker; it stems from cooperation itself (MEW 23, p. 349). Marx demonstrates this autonomous productive power using the following example: the overall production A of twelve collaborating persons with a combined workday of 144 h is greater than the overall production B of twelve separate workers, each of which works twelve hours; and is also greater than the overall production C of one worker who works twelve days long. The Δ A > B, C is the cooperation rent, which is not generated by the productivity of the respective workers, but by cooperation itself.

The collective productive power (cf. ibid.) expressed here is the result of cooperative teamwork and costs no additional capital; further, as a valorisation process for capital (cf. ibid., p. 351 The German category "Arbeits- und Verwertungsprozess des Kapitals" used by Marx is translated here as a combined labour and valorisation process.), it is also the result of the concentration of capital in factory work "as a power with which capital is endowed by Nature—a productive power that is immanent in capital" [own translation] (ibid., p. 353).

Therefore, according to Marx, the economic benefits, which we could just as easily call rent, of this immanent (without further factor services) productive power possessed by capital, but which are only produced by a cooperative form of labour process that it made possible, organised and hierarchically managed by the owner of the capital, the capitalist, cannot be attributed to the individual labourers. The rent does not belong to the labourers and is not a factor in their accumulation of value, because it cannot be generated before or without the labourers forming a team as a result of capital investments. According to Marx, then, it is generated as an immanent quality and outcome of a combined labour and valorisation process and as such, is appropriated by the capitalist free of charge as an additional, supernormal profit. The appropriation of rent from cooperative labour emanates from the capitalist's property rights and usage rights and from his/her role as organiser and leader of the cooperation process. In this regard, Marx embraces military vocabulary and speaks of hierarchies and the power of command. Therefore, the capitalist's appropriation of the rent at the dawn of industrialisation was due to the fact that capital supplied the technical and organisational (workspaces, machines, hierarchy, management) resources required for cooperation and attendant value creation and was therefore what created them in the first place. Or, from a slightly more technical perspective: at this point in the history of industrialisation, the ownership and usage rights to capital were the quintessential cooperation-specific resource.

At the same time, however, cooperation transformed the value creation process "into a social process" [own translation] (ibid., p. 354). According to Marx, cooperation as a form of "increasing the productive power of labour" [own translation] (MEW 24, pp. 143, 237) is one of the "three main aspects of capitalistic production"[own translation] (MEW 25, p. 276 f.), namely concentration, cooperation and the world market.

This developmental dynamic, Marx (1857) claims in the "Grundrisse", leads to the "highest forms of the economy, e.g. cooperation" [own translation] (ibid., p. 634). In this regard, from the outset, he considers cooperation as a social process to involve more than sharing and combining work in a team and to also include its relationalisation to other sectors of society—above all through the integration of the natural sciences in the production process (cf. Capital Volume II, MEW 24, p. 277). In this way, the economy of cooperation fosters the development of productivity, "of power, of capabilities of production, and hence both of the capabilities as well as the means of consumption" [own translation] (Marx, 1857, p. 599). It is this ability to initiate a social dynamic and prosperity that legitimates capital and its factor income profit as the most important, guiding element in the market economy. As such, capital was initially justified by upholding social responsibility, unlike today, where upholding social responsibility is justified by its contribution to economic success (for a detailed reconstruction of this discussion in economic theory-building cf. Heck, 2016).

For Marx, however, the cooperation rent is not simply a Ricardian natural quality of capital, which does not involve the need for societal property rights or to provide any additional investment and service. It is the capitalist owner who, by investing in organising and coordinating the material resources and personnel needed for a factory-like production process, makes it possible to generate a rent from cooperation of labour in the first place. As such, he considers it only logically consistent that this rent from the cooperation of the production factor 'labour' be immanently attributed to the production factor 'capital' and that it be wholly appropriated by capital as an extra profit. For Marx, capital is not merely an economic category but also a societal relation.

This state of the discussion would remain largely unchanged, to the best of my knowledge, until the 20th century. In the late 19th century, the previously mentioned Alfred Marshall had already argued that the standard "agents of production" cited in economic theory—land, labour and capital—could only very imperfectly represent the value-creating productive forces to be found in an economy. While he still defined capital as the result of private labour and private non-consumption in a book he co-authored with his wife (Marshall & Marshall 1879, cf. p. 14); in a later work, Principles of Economics, Marshall notes:

> Capital consists in a great part of knowledge and organization: and of this some part is private property and other part is not. (…) The distinction between public and private property in knowledge and organization is of great importance: in some respects of more importance than that between public and private property in material things; and partly for that reason it seems best sometimes to reckon Organization apart as a distinct agent of production. (Marshall, 2009, p. 115)

Here we can very clearly see the importance of the economic organisation's role as an autonomous agent of production that makes its own contribution to value creation, which must also be taken into account when it comes to disbursing the resultant factor incomes. Yet Marshall does not pursue the idea further, because he still considers the organisation to chiefly be a result of the division of labour. This discussion would only ultimately be opened by the argument that organisations are the embodiment of functional continuity.[1]

This was due in part to the rise and evolution of the *Modern Corporation and Private Property*, to quote the title of Berle and Means' book (1932), which is to say, to the advent of self-contained and de-personalised corporations. This changed the basis of legitimation for capital and its profits.

Capital was now seen as "a passive form of wealth" (ibid., p. xxxvii), which had largely emancipated itself from the individual saving behaviour of the firms' entrepreneurs. Berle and Means note the consequences of this historical caesura: "no

[1] Interestingly, Marshall considered his "principles" to be an epistemological and methodological expression of the "principle of continuity". Continuity, he claims, is a fundamental law of nature that, for example, precludes the meaningful conceptualisation of a static equilibrium for society as a whole. This can also be seen, he argues, in the chronological and ethical dimensions of economic activity. The foreword of the 1st edition largely revolves around this argument. However, Marshall does not link continuity with the purpose or mode of existence of economic organisations (for a more in-depth discussion cf. Martins (2013)).

large corporations, can take the view that their plants, tools and organizations are their own, and that they can do what they please with their own." Moreover, these corporations' revenues and profits "without a corresponding duty to work" (ibid., p. xxxv) can only be justified "on the ground that the community is better off" (ibid.).

Yet contrary to Marx's claims, this development clearly shows that de-personalised capital itself and in various forms is a resource, has a value and produces value. Berle and Means consider this to be the principal flaw in Marxian labour theory of value and surplus value theory and seeking to prove it is one of the main goals of their book. Yet this fact alone, the two authors claim, tells us nothing about who appropriates that value. For our purposes, the following statement is particularly relevant:

> The nature of capital has changed. To an increasing extent it is composed not of tangible goods, but of organizations built in the past and available to function in the future. (Berle & Means 1932, p. 45)

This twofold relationalisation of *organised relationships* on the one hand and of the focus on the theoretically infinite continuation of the firm's existence on the other makes private firms into *social institutions*; an *institutional economic revolution* that transforms firms into the "dominant institutions of the modern world" (ibid., p. 313). This elucidates the social character of the corporation as an organisational form, as an *autonomous and artificial* actor, as well as its importance for economic theory-building. This insight also has far-reaching ramifications for the meaning of the cooperation rent. If it is no longer the individual capitalist who (for the reasons explained by Marx) acquires the rent, but rather the organisation itself (the de-personalised organisation, *an entity in its own right*), it also means that every stakeholder who joins this organisation is not only entitled to a share of the organisation's earnings in the form of his/her factor income, but also to a share of the cooperation rent generated by and through an organisation. This is precisely why resource owners choose to join a given organisation: the return on investment as a combination of factor income and cooperation rent.

Let us recall that Barnard also addressed this new development, namely the organisation as a form of cooperation and made it the basis of his theoretical work *The Functions of the Executive*. Personalised capital is no longer the organiser of productive activities; the organisation as an independent system is. It is the organisation as a functionally differentiated form that makes economic cooperation and the resultant rent possible. It is the organisation as social form that stakeholders, including capitalists, use in order to pursue their interests; it is where the cooperation rent is produced; and it is where said rent is distributed by the (separate from capital) management, who are responsible for ensuring that stakeholders are given opportunities to participate (Cf. Berle & Means 1932, p. xxxix). The firm's senior management represents the organisation's interests and is authorised to make decisions on its behalf.

In practical terms, in industrialised Western societies, this redistribution of the economic rent is achieved either through tax-financed measures on the part of the welfare state or through various types of voluntary corporate benefit, although both terms are somewhat misleading. From this perspective, systematically speaking, the discussion over corporate social responsibility and creating shared value is rooted more in the cooperation rent produced by modern firms and less in the externalities of global value creation.

9.3 Rent from Cooperation and Appropriation

The theoretical situation subsequently—and, from a categorical perspective, quite logically—changes due to the fact that economic theory now views the labourer, which Marx portrayed as being dependent on the capitalist, as *human capital* (cf. Becker, 1964; Machlup, 1980), which is to say, as being in possession of capital. Accordingly, the qualities of this new form of capital resource have a direct impact on the amount of the cooperation rent that can be achieved and on its distribution.

With regard to cooperative team production, Alchian and Demsetz (1972) show that it is based on an inseparable production function in which the performance of the whole is greater than the sum of its parts (that is, the performance of the individual team members). Further, the two authors argue that the *residual claimant* should be responsible for managing the cooperation rent, which can especially be taken advantage of by shirking team members since he or she (as the actor with the *residual risk*) has the least incentive to shirk. Consequently, in this approach behavioural assumptions and incentives are of fundamental importance for the distribution of the cooperation rent.

In contrast, Molloy and Barney (2015) argue that the appropriation of the cooperation rent depends on the intensity of competition on the labour market and on the degree of specificity regarding human capital. It is the firm-specific nature of this resource that generates a quasi-rent. In contexts characterised by competitive labour markets and highly specific human capital, the firm and the owners of the human capital share the rent. In this regard, governance arrangements are called for in order to foster and protect specific investments on the part of stakeholders, offering them an incentive to invest in *capital based capabilities*.

Mahoney and Kor (2015) argue along the same lines by focusing on the difference between the first-best and second-best use of investments, which is to say, on generating a quasi-rent. Whereas in the first-best use context, human capital is developed in a firm-specific manner and is moreover co-specialised with complementary assets within the firm, in the second-best use case (at another firm in the same sector) it is precisely the latter condition—the co-specialisation within the firm—that is not fulfilled. Here, too, the question of who appropriates the rent naturally arises. As such, it remains open how, but not whether a cooperation rent will be distributed.

Arriving at a Pareto-optimal allocation of tangible and intangible factor incomes and of the cooperation rent, to all actors involved in a cooperative project at a certain equilibrium point poses a fundamental challenge. Olson (1968) astutely observed that a Pareto-optimal distribution of exclusively material goods cannot always be achieved in cooperative projects since each actor always has the choice of prioritising intangible goods over material ones. Thanks to an increased factor income, they may improve their standing in the cooperative relation without negatively impacting the standing of others; however, if they partially or completely lose moral goods like status or recognition in the process, that is no longer the case. This applies not only to employees' career planning but also to the representatives of NGOs in multi-stakeholder dialogues. This can result in a trade-off between different intangible goods, for example, when gaining recognition in the dialogue would mean losing political power within the organisation that the actor represents. Or, in more general terms:

> [...] an attempt to 'sub-optimize' by considering only material objectives could be meaningless, for a step that seemed efficient because it increased the output of material goods might, in fact, be inefficient because the social or political goods that had to be sacrificed were worth more than the material goods gained. There is thus no way of defining a situation as Pareto-optimal without taking all of the things people value into account (ibid., p. 101).

Accordingly, in relational contexts, Pareto-optimality, in which by definition the earnings must be greater than the costs, can and will chiefly be of transaction-specific relevance. However, it is not achieved throughout the entire cooperative network at any given point in time; instead, it is an ongoing process of adaptation that constantly creates new, temporary states of equilibrium.

In this context, it is also important to bear in mind that, as previously noted, modern value creation has long-since transcended the domain of intra-firm relations and (also) takes place in multi-firm networks. Lafontaine and Slade (2013) clarify the nature of the *quasi-rent* in *inter-firm contracts* as follows:

> [...] the rent that parties earn within their relationship, or the difference between the profits that they can expect if they remain in their relationship compared to what they could earn outside of it, can play a crucial role in the maintenance and day-to-day functioning of the relationship. (ibid., p. 998)

As such, what we are dealing with is a "rent from continuing their relationship. The rent can go to either party" (Malcomson, 2013, p. 1057).

Generally speaking, inter-firm networks are cooperative organisational arrangements, which can produce appropriable quasi-rents (cf. Klein, Crawford & Alchian 1978) on the basis of a long-term, network-specific investment. Stephan Duschek (2004) views them as interorganizational quasi-rents (cf. Duschek, 2004, p. 62) that are difficult to reconcile with the resource-based view of the firm:

> Mutual pooling of success potentials with the aim of creating unique and long-lasting value potential within the framework of cooperation, not only for individual companies, but also for partners in the cooperation [...] is hardly integrable into the logic of the resource- and competence-based approach of strategic management. (ibid., p. 59)

The challenge here, he argues, consists in the fact that the only basic unit of analysis in the resource-based view is the individual firm. In contrast, the relational perspective works under the assumption that the value-creating resources within a given network belong to and are controlled by, all partners involved (cf. ibid., p. 61). Accordingly, gaining a competitive edge through relationalisation can only be achieved by co-specialisation within the network of partners, which must also satisfy the condition of being, for all parties involved, a specific investment in its transactions and organisation. As such, I propose viewing the firm—as a relation of stakeholders for the purpose of completing specific transactions—as a firm-specific network, in which private and public organisations are also stakeholders. The fact that this will alternately be true for all firms participating in the network doesn't change the challenge of simultaneous co-specialisation and firm-specialisation in cooperative projects for the purpose of completing specific transactions. This places us squarely in the middle of the topic 'relational rent', in which the first priority must, of course, be to arrive at a theory of the relational economy.

9.4 Relational Rents and Networks

Whereas in the paradigm of market exchange, a rent can only be produced as the expression of natural scarcity or a monopoly, the rent generated by cooperation within and between firms is appropriated by the organisations. It manifests in the organisations' supernormal profit. In terms of the resource-based view of the firm, this profit is produced by the firms' service differentiation and by the heterogeneity and combination of their resources.

> Firms that are able to accumulate resources and capabilities that are rare, valuable, non-substitutable, and difficult to imitate will achieve a competitive advantage. (Dyer & Singh, 1998, p. 660 citing Barney, 1991; Dierickx & Cool, 1989; Rumelt, 1984)

Dyer and Singh (1998) have made an initial and substantial contribution to grasping the rents produced by networking firms' resources. They view firms as focal organisations, which create and manage networks, while simultaneously being embedded in them. When all stakeholders in the network make relation-specific investments (Cf. Dyer & Singh 1998, p. 661) and the focal organisation is capable of combining the invested resources in a specific and unique manner, then precisely this idiosyncrasy of intra-firm and inter-firm resources can "be a source of relational rents" (ibid., p. 661). With regard to the nature of these rents, they go on to say that:

> We define a relational rent as a supernormal profit jointly generated in an exchange relationship that cannot be generated by either firm in isolation and can only be created through the joint idiosyncratic contributions of the specific alliance partners. In summary, at a fundamental level, relational rents are possible when alliance partners combine, exchange, or invest in idiosyncratic assets, knowledge and resources/capabilities and/or they employ effective governance mechanisms that lower transaction costs or permit the realization of rents through the synergistic combination of assets, knowledge, or capabilities. (ibid., p. 662)

According to this view, relational rents are produced by the successful relationalisation of idiosyncratic resources and abilities via efficient governance structures. Transnational, global value creation chains facilitate the access to hard-to-imitate resources with unique characteristics. This shows once more the importance of transcultural skills (discussed in the previous chapter), which from this perspective directly contribute to the generation of relational rents, as they pave the way for new and idiosyncratic combinations of resources. Relational leadership is one such skill, because, as the outcome of a global social process and independent of organisational status or managerial authority, it is precisely tailored to the creation and activation of these resource combinations. Dyer and Singh (1998) explicitly underscore the importance of cultural leadership resources, given their ability to engender goodwill trust (cf. ibid., p. 669). They represent the firm's relational skills, namely its "willingness and ability to partner" (ibid., p. 672), to monitor agreements and, if need be, to enforce them using social oversight.

For Dyer and Singh (cf. ibid., p. 663 ff), the determinants of relational rents are:

(i) *Relation-specific assets*: the degree of specificity depends on the duration/permanency of the cooperation, on the possibilities for safeguarding resources and on the transaction volume.
(ii) *Knowledge-sharing routines*: the extent of knowledge sharing depends on the ability to productively absorb and implement knowledge within the organisation and on the incentives to do so in a transparent manner and to refrain from shirking.
(iii) *Complementarity of resources/capabilities*: this aspect depends on the quality of mechanisms for identifying and evaluating possible complementarities and their potential with regard to value creation.
(iv) *Effective governance*: in networks based on relational contracts, the effectiveness of self-enforcing, informal contracts is essential, given that their formal enforcement via third parties would be prohibitively expensive, if possible at all.

In turn, the two authors contend that the basic unit of analysis in the relational view is the network of firms (cf. ibid., p. 674 ff.). This insight may prove useful for the investigation of inter-firm relations, but for the firm as a relation of stakeholders, the relation itself would seem to be a more promising candidate. In both variants, the ownership/control problem and the combination of rent-generating resources represent challenges that must be overcome by the network as a whole. At the same time, this raises the question of how to allocate and distribute the resultant rents. Cooperation in the context of collective value creation goes hand in hand with competition in terms of the individual appropriation of said value creation (cf. Dyer, Singh & Hesterly 2018). What may be shared value creation from the perspective of the network is at the same time a process of appropriating quasi-rents by its nodes. Co-specialisation as a constitutive aspect of the network 'collides' with the stakeholder-specificity of the firm and each of its stakeholders.

9.5 Specificity and Relational Rents

The specific roles of firm-specialisation and co-specialisation as qualities of network resources have been explored in the economic literature for some time now. Building on the works of Dyer and Singh (1998), Gulati (1999), Lavie (2006) defines these assets as "external resources embedded in the firm's alliance network that provide strategic opportunities and affect firm behavior and value" (ibid., p. 638). The 'firm/network of firms' difference affects the competitiveness of all participating firms, which provide an environment for one another. For a firm that is connected to other firms, the chief task is to use its own internal organisation to achieve value creation with resources that it neither completely possesses nor completely controls (cf. ibid. p. 639). Amit and Schoemaker (1993) argue along similar lines when they state that the focus in viewing and analysing firms as networks of stakeholders shouldn't be on the resources that belong to and are controlled by focal organisations, but on those that they organise and manage. Lavie has taken this one step further and developed a concept for the different forms of rent produced by relational networks of firms, according to which the amount of the rent is fundamentally determined by the scarcity and value of the resources invested (cf. Lavie, 2006, p. 643). Drawing on this distinction, he then seeks to show that relational rents can only be generated by the partners' shared resources, whereas the internal rent is generated by the focal organisation's shared and non-shared resources alike. Since this, as previously mentioned, applies to all partners, according to Lavie this results in an inbound spillover rent, which flows from the network partners to the focal organisation; and to an outbound spillover rent, which is transferred from the focal organisation to its partners (cf. ibid. p. 664). In this regard, we can differentiate between four types of relational rent (cf. ibid. p. 664 ff.):

(i) *Internal rent*: is generated by the firm's internal resources and therefore belongs to and is controlled by the firm, can manifest in the form of a Ricardian rent (based on scarcity and/or monopoly) or a quasi-rent (based on the specialisation with regard to other firms). Appropriated by the focal organisation.
(ii) *Appropriated relational rent*: refers to the mutual benefit for all partners, produced by the combination of their resources. A number of factors determine the appropriation of this rent by the focal organisation and its allocation to the partners; the most important examples are the respective organisations' ability to absorb this type of rent, the scale and scope of resources, contractual agreements, opportunistic behaviour and bargaining power.
(iii) *Inbound spillover rent*: refers to the rent accumulated by the focal organisation from shared network resources. The factors influencing the appropriation of firm-specific, shared resources include opportunistic behaviour and bargaining power. However, isolating mechanisms are required for non-shared resources, so as to prevent their being exploited by partners.
(iv) *Outbound spillover rent*: is, as previously mentioned, the rent from the focal organisation's resources that is completely or partially distributed to its network partners. The allocation of this rent is determined, for example, by the relations within the network and by the specificity of the resources, including their imitability or substitutability.

These four types of rent are produced simultaneously (cf. ibid., p. 651.), though the balance between the inbound and outbound spillover rent can be regulated by a relational contract.

References

Alchian, A. A., & Demsetz, H. (1972). Production, information costs, and economic organization. *American Economic Review, 62*(5), 777–795.

Amit, R., & Schoemaker, P. J. H. (1993). Strategic assets and organizational rent. *Strategic Management Journal, 14*(1), 33–46.

Barnard, C. I. (1938). *The functions of the executive*. Cambridge, MA: Harvard University Press.

Barney, J. B. (1991). Firm resources and sustained competitive advantage. *Journal of Management, 17*(1), 99–120.

Becker, G. S. (1964). *Human capital: A theoretical and empirical analysis with special reference to education*. New York: Columbia University Press.

Berle, A. A., & Means, G. (1932). *The modern corporation and private property [Reprint: 1962]*. New Jersey: Transaction Publishers.

Dierickx, I., & Cool, K. (1989). Asset stock accumulation and sustainability of competitive advantage. *Management Science, 35*(12), 1504–1511.

Duschek, S. (2004). Inter-firm resources and sustained competitive advantage. *Management Revue, 15*(1), 53–73.

Dyer, J. H. & Singh, H. (1998). The relational view: Cooperative strategy and sources of interorganizational competitive advantage. *Academy of Management Review, 23*(4), 660–679.

Dyer, J. H., Singh, H. & Hesterly, W. S. (2018). The relational view revisited: A dynamic perspective on value creation and value capture. *Strategic Management Journal* (in Press).

Gulati, R. (1999). Network location and learning: The influence of network resources and firm capabilities on alliance formation. *Strategic Management Journal, 20*(5), 397–420.

Heck, A. E. (2016). *Gesellschaftliche Wertschöpfung und ökonomische Verantwortung: Genese, Form und Wesen der Verantwortung ökonomischer Akteure*. Marburg: Metropolis.

Klein, B., Crawford, R. G., & Alchian, A. A. (1978). Vertical integration, appropriable rents, and the competitive contracting process. *The Journal of Law & Economics, 21*(2), 297–326.

Lafontaine, F., & Slade, M. E. (2013). Inter-firm contracts. In R. Gibbons & J. Roberts (Eds.), *Handbook of organizational economics* (pp. 958–1013). Princeton, NJ: Princeton University Press.

Lavie, D. (2006). The competitive advantage of interconnected firms: An extension of the resource-based view. *Academy of Management Review, 31*(3), 638–658.

Machlup, F. (1980). *Knowledge: Its creation, distribution, and economic significance*. Princeton, NJ: Princeton University Press.

Mahoney, J. T., & Kor, Y. Y. (2015). Advancing the human capital perspective on value creation by joining capabilities and governance approaches. *Academy of Management Perspectives, 29*(3), 296–308.

Malcomson, J. M. (2013). Relational incentive contracts. In R. Gibbons & J. Roberts (Eds.), *The handbook of organizational economics* (pp. 1014–1065). Princeton, NJ: Princeton University Press.

Marshall, A., & Marshall, M. P. (1879). *The economics of industry*. Cambridge: Cambridge University Press.

Marshall, A. (1890). *Principles of economics*. Cambridge: Cambridge University Press.

Marshall, A. (2009). *Principles of economics: Unabridged* (Eight ed.). New York: Cosimo Classics.

Martins, N. O. (2013). Sraffa, Marshall and the principle of continuity. *Cambridge Journal of Economics, 37*(2), 443–462.

Marx, K. (1857). *Grundrisse der Kritik der politischen Ökonomie* [Reprint, o. J.]. Frankurt: Europäische Verlagsgesellschaft.

Marx, K. (1890). *Das Kapital*, Bd. 1 [MEW 23; 1972]. Berlin: Dietz Verlag.

Marx, K. (1893). *Das Kapital*, Bd. 2 [MEW 24; 1971]. Berlin: Dietz Verlag.

Marx, K. (1894). *Das Kapital*, Bd. 3 [MEW 25; 1970]. Berlin: Dietz Verlag.

Molloy, J. C., & Barney, J. B. (2015). Who captures the value created with human capital? A market-based view. *Academy of Management Perspectives, 29*(3), 309–325.

Olson, M., Jr. (1968). Economics, sociology and the best of all possible worlds. *The Public Interest, 12,* 137–162.
Ricardo, D. (1819). The works and correspondence of David Ricardo (Reprint by In P. Sraffa, Ed., 2004, Indianapolis, Ind.: Liberty Fund).
Rumelt, R. P. (1984). Toward a strategic theory of the firm. In R. Lamb (Ed.), *Competitive strategic management* (pp. 556–570). Englewood Cliffs, NJ: Prentice-Hall.

Chapter 10
Relational Rent and Societal Value Creation

10.1 Creating Shared Value (CSV) and Shared Value Creation (SVC)

Up to this point, our discussion of relational rents has focused on intra- and inter-firm relations, which is to say, exclusively on economic actors. However, in the course of the discussion I have also sought to show that, with regard to a transaction-based theory of the firm as a relation of economic and societal stakeholders, this perspective is necessary, yet insufficient. Value creation and growth through conducting business have always been based on societal value creation and societal growth, which can manifest in both tangible and intangible forms. The point of reference for this development is not the market, but the organisation, that is, the firm and its economic and societal stakeholders.

In this regard, Porter and Kramer (2011) have made a valuable contribution to the discussion with their industrial-economic proposal for the strategic management of firms based on *Creating Shared Value* (CSV) (cf. for this discussion and critique Beschorner, 2013; Crane, Palazzo, Spence & Matten 2014; Hartman & Werhane 2013; Heck, 2016; Porter, Hills, Pfitzer, Patscheke & Hawkings 2012; Wieland, 2017a, b; Wieland & Heck 2013). The core of their concept involves approaching the societal problems triggered by globalisation, which are addressed, for example, in movements for Corporate Social Responsibility (CSR) and Sustainable Development Goals (SDGs), as opportunities for growth with win-win options for firms and societies.

> More and more, companies are creating shared value by developing profitable business strategies that deliver tangible social benefits. This thinking is creating major new opportunities for profitable and competitive advantage at the same time as it benefits society by unleashing the power of business to help solve fundamental global problems. (Porter et al. 2012, p. 1)

For firms, this initially consists in identifying and prioritising societal challenges (boosting revenues, reducing costs), then defining the likely outcomes for the firm and society, weighing them against the costs and lastly, entering these parameters into their in-house calculation mechanisms and accounting systems. The authors believe

J. Wieland, *Relational Economics*, Relational Economics and Organization Governance,
https://doi.org/10.1007/978-3-030-45112-7_10

that pursuing this firm- and market-driven strategy could yield "the power to unleash the next wave of global growth" (Porter & Kramer 2011, p. 65), particularly if the firm in question succeeds in using innovation management, especially open innovation (cf. Chesbrough & Appleyard 2007) and social innovation (cf. Ehrenberger, 2017; Mulgan, 2006), to transform said societal challenges into growth strategies. Their proposal not only sparked a (largely critical) discussion in the academic world but was also (justly) positively received in political circles and society at large. That being said, the disadvantage of Porter's and Kramer's strategy for societal value creation is that the societal stakeholders, whose active participation is vital to these innovation processes, are at best included *ex-post* as a sounding board. As such, the integration of inside-out and outside-in practices (cf. ibid., p. 89) envisaged by Porter and Kramer (2006) can only be achieved on a very limited scale. Together with Andreas Heck, I have attempted to show that the strategy of integrating private and societal value creation through innovation cannot succeed solely as a market strategy of a firm and must instead be embedded in the continual governance of cooperative stakeholder relations. In this way, the *ex-ante* incorporation of relevant stakeholders via a multi-stakeholder dialogue produces a CSR evaluator (cf. Wieland & Heck 2013; Wieland et al. 2017), which, it is assumed, legitimates the societal character of the envisioned private value creation, while also making it visible and manageable.

In Fig. 10.1 "CSR evaluator and stakeholder management", this is achieved in a first step through the identification, prioritisation and organisation (dialogue, inter-sectoral management) of the stakeholders most relevant for the firm and its transactions. In a second step (Component I), the firm's stakeholder-specific services, such

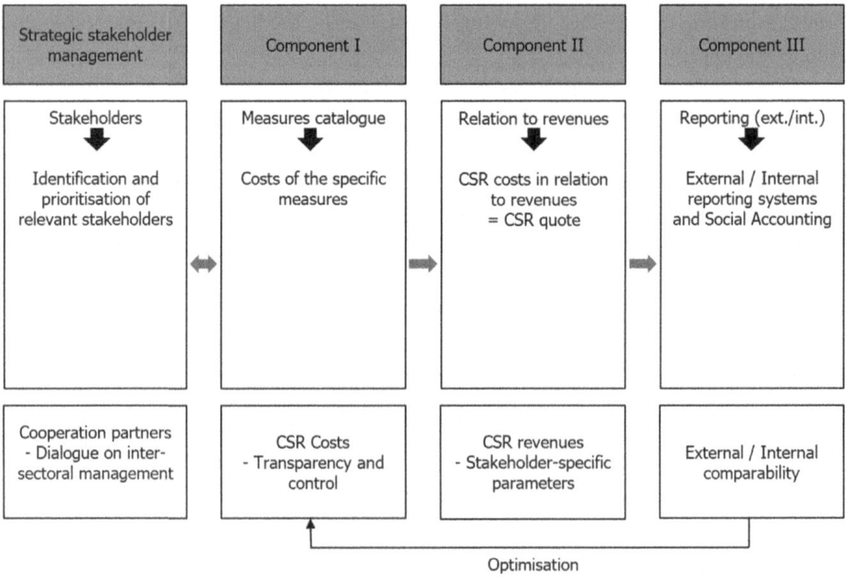

Fig. 10.1 CSR evaluator and stakeholder management

as the development of sustainable products and methods, but also direct services provided to employees, partners and investors, are presented in terms of their costs. In a third step (Component II), the costs and revenues of the firm's activities are compared, which yields as a proportion of cost and revenues the CSR quote for the firm in general and with regard to its specific stakeholder investments. Lastly, in a fourth step (Component III), the results of the CSR evaluator can be communicated, using the societal standard of reference in the process. This allows the firm's internal and external societal performance to be compared and optimised.

As a result, the firm's strategic management of its social responsibility not only becomes visible but also manageable on a stakeholder-specific basis.

Practising social responsibility as a voluntary investment and commitment on the part of firms is intended to produce a cooperation rent, which in turn makes it possible to provide stakeholders with dividends in addition to their factor incomes. *Shared Value Creation (SVC)* is not a market strategy of a firm; rather, it is an organisational strategy and the results it produces—the aforementioned factor incomes and cooperation rent—are from the outset the declared goal of competitive business activities and not the residual outcome of cooperation. Accordingly, the connection between the cooperation rent and Shared Value Creation (SVC) is that the latter refers to a firm's strategy and governance to transform possible cooperation opportunities into real cooperation benefits.

Shared Value Creation and to some extent Porter's concept of Creating Shared Value (CSV) as well, are attempts to operationalise Peter Drucker's (2011) dictum that firms should be led and managed "in the best-balanced interests of stakeholders" (Ibid., p. 80). The essential difference between the two is their being based on an Exchange Transaction approach (CSV) and a Relational Transaction approach (SVC), respectively. In the first case, the Creating Shared Value approach, the focus is on a discrete market economy, while in the second, the CSR evaluator approach, it is on a relational cooperative economy. In the next section, we'll take a closer look at how compatible this application-oriented instrument is with a theory of Relational Economics.

10.2 Willingness and Ability to Cooperate

Relational rents are produced by the successful cooperation of economic and societal actors, complete with their respective resources. Cooperation rents do not result from the use of additional production factors or, more generally speaking, from the use of additional resource inputs, but from their efficient, effective, or idiosyncratic relation. As Tollison (1982) has formulated this for economic rents, they occur as "excess returns" above the normal level. It is this cooperation, as we've seen in the discussion of Karl Marx's *Capital*, that has shaped the growth and dynamism of the modern market economy since its inception and currently drives it in the form of regional or global value chains (GVCs) and inter-sectoral networks. And cooperation projects, namely those of firms and society, are what—as clearly shown in the discussion of

Michael Porter's and Marc Kramer's shared value concept—continue to generate growth and prosperity in today's modern network economies.

The extraction of relational rents from cooperation requires, as our discussion of the works of Dyer and Singh and Lavie has shown, a type of governance that can accommodate all of these cooperative forms: in other words, one that can simultaneously process the behavioural and skills-based dimensions of networks, so that the difference between the revenues generated by cooperation and the costs of cooperation *surpasses normal returns* (cf. Dyer & Singh 1998) and a *supernormal profit* (cf. ibid.) is generated. Especially with regard to the costs side of the equation, this presupposes that the cooperation relations are free of any (or at least have very few) frictions.

With regard to the assumptions of the economy of discrete exchanges, friction-optimality is only possible when (i) the partners' views regarding the cooperation are symmetrical prior to their signing the contract; (ii) all partners are risk-neutral and therefore (iii) can be bound to fulfil their contractual obligations without incurring any additional costs; and (iv) the partners' individual contributions are clearly identifiable and separable, allowing them to be attributed to the correct actor (cf. Wieland, 1996, p. 195 ff.). Although such situations aren't impossible, they can be systematically ignored for the purposes of modern and global economies. Why? Because cultural diversity, differing risk preferences, contracts that cannot be formally enforced and resource revenues that cannot be separated (or only at a prohibitive cost) are the immutable preconditions for global cooperation and economic networks. In other words: fundamentally speaking, we have to assume that we are dealing with relational transactions, the constitution and continuation of which require adaptive governance structures that credibly signal (*ex-ante*) and implement (*ex-post*) the partners' willingness and ability to cooperate. The number of opportunities for cooperation that a given network has depends on the quality of development processes for *dynamic capabilities* (cf. Dosi, Nelson & Winter 2000; Teece, Pisano & Shuen 1997), which is to say, on its potential for value creation (cf. on this point and the next Wieland, 1998, p. 24 ff). Dyer & Singh 1998 also address the "willingness and ability to partner" (p. 672), but do not detail these aspects methodologically.). It is this relation—between (i) willingness, (ii) ability and (iii) chances—that determines the corridor for value-creating cooperation.

The (i) *willingness* to cooperate refers to individual and collective actors' readiness to take part in a long-term cooperative relation intended to be mutually advantageous. At the level of the individual, it has a mental and a behavioural dimension, both of which have been discussed using the example of trans-sectoral transactions. There is also an organisational dimension, which can either foster or hinder the individual willingness to cooperate.

The (ii) *ability* to cooperate refers to individual and collective actors' ability to actually and successfully cooperate with one another. It is fundamentally determined by the specific usefulness or productivity of a given resource, which is to say, by whether or not it can contribute to value creation with regard to the cooperation project. The ability to cooperate, too, has both individual and organisational components. Although both the individual and organisation have resources at their disposal that present opportunities for cooperation, their behavioural preferences, management culture or organisational structure prevent them from capitalising on these opportunities.

Lastly, (iii) *chances* for cooperation refer to the number of potential transactions that a team or network of teams can achieve through cooperation, which depends on their willingness and ability to cooperate. Chances for cooperation are not a quantity to be maximised; rather, they should be appropriate for the respective societal rules and for the strategy and abilities of the organisation in question. Opportunities for cooperation that are tainted by corruption or human rights violations must be passed up; the same is true for projects that would overwhelm the organisation's management abilities and therefore its growth corridor (cf. on the latter point Penrose, 1959).

In the next step, this distinction will be illustrated using the previously identified success-critical factors for relational contracts and cooperation projects.

10.3 Relational Contracts and Behaviour

In Part I of this book, 'Transaction and Contract', the requisite behavioural principles for relational contracts as identified by Macaulay (1963), Macneil (1980, 1981, 1983) were discussed. Viewed in relation to the willingness to cooperate and ability to cooperate, we arrive at the following Fig. 10.2.

Based on the points discussed in Part I, the table should be self-explanatory; moreover, it should be evident that a preference for continuity, contractual loyalty and a readiness to live up to social responsibilities are essential to signalling the willingness to cooperate, just as joint planning mechanisms and flexibility are to the ability to cooperate.

The picture changes somewhat when we refine the distinction to include the dimensions of the individual and the organisation (Fig. 10.3).

As the figure shows, the relational contract theories discussed tend to focus on individual virtues and especially the organisational willingness to cooperate is largely neglected. This becomes even more apparent when we compare it with the outcomes of the discussion on relational rents in the context of the resource-based view of the firm, as explored by Dyer and Singh (1998) and Lavie (2006) (Fig. 10.4).

Here the focus is (not surprisingly) on organisational factors, while the willingness to cooperate is largely overlooked. By combining and condensing this view with the discussion of Relational Economics up to this point, we arrive at something more like Fig. 10.5.

Here we can very clearly see the constitutive role and significance of relational behavioural assumptions concerning pro-social abilities. These success-critical resources for economic cooperation—continuity, reciprocity, ethical standards of conduct, social responsibility, integrity, the ability to find consensus and transcultural skills—should be understood as the manifestations of pro-social abilities in modern, relational economies.

	Macaulay	Macneil
Willingness to cooperate	Preference for continuity Living up to obligations Keeping your word	Reciprocity Contractual loyalty Continuity Contractual fidelity Social responsibility
Ability to cooperate	Joint planning Professionalism Risk management Internal sanctions Ability to form internal/external relations	Integrity Ability to find consensus Ability to resolve conflicts Flexibility Propriety

Fig. 10.2 Behavioural principles for relational contracts (Created by the author, drawing on Macaulay, 1963; Macneil, 1980, 1981, 1983)

	Individual	Organisational
Willingness to cooperate	Preference for continuity Reciprocity Internal/external relations	Social responsibility
Ability to cooperate	Professionalism Integrity Consensus Flexibility Propriety	Integrity Risk management Joint planning Internal sanctions Balance of power

Fig. 10.3 Individual and organisational relational norms

	Individual	Organisation
Willingness to cooperate	Opportunism	Continuity
Ability to cooperate	Resource-specificity	Ability to absorb Resource-specificity (productivity, imitability) Resource protection Sharing routines Transparency Bargaining power

Fig. 10.4 Determinants of relational rents

Discussing the factors in Fig. 10.5 more deeply, we find that, with regard to *individuals' willingness* to cooperate, the following factors are success-critical:

Continuity: This refers to the preference for long-term participation in a cooperation project. If questions or controversies arise, they do not promptly result in an endgame or exit options; there is still a willingness and sincere desire to find a mutually acceptable solution. As such, continuity focuses on preserving opportunities for cooperation and reducing the transaction costs resulting from formal conflict resolution and enforcement procedures (courts of law, assessors) and the subsequent processes (searching for and negotiating with new partners) that they entail (cf. Williamson, 2005). Without this factor, the informal side of contractual agreements is untenable.

Reciprocity: The condition that there be a balance between services and services in return—not at every point in time, but generally speaking, throughout the cooperation—is a fundamental characteristic of social interaction. Without the willingness to maintain this balance, cooperating for the mutual benefit of all parties and therefore also ongoing cooperation, are impossible. Not only does this approach not exclude the pursuit of individual interests; it makes that pursuit possible to begin with. What it does exclude, however, is the maximisation of individual benefits at others' expense.

With regard to *organisations' willingness* to cooperate, the following factors—in addition to the previously mentioned factor 'continuity'—are especially relevant:

Ethical standards of conduct: An organisation's Code of Ethics or Code of Conduct does not represent the sum total or the weighted average of its members' moral values; rather, it codifies the values of the collective actor, on the basis of which it is

	Level	Manifestation	Description
Willingness to cooperate	Individual	Continuity	- Preference for long-term relations - Reducing transaction costs
		Reciprocity	- In the long term, there must be a general balance between services, and services in return
	Organisation	Ethical standards of conduct	- Basis for cooperation with stakeholders - Signal for morally acceptable behaviour in day-to-day business
		Continuity	- Preference for long-term relations - Reducing transaction costs
		Social responsibility	- Simultaneously achieving private and societal value creation as a corporate goal
Ability to cooperate	Individual	Integrity	- The ability to implement values in actual practice (e.g. by choosing not to engage in opportunistic behaviour)
		Ability to find consensus	- Willingness to engage in long-term reciprocal behaviour
		Resource-specificity	- The imitability and substitutability of a given resource, which determine its relevance in the resources pool
		Transcultural competence	- The ability to cope with cultural differences in GVCs
	Organisation	Integrity and compliance management	- Ensuring the effectiveness of established management systems - Relationalising the components 'integrity' and 'compliance'
		Sharing routines	- Implementing organisational learning processes within the firm in order to establish sharing routines
		Transcultural competence	- The ability to cope with cultural differences in GVCs

Fig. 10.5 Success-critical resources for economic cooperation

willing to cooperate with its stakeholders. It signals a preference for morally acceptable behaviour in day-to-day business, obligates the organisation and its stakeholders to uphold the codified values and, in the process, places certain conditions on the collective actor's willingness to cooperate, which results in a selection (preference for, acceptance or rejection) of potential partners (cf. Wieland, 2014; Wieland & Heck 2013).

Social responsibility: The self-obligation to adhere to and principal willingness to accept, social responsibility reflects the societal character of those organisations for which simultaneously achieving private and societal value creation is a corporate goal. This stance has consequences for a firm's strategy, portfolio of products and services and governance structures and can only be credibly (internally and externally) conveyed as a willingness to engage in responsible conduct and practices via these outlets.

In turn, *individuals' ability* to cooperate requires the following:

Integrity: This refers to a virtue that encompasses moral qualities like honesty, dependability and contractual loyalty, which the actor him- or herself chooses to exhibit. Unlike values, virtues are not attitudes; rather, they represent the ability to implement values in practice. For example, without the ability to refrain from opportunistic behaviour, the continuity essential to cooperation is unattainable.

Ability to find consensus: This is a necessary consequence of the readiness to engage in long-term reciprocal behaviour. Understanding and assessing the interests of others and properly 'ranking' one's own interests in relation to them are important expressions of this ability. In this regard, both flexibility in the pursuit of personal interests and exercising restraint when it comes to exploiting one's own bargaining power, are also important aspects.

Resource-specificity: This refers to the specific productivity of a given resource in a network of resources. On the one hand, this has to do with its professional quality; on the other, with its imitability and substitutability. Taken together, these two aspects define the resource's relevance in a pool of resources, which in turn determines the corridor of opportunities for joining cooperation projects and the degree of mutual dependency (resource owner/team).

Transcultural competence: This refers to the ability to cope with cultural differences and diversity and is a constitutive element (not only, but especially) of global value chains. These differences can stem from individual, professional, organisational, regional and national cultural patterns. In addition to the ability to recognise and accept such differences, transcultural competence can be seen in the successful creation of new, shared horizons for defining problems; new ways and means of solving them; and new forms of cooperative community.

In addition to integrity and transcultural competence, *organisations' ability* to cooperate also requires the following:

Integrity and compliance management: This ability does not stem from the existence of formal procedures and instruments, but from the actual effectiveness of established management systems. Initially, it is primarily shaped by the successful relationalisation of the components 'integrity' and 'compliance', which is to say, of personal motivation and structured governance. In addition, it is based on a transaction-specific risk management system, which identifies and prioritises the risks of cooperation in order to create a risk management plan that is used to determine the level of risk acceptance and devise suitable prevention strategies for mitigating risks (cf. Wieland, Steinmeyer & Grüninger 2014).

Shared routines: The productivity and success of the cooperative use of resources are not only jeopardised by opportunism on the part of individual partners, a risk that can be mitigated with the aid of integrity and compliance management. (In this regard, conflict resolution mechanisms and building trust—which can only be achieved by means of transparency—are vital.) Equally important for success is the organisation's ability to absorb, in other words, its ability to appropriate and capitalise on the expertise and know-how from shared resources. In this regard, organisational learning processes (intra-firm, inter-firm and in societal networks) are of fundamental importance (cf. Lavie, 2006, p. 645).

Achieving these success-critical factors for economic cooperation (and therefore, the available corridor of cooperation opportunities and the size of achievable cooperation rents) is closely linked to a theoretical grasp of the economy, the firms operating within it and their managers and leaders. I laid the foundations for addressing these aspects in Parts I and II. In Part III, which covered trans-sectoral stakeholder management, relational leadership theory and transcultural management, the concepts, processes and instruments of Relational Economics were then discussed, both systematically and on the basis of selected examples. In the next step, the final chapter of Part IV, our focus will be on the costs of value creation based on the relationalisation of stakeholders; after all, managing costs is one of the most fundamental processes for any economic organisation. The revenues that a given firm can achieve are systematically determined by successful market transactions and organisational transactions in its environment; its costs, however, are (also systematically) determined by the firm itself.

References

Beschorner, T. (2013). Creating shared value: The one-trick pony approach. *Business Ethics Journal Review, 17*(1), 106–112.

Chesbrough, H. W., & Appleyard, M. M. (2007). Open innovation and strategy. *California Management Review, 50*(1), 57–76.

Crane, A., Palazzo, G., Spence, L. J., & Matten, D. (2014). Contesting the value of "Creating Shared Value". *California Management Review, 56*(2), 130–153.

Dosi, G., Nelson, R. R., & Winter, S. (Eds.). (2000). *The nature and dynamics of organizational capabilities*. Oxford, UK: Oxford University Press.

Drucker, P. F. (2011). *Managing for the future*. New York: Routledge.

Dyer, J. H., & Singh, H. (1998). The relational view: Cooperative strategy and sources of interorganizational competitive advantage. *Academy of Management Review, 23*(4), 660–679.

Ehrenberger, M. (2017). *Corporate social entrepreneurship: Prozess und form ökonomischer organisation zur Kreation sozialunternehmerischer opportunitäten*. Marburg: Metropolis.

Hartman, L. P., & Werhane, P. H. (2013). Proposition: Shared value as an incomplete mental model. *Business Ethics Journal Review, 1*(6), 36–43.

Heck, A. E. (2016). *Gesellschaftliche Wertschöpfung und ökonomische Verantwortung: genese, form und Wesen der Verantwortung ökonomischer Akteure*. Marburg: Metropolis.

Lavie, D. (2006). The competitive advantage of interconnected firms: An extension of the resource-based view. *Academy of Management Review, 31*(3), 638–658.

Macaulay, S. (1963). Non-contractual relations in business: A preliminary study. *American Sociological Review, 28*(1), 55–67.

Macneil, I. R. (1980). *The new social contract*. New Haven, CT: Yale University Press.

Macneil, I. R. (1981). Economic analysis of contractual relations: Its shortfalls and the need for a "Rich Classificatory Apparatus". *Northwestern University Law Review, 75*(February), 1018–1063.

Macneil, I. R. (1983). Values in contract: Internal and external. *Northwestern University Law Review, 78*(2), 340–418.

Mulgan, G. (2006). The process of social innovation. *Innovations: Technology, Governance, Globalization, 1*(2), 145–162.

Penrose, E. (1959). *The theory of the growth of the firm*. New York, NY: Wiley.

Porter, M. E., & Kramer, M. R. (2006). Strategy and society: The link between competitive advantage and corporate social responsibility. *Harvard Business Review, 84*(12), 78–92.

Porter, M. E., & Kramer, M. R. (2011). Creating shared value. *Harvard Business Review, 89*(1/2), 62–77.

Porter, M. E., Hills, G., Pfitzer, M., Patscheke, S. & Hawkings, E. (2012). Measuring shared value: How to unlock value by linking business and social results. FSG. Visited: 20th December 2017. http://www.fsg.org/publications/measuring-shared-value.

Teece, D. J., Pisano, G., & Shuen, A. (1997). Dynamic capabilities and strategic management. *Strategic Management Journal, 18*(March), 509–533.

Tollison, R. D. (1982). Rent seeking: A survey. *Kyklos, 35*(4), 575–602.

Wieland, J. (1996). *Ökonomische organisation, allokation und status*. Tübingen: Mohr Siebeck.

Wieland, J. (1998). Kooperationsökonomie. Die Ökonomie der Diversifität, Abhängigkeit und Atmosphäre. In G. Wegner & J. Wieland (Eds.), *Formelle und informelle Institutionen der Ökonomie*. Genese und evolution (pp. 14–43). Marburg: Metropolis.

Wieland, J., & Heck, A. E. (2013). *Shared value durch stakeholder governance*. Marburg: Metropolis-Verlag.

Wieland, J., Steinmeyer, R., & Grüninger, S. (Eds.). (2014). *Handbuch compliance-management: Konzeptionelle Grundlagen, praktische Erfolgsfaktoren, globale Herausforderungen*. Berlin: Erich Schmidt Verlag.

Wieland, J. (2014). *Governance ethics: Global value creation, economic organization and normativity* (Vol. 48). Cham: Springer International Publishing.

Wieland, J. (Ed.). (2017a). *Creating Shared Value – Concepts, Experience, Criticism*. Heidelberg: Springer.

Wieland, J. (2017b). Shared value—theoretical concepts, practical challenges. In J. Wieland (Ed.), *Creating shared value—concepts, experience, criticism* (pp. 9–26). Heidelberg: Springer.

Wieland, J., Baumann Montecinos, J., Heck, A. E., Jandeisek, I., & Möhrer, M. (Eds.). (2017). *CSR performance: Managen und messen*. Marburg: Metropolis.

Williamson, O. E. (2005). The economics of governance. *The American Economic Review, 95*(2), 1–18.

Chapter 11
Relational Costs and the Logic of Relational Economics

11.1 Earnings and Costs in Relational Economics

The basic unit of analysis for the Relational Economics developed in this book is a commercial transaction characterised by more than two actors and by multiple decision logics and decision-making contexts. Although these actors are occasionally competitors, from a theoretical standpoint, solving the problem of how to cooperate for the benefit of all parties concerned is of primary interest. The execution of a relational transaction (RT) involves individual (I) and collective actors (O), as well as the societal informal (SII) and societal formal (SFI) institutions of one or more societies, which engage with one another interactively and recursively. This initially produces a process of constant change, followed by a stabilisation of relations in the form of a new, temporary equilibrium. Change can be sparked by the classic driver—economic innovation—or by a transaction being socially reformatted, which is to say that the conventional economic decision logics involved are supplemented by new political, social or moral decision logics. Thanks to the recursive nature of the events, the character of the transaction itself is changed and, in turn, the logics concerning the transaction and the actors are reformatted.

The epistemological focus of Relational Economics is on the process of cooperative private and societal value creation, the scale and scope of which are determined by the actors' chances for cooperation. These chances systematically depend on the twelve previously described success-critical resources for promoting the willingness and ability to cooperate and, together with the factor incomes, determine the distribution of the available cooperation rent. This extraction and distribution are chiefly shaped by stakeholder management, a relational leadership process and the actors' transcultural skills. The strategies, concepts, organisational structures, procedures and instruments that need to be developed for this purpose are relation-specific: for a specific transaction and/or organisational form. That being said, the degree of specificity also has an influence on the size of the rent. But the development and implementation of these resources also produce costs, whether at the level of the individual actors, as firm- or network-specific human capital, or at the level of the

J. Wieland, *Relational Economics*, Relational Economics and Organization Governance,
https://doi.org/10.1007/978-3-030-45112-7_11

collective actors, as investments in production goods or structures. Specific investments can easily produce hold-up situations, which have to be avoided by means of governance arrangements, so that high-risk investments are ventured in the first place.

After all, to say it once again, the reference system for Relational Economics is not the market, but the organisation and above all the firm and its stakeholders. The guiding difference for firms, which they use to assess all events, though not to decide on every single transaction, is that between the earnings and costs involved in the transaction and the continuation of cooperation. Ensuring that the outcome of the equation $E - C > 0$ is and remains a positive one is the goal of the firm, together with disbursing factor-incomes and potentially distributing a rent, a supernormal profit. In order to generate revenues, the firm's relational transactions are transformed into market transactions, which result in payments when they satisfy consumers' expectations concerning the good's or service's benefits and the requirements of societal normativity. It is in precisely this way that a given firm's transactions produce payments. As previously discussed, the continuity of the pairs "payment—non-payment" and "earnings—costs", the components of which are mutually dependent, is vital to the economy and the firms operating within it, as well as all other types of organisation in society. The following also bears repeating: every organisation engages in economic activities, but not every organisation is an economic organisation.

11.2 Transactions, Adaptation and Cooperation Costs

Unlike transaction cost theory or governance economics, which are primarily based on the works of Oliver E. Williamson, the epistemological focus of Relational Economics and the goal of the firm is not merely *economising on transaction* costs, but on *shared value creation*. This stems from the decision logic of commercial organisations: achieving a positive difference between costs (for example, innovation costs and transaction costs) and earnings (for example, from smart products or reduced energy consumption) that produces factor incomes and a cooperation rent.

In this regard, in the economic discussion of business organisations to date, a distinction has been made between different types of cost, namely transaction costs, adaptation costs and cooperation costs:

1. Transaction costs: The theoretical design developed by Williamson (cf. Tadelis & Williamson, 2013; Williamson, 1979, 1985, 2005) defines transaction costs as the costs produced by the initiation, implementation and monitoring of contracts. In this theoretical approach, foresighted planning, situational adaptation and effective monitoring are essential aspects. Based on the assumptions of bounded rationality and that actors are prone to opportunistic behaviour, on the degree of specificity of the investments involved in a given transaction and on the contingency inherent to the execution of transactions, taking precautionary steps to identify and quash opportunistic behaviour on the part of the contractual partners

is a key priority in transaction cost theory. This can be achieved with the help of efficient governance structures, which economically combine incentives for the actors to provide services in a contractually compliant manner, conflict resolution mechanisms and monitoring for inappropriate behaviour. Although this aspect certainly constitutes a major component of managing stakeholder relations, it alone cannot sufficiently explain the costs involved in creating and developing those resources that are success-critical from a motivational and structural standpoint: the willingness to cooperate and ability to cooperate at both the individual and organisational level. Transcultural competence and the commitment to take on social responsibility are further aspects that can only to a very limited extent be seen as means of avoiding opportunism in contractual arrangements.

2. Adaptation costs: Birger Wernerfelt (for a compilation and summary of the most important works cf. Wernerfelt, 2016) developed a theory of adaptation costs (AC) as a micro-foundation of the Resource-based View of the Firm. Simply put, the focus is less on the structure of incentives for the actors and more on the bargaining costs involved in adapting the resources from previously existing contracts to new circumstances. These can include the communication and coordination costs that arise, but, fundamentally speaking, can also encompass all types of bargaining costs, including those stemming from cultural diversity (ibid., p. 33).

   We have already discussed (see Chap. 8) a number of drawbacks in the practical application of Intercultural or Cross-Cultural Management. Here we can see another advantage of transcultural competence over intercultural competence. Whereas both involve specific cultures, only the former is a generalised competence with a sizable sub-additive excess capacity, which reduces the adaptation costs for every transaction.

   In this regard, what is especially interesting for Relational Economics is the premise that a given organisation's unique resources, despite being productive assets, are not 'for sale'. They are the firm's strategic strengths and cannot be bought or sold on the market. This, in turn, means they have *excess capacity*, which is to say, they offer additional benefits at no additional cost. Examples of such assets include know-how, product brands, business contacts and cultural expertise, not to mention critical factors like relational contracts and value creation. Once generated and in place, they can be employed in further, related transactions. To use Wernerfelt's terms, they are sub-additive, because changed or new transactions do not incur additional bargaining costs. "So it is logical to ask whether bargaining costs are sub-additive, such that parties can economize on them by pooling several bargains into one" (Ibid., p. 15). Adaptation costs can be either material or non-material: "AC theory looks for mechanisms that minimize the sum of adaptation costs associated with price-determination and production" (Ibid., p. 75).

   These aspects play a significant part in arranging contracts for cooperative networks, since these contracts are intended not for one-time but for continuous transactions, which, due to the emergence and blending of new decision logics, are subject to a process of permanent adaption to change. Clear, adequate communication and shared values can help to avoid the need for amending contractual specifications and the accompanying adaptation costs.

A network represents a bundle of resources, which are in a continuous process of combination and recombination. The costs produced by the mutual need to adapt resources and decision logics can be substantially reduced with the aid of sub-additive and unique cooperation resources. In the context of Relational Economics, these resources' *excess capacity* can also produce leverage effects that transcend a firm's internal operations—though it should be noted that this assumption contradicts Wernerfelt's argumentation that these effects only manifest "inside the boundary of the firm" (Ibid., p. 110). Networks boost the economic leverage effect of these resources and economise the adaptation costs. Although we "still know very little about how to identify them, measure them, and most efficiently share them across businesses" (Ibid., p. 111), I believe the identification of success-critical, relational resources as described above represents a valuable step in precisely this direction. If the costs for stakeholder processes become higher than the achievable cooperation rent due to the total lack of (or inadequate) transcultural management, together with a failure in leadership, networks cannot be formed. This is especially true for global value creation chains.

3. Cooperation costs: White and Siu-Yun Lui (2005) have proposed drawing a distinction between the costs of cooperation and transaction costs as defined by Williamson, which they argue are too unilaterally determined by the presumption of opportunism.

   "Cooperation costs are those incurred in order to undertake a collaborative activity with a partner, separate from those incurred in reducing the threat of opportunism from that same partner." (Ibid., p. 914)

   Their point of reference isn't a certain transaction or sequence of transactions; rather, in their view cooperation costs are essentially a natural element of social cooperation, resulting firstly from the coordination of joint efforts (*task complexity*) and secondly from the need to accommodate differences (*interpartner complexity*) (ibid., p. 915). For the authors, the latter aspect especially includes cultural differences and differences in the actors' values and perceptions. The complexity produced by information processing and diversity in terms of corporate goals and corporate cultures is among the direct causes of cooperation costs. In an empirical study, White and Lui demonstrate that, even in cases where there is no opportunistic behaviour and the transaction costs are zero, cooperation costs are still incurred—an important insight that reveals the limits to which transaction cost theory can be generalised.

11.3 Relational Costs and Cooperation Corridor

These discussions offer a good point of departure for the next topic because the costs of cooperation are also of interest with regard to the categorical context developed here. More precisely, the question of how and at what price a corridor of chances for cooperation can be created by the willingness and ability to cooperate is of interest. I refer to these costs as relational costs. Generally speaking, they are the costs that a given organisation has to pay in order to continually fulfil the purpose of its existence, namely interacting with stakeholders and their resources. More specifically, they are the costs incurred by generating and maintaining the willingness and ability to cooperate.

Figure 11.1 in the previous chapter draws a distinction between the individual and organisational levels of motivational and structural resources; costs are incurred in the creation and development of these resources. For example, creating and maintaining the individual willingness to cooperate, which tends to manifest in a preference for continuity and reciprocity, incurs costs in connection with selecting personnel and their continuing training. The same is true for fostering the individual ability to cooperate in terms of promoting integrity, the ability to find consensus and (trans) cultural competence, which entails costs for partner screening and communication.

With regard to the organisational willingness to cooperate, costs can, for example, be produced by the development and communication of a value management system, or by maintaining a multi-stakeholder dialogue. At this level, fostering the ability to cooperate includes the costs of implementing routines for sharing knowledge among the partners, of compliance management and of transcultural competence training.

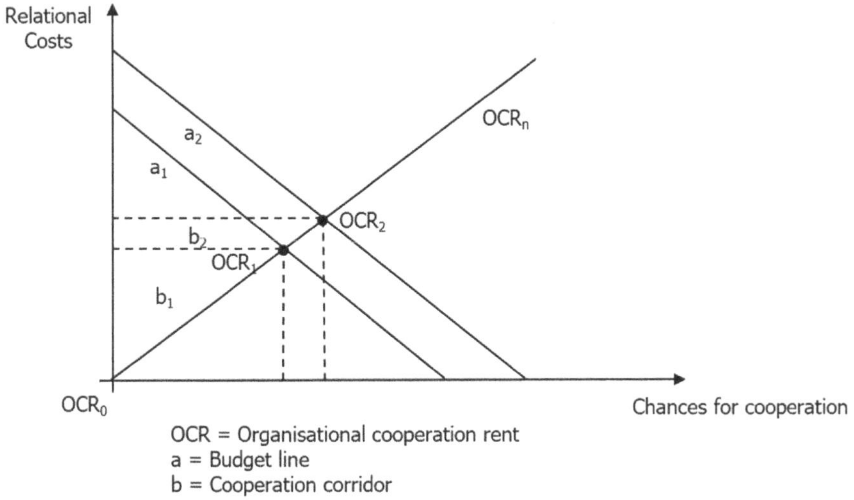

Fig. 11.1 Organisational cooperation rents and corridors

Lastly, relational costs include the costs incurred by using chances for cooperation, or more precisely: the shaping of and capitalising on these chances on the part of the leadership. Seizing chances for cooperation not only involves the previously mentioned *agency costs* (contract, monitoring and privilege-related costs) but also and especially team-building costs. In addition, there are the costs produced by deviating behaviour on the part of leaders, whether in the form of illicit actions, staff turnover, or the loss of customers and/or reputation.

Relational costs differ from the transaction, adaptation and cooperation costs proposed in other concepts in terms of their exclusive connection to specific relational transactions and the corresponding contracts. Another difference is their trans-sectoral influence. Their point of reference is the firm, especially with regard to its stakeholder management, leadership and transcultural nature. All activities related to these three fundamental areas of the relational economy generate costs, though we still know comparatively little about how they arise or are recorded in firms and other organisations. Here are a number of examples to help characterise relational costs.

Stakeholder management costs: These include costs for programmes that encourage practising societal responsibility in connection with social standards, human rights and sustainability. Multi-stakeholder dialogues and supplier management are prime examples. This category also includes the costs resulting from a suboptimal process dynamic for innovation with regard to disruptive or sustainable production innovations.

Leadership costs: I have previously described relational leadership as a social exchange process designed to ensure that employees voluntarily follow their leaders and have argued that leadership is a dynamic phenomenon that can be found at all levels of a given organisation or network. Accordingly, in relational transactions, leadership cannot be reduced to an agency function; in other words, it entails more than superiors who possess certain decision-making powers and the authority to give directives. There are also agency costs: pecuniary and non-pecuniary privileges like company cars, company housing and costs for insurance to cover illegal or illegitimate decisions and their financial (penalties) and non-financial (reputation, trust) consequences. Leadership costs, which are not to be confused with agency costs, include the following aspects.

From a resource perspective (character, creativity, culture), these costs can include the loss of productivity in a given team due to inappropriate leadership methods. Employees doing the bare minimum, a lack of enthusiasm, inner resignation, frequent absences due to illness and unusually high staff turnover are typical symptoms.

From a transaction perspective (goal-setting, coordination, absorbing uncertainty, forming and reinforcing a team identity), leadership costs include those produced by meetings, team-building and coaching. As previously shown, the various costs stemming from poor communication—central to any concept of leadership—are completely ignored in the relational contract theory put forward by Macneil. Lastly, from a governance perspective on leadership (the creation of adaptive governance structures), apart from agency costs there are, for example, the costs of integrity management and those involved in establishing a suitable leadership culture.

Transcultural management costs: these can include, for example, costs produced by diversity programmes, continuing education and global team-building.

In my estimation, today's corporate cost-accounting systems either fail to reflect the costs discussed above or reflect them using very general cost categories. A study on German firms revealed that the costs they incur in connection with following a societal responsibility strategy via stakeholder management and transcultural management are neither completely nor systematically recorded (cf. Wieland & Heck, 2013; Wieland, Baumann Montecinos, Heck, Jandeisek, & Möhrer, 2017). Leadership costs are often mistaken for agency costs; moreover, they are at best reflected as the costs of staff turnover and loss of customers resulting from the conduct of the leadership.

In a nutshell: generating and fostering the individual and organisational willingness and ability to cooperate is what defines the available corridor for a given firm and its stakeholders: the quantity and quality of chances for cooperation. In turn, the quantity and quality of these chances are what determine the size of the maximum achievable cooperation rent. The previous illustration (Fig. 11.1) helps to clarify these connections.

Let us assume that the trade-off between costs and chances can be modelled as a constant function for generating the cooperation rent and that the investments made in order to access chances for cooperation are limited by the scarcity of available resources and accordingly have a declining marginal benefit in economic practice, which is not reflected in the graphic. Here the point is merely to show that not all chances theoretically made available to a firm by willingness and ability *will* ever be capitalised on, nor *can* they ever all be capitalised on. The same applies to chances for cooperation. For example, potential transactions on markets that are high-risk in terms of corruption, human rights or sustainability and which would violate legal regulations, societal standards, corporate values, or the organisation in question's code of ethics or code of conduct, have to be rejected. Put another way, a firm's ability to cooperate also includes the willingness and ability to turn down chances for cooperation.

Under these conditions, the budget line a_1 limits the maximum chances for cooperation available to an organisation, regardless of the costs they entail. The expansion line OCR represents the organisation's learning process, which generates an optimal cooperation rent at the point OCR_1. The actually achievable cooperation corridor lies in the field b_1. All points on the line between OCR_0 and OCR_1 will produce suboptimal rents.

Further, for the sake of argument let us assume that, as a result of either an external (for instance, the opening of new global markets thanks to political decisions) or internal (for instance, a firm's introducing an effective compliance or CSR management system in global value creation chains) development, the scope of potential chances for cooperation expands, with appropriate changes in costs. This field is demarcated by the budget line a_2, with the increased rent OCR_2 and the larger corridor b_2. Just as in the first example, all points between OCR_1 and OCR_2 are suboptimal.

11.4 Relational Value Creation and Governance Forms

Marx essentially portrays the cooperation rent as a natural feature of capital and its added value production. Let us follow in the footsteps of Berle and Means, not to mention Barnard and approach it as a characteristic of organising cooperation, not by individuals but by organisations; then the generation of this rent, very much in keeping with Drucker's dictum, is accompanied by costs. This side of the organised interaction of actors is an aspect we've just discussed as the costs of relation and one that we have specified using the causal chain 'willingness to cooperate → ability to cooperate → chance for cooperation → cooperation rent'.

This discussion can also be summarised in a schema of relational value creation (Fig. 11.2).

The governance form 'market' and its discrete exchange transactions (ET) do not yield cooperation rents. Only natural scarcities and monopolies allow individual participants on the market to generate a monopoly rent MR >0. The willingness and ability to cooperate and with them, the relational costs (RC) have a value of 0 and therefore produce no chances for cooperation (CR = 0).

On the horizontal axis, relational governance, the next point is the neoclassical firm, which completely adapts to developments on the market and exclusively does business via a series of short-term contracts. Its cooperation indicators (willingness, ability and chances) and costs of organising and monitoring are >0. Through relational transactions (RT_1), an intra-firm rent from cooperation is generated, resulting from team production as defined by Alchian and Demsetz (1972) and is appropriated by the *residual claimant*. However, in order for this to occur, the relational costs (RT_1) required to generate the cooperation rent CR_1 must be taken into account, especially the search and selection costs involved in forming and maintaining the team, as well as the costs of monitoring to prevent shirking and other opportunistic behaviours.

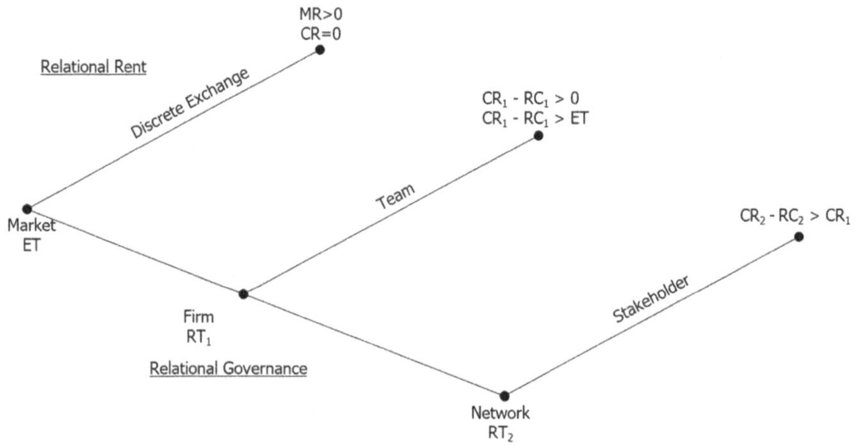

Fig. 11.2 Schema of relational value creation

The residual rent from cooperation (CR_1-RC_1) must be positive and also higher than the accessible profit by doing this transaction as an Exchange Transaction (ET).

The next point (RT_2) to the right on the horizontal axis leads to the firm as a relation of stakeholders, which forms a network of resources. Networks will continue to form, provided the cooperation rent CR_2 is larger than the rent at the point CR_1. At this point, the cooperation rent, though not based on additional performance, is not free of costs: the costs of relation, relational costs (RC_2), must be taken into account. If we assume that RC_2 is greater than RC_1, then networks will only be formed if the change in the cooperation rent is greater than the change in the relational costs.

This schema helps to explain why the *next wave of growth* in and through globalisation remains a distinct possibility, though it will only come to pass if earnings remain higher than the unavoidable transaction costs and relational costs.

References

Alchian, A. A., & Demsetz, H. (1972). Production, information costs, and economic organization. *American Economic Review, 62*(5), 777–795.

Tadelis, S., & Williamson, O. E. (2013). Transaction cost economics. In R. Gibbons & J. Roberts (Eds.), *Handbook of organizational economics* (pp. 159–189). Princeton, NJ: Princeton University Press.

Wernerfelt, B. (2016). *Adaptation, specialization, and the theory of the firm: Foundations of the resource-based view*. Cambridge, UK: Cambridge University Press.

White, S., & Siu-Yun Lui, S. (2005). Distinguishing costs of cooperation and control in alliances. *Strategic Management Journal, 26*(10), 913–932.

Wieland, J., Baumann Montecinos, J., Heck, A. E., Jandeisek, I., & Möhrer, M. (Eds.). (2017). *CSR performance: Managen und messen*. Marburg: Metropolis.

Wieland, J., & Heck, A. E. (2013). *Shared value durch stakeholder governance*. Marburg: Metropolis-Verlag.

Williamson, O. E. (1979). Transaction-cost economics: The governance of contractual relations. *The Journal of Law and Economics, 22*(2), 233–261.

Williamson, O. E. (1985). *The economic institutions of capitalism: Firms, markets, relational contracting*. New York, NY: The Free Press.

Williamson, O. E. (2005). Transaction Cost Economics. In C. Menard & M. M. Shirley (Eds.), *Handbook of new institutional economics* (pp. 41–65). New York, NY: Springer.

Chapter 12
Conclusion: Epistemology and Method

12.1 Taxonomy and Mechanism

Let's begin with a brief summary of the research agenda of Relational Economics. In this book, I have sought to develop a categorical taxonomy for private and public value creation, one based on the effective and efficient interlinking of and interaction between multiple resources and abilities. The chief categories involved in an economic theory of the relations between events are relational transactions and their governance, polycontextual cooperation and the factor incomes and relational rents that it produces.

A discrete and (initially) purely economically motivated exchange of goods and services becomes a relational transaction when, in addition to a purely economic rationality, other social rationalities and actors—for example, law and the courts, morality and civil society, or politics and governments—are docked to it and consequently have to be considered in terms of their interrelations and respective proportionalities. This also means that the process does not aim at constraining purely economic transactions, but at making such transactions possible, boosting their productivity and creating value. Viewed in this light, a transaction is a gathering place (see also Priddat, 2016, 2018) for multiple social contexts, a dynamic attractor and an interaction of polyvalent contexts and decision logics necessary for value creation under conditions of uncertainty and competition. As such, it hardly represents an exception to the rule but is instead characteristic of modern economies and the global grids connecting them.

From an economic perspective, this makes it necessary to create a suitable, efficient and effective regime by means of relational contracts and forms of governance. The identities, subjective and collective perceptions and behavioural preferences of the actors involved are just as important as mechanisms for governing cooperation and cost-effective conflict resolution. Both relational contracts and their governance require and create a high degree of flexibility, which in turn allows the transaction partners to adapt to unavoidable frictions and contingencies. Managing the stakeholders involved in a given transaction is just as important as leading them at all

J. Wieland, *Relational Economics*, Relational Economics and Organization Governance,
https://doi.org/10.1007/978-3-030-45112-7_12

levels and in various cultures. These mechanisms of adaptation and flexibility come at a price, in the form of transactional and relational costs; however, these costs are balanced by the earnings produced by the continued (market) transactions that the mechanisms make possible.

These earnings include not only a continual stream of factor incomes for the contractual partners involved but also the generation of a revenue that is not based on additional performance, namely the rent resulting from the cooperation, for all parties. This is the value-creation aspect of Relational Economics, which encompasses the creation and distribution of tangible and intangible benefits in return for the resources invested by all stakeholders, as well as a portion of the cooperation rent based on a given stakeholder's respective, specific investment. The size of this rent depends on the actors' individual and collective willingness and ability to cooperate, which in turn define the scope of chances for cooperation.

With regard to value creation, the mechanism of Relational Economics can be classified into the following categories:

- Relational value creation: refers to the total amount of new value created by the cooperation of production factors.
- Production factors: are the economic and societal stakeholders and their resources, that are involved in a transaction or in an organisation as a continuum of transactions.
- Factor incomes: are the monetary incomes generated for stakeholders in a given timeframe and in return for their invested resources (wages, fees, interest, rent, consulting fees, shared earnings, etc.).
- Relational rent: refers to the positive difference between the value-creating performance of a relational cooperation project and the next-best, competing cooperation project or a market-mediated, simple exchange transaction. Relational rents can be monetary or non-monetary in nature.

The dynamic capacity of a given firm's leadership—of its governance structures and management—is what allows it to identify, acquire, combine and monitor the specific resources needed (with regard to a transaction or organisation) in order to transform potential opportunities for cooperation into real and shared cooperation dividends. In this regard, as we've seen in the first part of this work, the most critical parameters are the ability to couple relational transactions with exchange transactions, the uncertainty, specificity and productivity of a given resource and the mechanisms used to allocate the cooperation rent.

We refer to the strategy and governance that a firm needs in order to achieve this transformation as *shared value creation*, that is, as the integration of business into the social matrix.

That is, in a nutshell, the world of Relational Economics.

12.2 Epistemological and Methodological Categories

The basis for the methodology applied in this book is the conviction, shared with Pierre Bourdieu (1998), that all things real are also relational (p. 15). Being is being in a relation. Unlike the methodology employed in textbook economies, Relational Economics does not rest on the assumption that everything in our world is a discrete event and can theoretically be understood and explained accordingly. Polycontextuality, polycontexturality and polylingualism, as marks of a relational society, are central epistemological and methodological categories of relationalism. However, the holistic maxim that everything is somehow related to everything else has no immediate implications for the scientific study of these relations. Its goal is to constrain and sharpen the epistemological interest and cognisance. In doing so, the hope is to arrive at a theoretical grasp of the effects of the practical functions of local mechanisms, as well as the trade-offs between them and other mechanisms. A transaction is one such local mechanism and we have dubbed the trade-offs concerning it as 'relations'. The relations are not necessarily causal, because an event may or may not be attracted by a transaction. Societal Relations are the result of a dynamic and self-unfolding process (cf., von Müller & Zafiris, 2018), the continuity of interactions of what Georg Simmel called "Wechselwirkung" and Penrose (1959, p. 1) the "result of a continuous on-going or 'unfolding' process". Understanding and explaining a given event in this context equates to positioning it and gauging its proportionality with regard to other events.

At the beginning of its success story in the social sciences, economic theory, very much in the tradition of the classical natural sciences, was predicated on a subjectless universe characterised by the interaction of things, of goods and by their exchange values. Here, in the market, supply meets demand and their interaction through the medium of money determines the prices of goods; in turn, the essentially strict adaptation mechanism of Homo economicus is oriented on these prices. Homo economicus is no active social subject, nor did economists ever intend him to be. He is an abstraction, a hypothetical figure used to model economic calculations and rational assumptions regarding human behaviour. This has certainly changed over the past few decades, especially in those approaches to economic research that are oriented on behavioural psychology; nevertheless, I feel that Günther's (1979) statement that "a subjectless Universe presents us with a rigorously mono-contextural structure" (ibid., p. 304) remains largely true today in terms of economic theory-building. Accordingly, in epistemological terms, anyone who is interested in actors who consciously perceive their surroundings and who have their own social preferences and individual or collective moral convictions, must assume that our world is polycontextual and polycontextural. In such cases, to cite Günther once more, we see the "mono-contextural concept of Reality [...] abandoned and replaced by a poly-contextural theory of Existence which makes room for the phenomenon of Life within this Universe" (ibid.).

Here it's all about—very much in keeping with both Greek thought and process philosophy—the relations between the actors, between the actors and their respective environments and between these environments. Economy and society, economic theory and social theory are topics in the relation of relations. The fact that my own work draws on the philosophies of Aristotle and Whitehead is due in no small part to the influence that their epistemological theories have had on theory-building in institutional and organisational economics.

Accordingly, I wish to close the book by following this tradition and discussing a number of epistemological and methodological fundamentals of Relational Economics. It may come as a surprise that this discussion appears so late in the book and not in the introduction, yet it seemed more advantageous to me to first develop the subject matter and goals that such a philosophical reflection refers to. This is all the more sensible because, in the course of the argumentation, there have been several aspects that I have only briefly (in some cases, perhaps too briefly) touched upon.

12.3 Economic Form and Organisational Process

The deliberations regarding Relational Economics presented in this book are oriented, from an epistemological standpoint, on the process philosophy put forward by Alfred N. Whitehead (the following passages represent a slightly modified version from Wieland, 2016, pp. 289–298). In this context, process and form are central epistemological concepts with methodological consequences. They encompass both their object of study and the perspective on it. As such, I feel it is worthwhile, as a closing reflection, to discuss these epistemological concepts, together with the methodological consequences they entail for their object of study, namely the relational economy. To do so, I will concentrate, as I have up to this point, on the level of relational transactions and on the governance structure of organisational systems, or to be more precise: on the economic form of the 'firm' as a governance structure for the processes of its transactions.

The firm, as an autonomous economic form, as an 'entity in its own right', is, as previously established, a societal organisation. It is not a causal consequence of market activities, whether they be attempts to create a monopoly, to economise on transaction costs, or to govern incomplete contracts. Rather, it is the result of legal, political and societal communication regarding the organisation of a given society's economic affairs. Within it can be seen a form of organising the economic interests and resources of its stakeholders for the purpose of creating public and private prosperity. The famous claim that 'the business of business is business' is only accurate in the context of specific economic categories and theories, which do not permit a differentiation in form between market and organisation, because they predominantly use the price form of the market as a model for explaining firms' value creation process. Here, the process dissipates into the form and, in turn, the form 'firm' is supplanted by the form 'market', the object of study for these theories. Made in the 1960s, Fritz Machlup's classic, straightforward and pointed observation that in price theory the firm only exists as a 'theoretical link'—which is to say, not at all—is just as true today:

> The model of the firm in that theory is not, as so many writers believe, designed to serve to explain and predict the behavior of real firms; it is designed to explain and predict changes in observed prices [...]. In this causal connection the firm is only a theoretical link, a mental construct helping to explain how one gets from the cause to the effect. (Machlup, 1967, p. 9)

Similarly, the introductory statement made by Robert Gibbons and John Roberts in 2013 has lost none of its validity: "organizational economics is not yet a fully recognized field in economics" (Gibbons & Roberts, 2013, p. 1).

The economic discussion regarding The Nature of the Firm is a paradigmatic case that demonstrates how a static definition of form can both foster and hinder the evolution of research into organisational value-creation processes for several decades and, with regard to the nature of the firm, can steer said research in a direction that is of only limited epistemological value. Paving the way for new process-related insights can only be achieved by changing the "defining characteristics" (Whitehead) of form and this, in turn, calls for new ways of approaching form. Today there are multiple approaches that view the firm as an 'input-output relation', as a 'nexus of contracts', as a structure for 'economising on transaction costs', as 'resource- or capability-based', as a 'network of stakeholder resources' and so on.

Yet in all of these cases, the abstract objects of different theoretical approaches cannot be seen as representing the reality per se. This is an example of what Whitehead dubbed the 'fallacy of misplaced concreteness', which cannot stand up to empirical scrutiny. Whitehead's process philosophy seeks to avoid this fallacy by viewing the firm—or more generally, the organisation—as a 'society' and not a 'theoretical link' or a 'perspective':

> A 'society', in the sense in which that term is used, is a nexus with social order [...]. A nexus enjoys 'social order' where (i) there is a common element of form illustrated in the definiteness of each of its included actual entities, and (ii) this common element of form arises in each member of the nexus by reason of the conditions imposed upon it by its prehensions of some other members of the nexus, and (iii) these prehensions impose that condition of reproduction by reason of their inclusion of positive feelings of that common form. Such a nexus is called 'society' and the common form is the 'defining characteristic' of the society. (Whitehead, 1929/1941, p. 50)

Forms determine the character of events related to them; events reproduce the form as a shared trait. Accordingly, for process philosophy, a firm would be the unity of form (a shared point of reference), relation (of the events) and reproduction (through information and identification), in which the three elements are intertwined through their interactions and which exist and are newly formed in this way.[1] Here, process means: becoming, being and being related (to something else).

> In the philosophy of organism it is not substance which is permanent, but form. Forms suffer changing relation; actual entities 'perpetually perish' subjectively, but are immortal objectively. (Whitehead, 1929/1941, p. 44)

[1]Dirk Baecker (1993) portrays the form of the firm [*Die Form des Unternehmens*] as a cognitive mechanism, as a process that generates communicable distinctions, any by doing so, stabilises itself as a system. Mark R. Dibben, drawing on the work of Joseph Bracken and adopting a process philosophy perspective, suggests that we view organisations as societies in the sense of being structured and structuring, existing and emerging fields of activity (cf. Dibben, 2008, p. 102).

12.4 Form and the Fallacy of Misplaced Concreteness

Whitehead's terminology is a product of his cosmology. The terms 'actual entities' and 'actual occasions' refer to physical micro-events, which are difficult to fruitfully apply in the social sciences—unlike the term 'event', which entails a process philosophy approach and accordingly, in my view, offers a promising 'basic unit' for dynamic economic analysis. "I shall use the term 'event' in the more general sense of a nexus of actual occasions, inter-related in some determinate fashion in one extensive quantum" (Whitehead, 1929/1941, p. 73). I surmise that this is also the reason Commons (1934/1990, p. 619) chose to base his institutional economics on the term 'event'.

Actual entities or—better suited to the social sciences—'events'[2] are subject to change, yet are in an objective sense eternal and in this way form the basis for dynamism, creativity and the new. As organisations, firms represent an intelligible form of the relation of empirical events, one that is the result of individual, collective and last but not least, philosophical thought. This form-creating process is a striving for "satisfaction" (Whitehead, 1929/1941, p. 130) and "limitation" (Whitehead, 1925/1967, p. 177 f.) and as such, in the real world it is endowed with a certain behaviour-guiding power as 'abstraction' (Whitehead, 1929/1941, p. 11), which is to say, it is ascribed values and normativity (cf. also Neesham & Dibben, 2012, p. 72). Yet this is also precisely the process that the 'fallacy of misplaced concreteness' refers to (Whitehead, 1984, p. 39).

> This fallacy consists in neglecting the degree of abstraction involved when an actual entity is considered merely so far as it exemplifies certain categories of thought" (Whitehead, 1929/1941, p. 11). Or, as he aptly summarises the point, an "imaginary terrier" can't kill a "real rat." (cf. Whitehead, 1929/1941, p. 348)

In turn, Chester I. Barnard pointed out the following: "executive functions [...] have no separate concrete existence [...]. They are part or aspects of a process of organization as a whole" (Barnard, 1938/1968, p. 235). When we contemplate and theorise on the practice of leadership and decision-making within organisations, Barnard claims, the risk of 'misplaced concreteness' is great because the 'analysis is not the end but the beginning of purposive action' (Barnard, 1938/1968, p. 239). The sheer complexity of everyday life and its decision-making situations systematically implies that all leadership theories are ultimately doomed to fail and helps to explain why there are so many and why they come and go like fashion.

Karl Weick explored this aspect with regard to organisation theory, in the course of which he stated, very much in keeping with process philosophy, that:

> Most 'things' in organizations are actually relationships, variables tied together in systematic fashion [...]" and, in similar vein: "The word organization is a noun, and it is also a myth. If you look for an organization you won't find it. What you will find is that there are events, linked together, [...] and their timing are the forms we erroneously make into substances when we talk about an organization. (Weick, 1979, p. 86)

[2]This idea stemmed from a discussion with Michael Schramm, who I'd like to take this opportunity to thank.

The difference between form and process of organising can only be eliminated at the cost of both the form-specific nature of the process and the process-specific nature of the form—not to mention the dynamic character of their interactions—being completely ignored as objects of analysis. As it is the case in conventional economics, organisations then become markets and markets become organisations. I have illustrated and discussed the consequences of doing so in this conclusion and elsewhere throughout this book. When the line between form and process becomes blurred, both phenomena tend to disappear from theoretical categories.

12.5 Events and Form

However, the philosophical and methodological reflection on the governance of economic transactions can be coupled with the process of defining the economic form and its relation to 'events'. Not only as a history of thought-forms but also with explorations of the adjacent yet driving elements of a creative process from which the world establishes itself through self-causation and transcendence (Whitehead, 1929/1941, p. 336). Economic thought-forms are the product of a discursive and evolutionary process and are historical, which is to say, real and contingent. Whereas the organisation of economic activity was simultaneous with human life and human culture, the same most likely cannot be said for the process of identifying the defining characteristics of their form, or the latter's relation to economic practice, at least not in my estimation. By focusing on the defining characteristics of the form of relations, I am following in the footsteps of a "theory of the relationship between events [...]" (Whitehead, 1925/1967, p. 122), which is epistemologically based on a "primacy of relations" (Lachmann, 1990, p. 45), the abstract economic form in the relational context of individual actual economic events (cf. Whitehead, 1925/1967, p. 159 f.).

In this regard, the goal is to understand the economy as the sum of the concrete and empirical individual economic acts and to approach economics as the intellectual structuring and classification of these acts as a form of cultural and civilized existence. It is the philosophy, so Whitehead, which "seek(s) to express that ultimate good sense which we term civilization. In each case, there is reference to form beyond the direct meanings of words" (Whitehead, 1938/1968, p. 174). The philosophy achieves this by rationalising the mythical world, "not by explaining it away, but by the introduction of novel verbal characterizations, rationally coordinated" (Whitehead, 1938/1968, p. 174).

The Greek philosophers are the first who sought to distil the form of economic organisation from the myth (cf. Biervert & Wieland, 1986, 1987, Biervert, Held, & Wieland, 1990, Wieland, 2012, Priddat & Seele, 2008). Aristotle's theory of the *oikonomia* is intended as a relational theory for all human and material resources of the *oikos* and the form that provides the *oikos* with both meaning and structure is that of hierarchical relations: the *oikonomike* is a science of "examin[ing] the proper constitution and character of each of these three relationships, I mean that of mastership, that of marriage [...], and thirdly the progenitive relationship [...]. Let us then accept these three relationships that we have mentioned" (Aristotle, Pol. I, 1253b 10). In turn, this perspective on the social community raises the question as to "that [a community] is to be well ordered" (Aristotle, Pol. II, 1261a 1). Under the primacy of personal relations, the adequate order of the economic sphere[3] with its concrete-practical side and ethical-normative side leads, through the integration of the *technai* (the proper disposition of assets and personnel), to the emergence of an initial intelligible form of economic organisation, the *oikonomia*. It was the discursive work concerning the categories of production (nature—*physis*, labour/creation—*ponos/ergon*), circulation (market—*agora*, exchange—*metabletikos*, competition—*philoneikeo*) and pursuit (money—*nomisma*, value—*axias*, utility—*ophelia/chresimos*, scarcity—*chreia*, desire—*epithmya*) that defined the private and public economic sphere, the differentiation of the actors (master/owner—*oikonomos*, manager—*oikonomikos*) and the specific expertise of a behaviour-guiding *techne* (*oikonomike*) that established the Greek economy as a societally differentiated relation from mythical thought. Though Aristotle was quite familiar with the *oikonomia* as a specialised form of Greek economic organisation and corresponding expertise (*techne*), he felt its essence was to be understood as a hierarchical personnel relation, not as a relation of things. To put it in more modern and perhaps slightly overstated terms, Aristotle was the first to pose and answer the question "What is the nature of the firm?".

12.6 Fundamental Transformation and Selective Interaction

In Relational Economics, the concept of organisation is developed as the unity of difference of the form 'organisation' and the process of 'organising' (cf. Wieland 2001, esp. Sect. 12.2). As a result, economic transactions can be executed by a market, hierarchy or hybrids, which are three different forms of governance and accordingly permit and require different processes (such as a pricing mechanism or long-term contracts). Abstract forms have practical consequences. In the context of a perfect, exclusively price-driven competitive market, the process of fostering and cultivating moral business principles is neither representable nor possible; conversely, in a continuity-oriented organisation, managing moral values is indispensable. In the language game of prices, morality produces communicative white noise. In the organisation, morality is a language game that is understood and permissible and one that must confer with the language of prices, of profitability, of law, of engineering, of aesthetics and so on.

In this interrelation, the form influences the process, just as the process reproduces the form. Oliver E. Williamson coined the governance economic term "fundamental transformation", which, driven and shaped by economic transactions' type and degree of specificity, leads to the "impossibility of selective intervention" (Williamson, 1985, p. 61 ff., p. 133 ff.). The process (structures, transaction costs) yields the

[3]On the *kataskeuazesthai* of the *oikonomia* cf. Wieland (2012, p. 209).

change of form (from market to organisation), while the form (organisation) produces changed processes (structures, transaction costs). The point that Williamson is trying to make is the following: market processes can't be used to efficiently steer an organisation, just as the governance structures for organisations can't be used to steer a market. "Market and Hierarchy" (cf. Williamson, 1975) are two separate and distinct forms of governance for economic transactions and cannot be dissolved into one another. A comparative study on the theory and practice of 'planned economies' on the one hand and the practical implementation of theories on 'internal markets in firms' on the other, could offer valuable insights into the limits of such attempts at selective intervention. The combination of 'fundamental transformation' and the 'impossibility of selective intervention' is what forms the dynamic, driving force in Relational Economics (cf. Williamson, 1975, 1996, 2005). It is this interplay as the unity of difference of form and process that is demarcated within and by means of a discrete economic transaction.

12.7 Continuation and Going Concern

As such, the fact that process philosophy also influences the theoretical references of Relational Economics should hardly come as a surprise. Whitehead's *Process and Reality* was published in 1929, John R. Commons' *Institutional Economics* in 1934 and Chester I. Barnard's *The Functions of the Executive* in 1938.

Michael Schramm has (in my opinion, quite correctly) argued that John R. Commons' institutional economics can be understood as being "analogous to Whitehead's cosmological metaphysics" [own translation] (cf. Schramm, 2016, p. 48, 2008, 2014). Or, to quote Commons himself:

> But the mechanism itself is 'organic' in that it is a kind of prolonged interweaving of changing events, having, as Whitehead says, a past, a present realization and a future life in its present events. (Commons, 1934/1990, p. 619)

In his view, organisations are forms of collective action that permit societal transactions of various kinds ("managerial, bargaining, rationing, moral, economic, sovereign") to be executed (Commons, 1934/1990, p. 748 ff.)

> The economic concerns are those, such as business organizations, labor unions, farmers' cooperatives, produce or stock exchanges, in so far as they rely on the economic sanctions of coercion by protecting gains or imposing losses, through participation in, exclusion from, or non-interference with, transactions. (Ibid., p. 749).

Each of these organisations becomes an "economic concern" through its relation to and reference to the guiding difference for economic organisations: 'earnings–costs'. This difference determines whether economic transactions are included in or excluded from the form 'organisation'. According to Commons, the effectiveness and efficiency of economic organisation processes led to their being portrayed as "the machine" among the public in the early twentieth century, though doing so neglects the form-process difference.[4]

> In the proportion to which organization reaches this smooth perfection we give to it, not the physical name 'machine,' not the biological name 'organism,' nor even the indefinite name 'group,' but the social activity name 'going concern.' The distinguishing character of a perfected going concern is its capacity to continue with changing personalities and changing principles, not depending upon any particular person or any particular principle. (Commons, 1934/1990, p. 750)

Firms, farms, labour unions, stock exchanges and so on are, in terms of form, 'societal activities'; they are forms used by society to manage its economic affairs (products, food, finance, income etc.). For Commons, then, firms are organisations within society: not just historically-genetically, but also conceptually and not for socio-political reasons, but because they permit the continuity of economic cooperation. Williamson would later underscore the importance of this aspect as the systematic basic assumption of governance economics.

> As against simple market exchange, governance is predominantly concerned with ongoing contractual relations for which continuity of the relationship is a source of value. (Williamson, 2005, p. 2)

It is the abstraction of all concrete persons and processes that constitutes the infinite permanence of the firm as an economic form and which reflects its characteristic as a 'going concern', as the continuation of societal value creation and as value creation from continuity. Accordingly, the nature and purpose of the firm as a 'going concern' do not consist in personal relations, the production of investment or consumer goods, maximising profits for the owners or shareholders, or generating shared value for stakeholders; the nature and purpose of the firm exclusively lie in the continuation of its own existence, in the permanence of its existence as a medium for private and societal value creation. The firm as a production function, or as a vehicle for maximising profits or strategically generating shared value—from the standpoint of Relational Economics, these are all contingent process descriptions that, although not residing on the abstract level of the defining characteristics of the form, can nonetheless certainly serve as expressions, results or conditions for reproducing the 'going concern'. The idea championed by neoclassical and mainstream economists, namely that of defining the firm as a price mechanism for achieving equilibrium and therefore subsuming it as a market form, fails from an empirical standpoint, due to the non-arbitrary consequences of this 'fundamental transformation' and the 'impossibility of selective intervention'. The form 'organisation' realises its character as a *society of events,* not as a societal entity per se. This realisation is carried out through the process of cooperation among stakeholders via this form, which they use to relationalise resources and interests in connection with executing economic transactions. Consequently, the societal responsibility of firms is an abstraction linked to a form that, as process events of the *going concern*, combines stakeholder discourses,

[4]Cf. for example Charlie Chaplin's film *Modern Times* from 1936. For a critical discussion on the neoclassical theory of the firm in this regard cf. Schramm, 2016.

standards, compliance, risk management and values management and in this context underscores societal responsibility in a local, material manifestation.

For the epistemological discussion, however, the task of determining the consequences of this process in connection with defining the form of economic organisation remains.

12.8 Societal Matrix and Political Economy

Commons' suggestion that we view the firm as a "going concern existing in its transactions" (Commons, 1934/1990, p. 53), as a form that exists in its transaction processes and which is reproduced by them as an abstraction, is sound from a process philosophy perspective. Situating the firm within society, embedding the economy in the society and the society in the economy, is produced and reproduced in each and every economic transaction. In the process, the transaction becomes an event, becomes a starting point and end point in the infinite continuity of the societal nature of the firm. Accordingly, for Commons it goes without saying that the transaction and the actors involved, which form the 'basic unit' of the economic process, are also the 'basic unit' of institutional economics (for an interesting, more recent discussion of this idea cf. Priddat, 2015), because the transaction, with its three dimensions—legal, economic and moral—and three principles—conflict, mutual dependence and order—is the shared point of reference for socially and economically relevant and distinct actors, as well as their respective decision logics (Commons, 1934/1990, p. 57). Therefore, polycontextuality and polycontexturality are constitutive characteristics of the transaction as the basic unit of relational economic analysis. Here let us recall once more Commons' previously mentioned, classic definition:

> Thus the ultimate unit of activity, which correlates law, economics, ethics, must contain in itself the three principles of conflict, dependence, and order. This unit is a transaction. A transaction, with its participants, is the smallest unit of institutional economics. (Commons, 1934/1990, p. 58)

One question that remains open is how and to what extent the thought of Chester I. Barnard was influenced by Commons' Institutional Economics; in any event, Barnard knew and maybe read the book (cf. Barnard, 1938/1968, p. 202 ff.). However, we do know that his organisational and management theory was informed by Whitehead's ideas, as can be seen in the following footnote:

> I am under the impression that in a general way both the form of expression and the concepts stated in the next several paragraphs were derived from or influenced by A. N. Whitehead's Process and Reality. (Barnard, 1938/1968, p. 195 f.)

Accordingly, he somewhat casually refers to organisations as groups of persons or members, although he knows that, technically speaking, such definitions are inadequate. Organisation refers to activities and events and to processes of abstraction and of defining cooperative relations. "I define an organization as a system of cooperative activities of two or more persons—something intangible and impersonal, largely a matter of relationships". (Barnard, 1938/1968, p. 75)

The societal nature of economic organisation as a form of cooperation; the constitutive polyvalence of the transactions and actors involved in this collaborative project; the polylingualism of their discourse as an immanent resource for these collaborations; the establishment and reinforcement of robust governance structures or order, transcending conflict and mutual dependence; the relations between individual and collective actors and between transactions and actors; the integration of fragmented and temporalised events at the levels of the economic transaction, of the individual person and of the form 'person'; the processes and form of the organisation and of the market as an intelligible form; and lastly, the societal totality as the appearance and disappearance of the successful simultaneity of different decision logics—all these aspects are not only developmental stages in an abstraction that increases the risk of 'misplaced concreteness'; in this form, they are also process- and relation-based building blocks in the development of a social-theory-oriented '*General Theory for the Governance of Relational Economic Transactions*'. The "societal matrix" of Relational Economics as a Political Economy is a relational society.

What are the next steps? It is readily apparent that any theory on the dynamics of economic transactions and the corresponding processes of socialisation (*Vergesellschaftung*) and one that is intended as a theory, cannot be viable without a theory of money. After all, the financial and capital markets are what determine the dynamics of transactions. From an epistemological perspective, the point of departure for a theory of money with a social theory focus should be the relational '*Philosophy of Money*' put forward by Georg Simmel. For Simmel, money has a function of "expressing the economic relations between objects—or the relations that render things economically valuable" [own translation] (Simmel, 1901/1989, p. 131). In Simmel's work, 'relation' refers to the fact that "things receive their meaning through each other" (Ibid., p. 136). For him, this is the quintessential characteristic of all existence, which is expressed in the "dual role of money". On one hand, money is the medium of transaction for economic goods and services (commodity–money–commodity); while on the other, it is itself the origin and purpose of financial-economic transactions (money–money). "Money is therefore one of those normative ideas that obey the norms that they themselves represent" [own translation] (Simmel, 1901/1989, p. 126). In this dual role, money becomes the ultimate "symbol of a relation" [own translation] (von Flotow, 1995, p. 40) linking the economy and society.

I indicated in the introduction that the economics of governance, with which the current investigation shares a common theoretical point of departure, generally limits its focus to the area of private ordering; however, the shift of focus from the analysis of private ordering regimes to polyvalent transactions and their relations to other contexts within society makes the economics of other modes of governance of fundamental interest. This includes the area of government policy, distributive justice and welfare, which have a significant influence on private and societal value creation. Explorations concerning government policy, distributive justice and welfare and towards a theory of money are desiderata of Relational Economics as a Political Economy that warrant further research.

Further essential steps on the way to a Relational Economics include empirical research and case studies on the governance mechanisms of economic transactions that were proposed and developed in this book. In addition, the ideas presented here no doubt require critical theoretical refinement and formalisation; in this regard, certain initial models (discussed in the text) are already available. An important contribution with regard to the epistemological and methodological foundation of relational economics as a network theory can be found in the book *Relational Methodologies and Epistemology in Economics and Management Sciences* by Biggiero et al. (2016). But this refinement and formalisation will be virtually impossible without a categorical taxonomy of Relational Economics, one that affords us a different perspective on economic transactions. By writing this book, my intention was to bring us closer to achieving that goal.

References

Aristotle. (1959). *Politics*. Cambridge, MA: Harvard University Press.

Baecker, D. (1993). *Die Form des Unternehmens*. Frankfurt a. M.: Suhrkamp.

Barnard, C. I. (1938). *The functions of the executive*. Cambridge, MA: Harvard University Press.

Biervert, B., Held, K., & Wieland, J. (1990). Gegenstandsbereiche und Rationalitätstypen in Ökonomie und Ökonomik. In B. Biervert, K. Held, & J. Wieland (Eds.), *Sozialphilosophische Grundlagen ökonomischen Handelns* (pp. 7–32). Frankfurt a. M.: Suhrkamp.

Biervert, B., & Wieland, J. (1986). *Ansatzpunkte einer Analyse ökonomischer Denkformen und Kategorien*, Diskussionspapier 2/1986 der Forschungsgruppe Sozialökonomischer Wandel. Bergische Universität-GH Wuppertal.

Biervert, B., & Wieland, J. (1987). Der ethische Gehalt ökonomischer Kategorien – Beispiel: Der Nutzen. In B. Biervert & M. Held (Eds.), *Ökonomische Theorie und Ethik* (pp. 23–25). Frankfurt a. M.: Campus.

Biggiero, L., Angelini, P. P., Basevi, M., Carbonara, N., Mastrogiorgio, A., Pessa, E., et al. (2016). *Relational methodologies and epistemology in economics and management sciences*. Hershey, PA: IGI Global.

Bourdieu, P. (1998). *Praktische Vernunft: Zur Theorie des Handelns*. Berlin: Suhrkamp.

Commons, J. (1934). *Institutional economics. Its place in political economy* (Vol. 1). New Brunswick, NJ: Transaction Publishers.

Dibben, M. R. (2008). Organisations and organising: Understanding and applying Whitehead's processual account. *Philosophy of Management, 7*(2), 13–24.

Gibbons, R., & Roberts, J. (Eds.). (2013). *The handbook of organizational economics*. Princeton, NJ: Princeton University Press.

Günther, G. (1979). *Beiträge zur Grundlegung einer operationsfähigen Dialektik* (Vol. 2). Hamburg: Meiner.

Lachmann, R. (1990). *Ethik und Identität: der ethische Ansatz in der Prozessphilosophie. A.N. Whitehead und seine Bedeutung für die gegenwärtige Ethik*. Freiburg/München: Karl Alber.

Machlup, F. (1967). Theories of the firm: Marginalist, behavioral, managerial. *American Economic Review, 57*(1), 1–33.

Neesham, C., & Dibben, M. (2012). The social value of business: lessons from political economy and process philosophy. In M. Schwartz & Howard Harris (Eds.), *Applied ethics: Remembering Patrick Primeaux (Research in Ethical Issues in Organizations* (Volume 8, pp. 63–83). Bingley, UK: Emerald Group Publishing.

Penrose, E. (1959). *The theory of the growth of the firm*. New York, NY: Wiley.

Priddat, B. P. (2015). *Economics of persuasion: Ökonomie zwischen Markt, Kommunikation und Überredung*. Marburg: Metropolis.

Priddat, B. P. (2016). Transaktion als Juxtaposition und als Kooperation: Differente Interpretationen des Marktes. In Discussion Papers Fakultät für Wirtschaftswissenschaft Universität Witten/Herdecke New Series 2010 ff. No. 38. Witten/Herdecke: Universität Witten/Herdecke.

Priddat, B. P. (2018). *Vertrag als Kooperation*. Unveröffentlichtes Manuskript: Über die implizite Ethik der Transaktion.

Priddat, B., & Seele, P. (2008). *Das Neue in Ökonomie und Management: Grundlagen, Methoden, Beispiele*. Wiesbaden: Gabler.

Schramm, M. (2008). Transaktions-Rhizome. Ontologie und Ethik eines mikroanalytischen Stakeholder-Managements. In J. Wieland (Ed.), *Die Stakeholder-Gesellschaft und ihre Governance. Management, Netzwerke, Diskurse* (pp. 39–64). Marburg: Metropolis.

Schramm, M. (2014). Business metaphysics. *Forum Wirtschaftsethik, 22*, 51–58.

Schramm, M. (2015). Business metaphysics: Konturen eines Forschungsprogramms. In R. Neck (Ed.), *Wirtschaftsethische Perspektiven XI, Schriften des Vereins für Socialpolitik* (pp. 1–62). Berlin: Duncker & Humblot.

Schramm, M. (2016). Wie funktioniert die Geschäftswelt wirklich? Business Metaphysics und Theorie der Firma. *Ethica, 24*(4), 311–360.

Simmel, G. (1901/1981). *Philosophie des Geldes*. Frankfurt a. M.: Suhrkamp.

Von Flotow, P. (1995). *Geld, Wirtschaft und Gesellschaft. Georg Simmels Philosophie des Geldes*. Frankfurt a. M.: Suhrkamp.

von Müller, A., & Zafiris, E. (2018). *Concept and formalization of constellatory self-unfolding*. Cham: Springer.

Weick, K. E. (1979). *The social psychology of organizing* (2nd ed.). New York, NY: McGraw-Hill.

Whitehead, A. N. (1941). *Process and reality*. New York, NY: The Free Press.

Whitehead, A. N. (1967). *Science and the modern world*. New York, NY: The Free Press.

Whitehead, A. N. (1968). *Modes of thought*. New York, NY: The Free Press.

Wieland, J. (2001). Eine Theorie der Governanceethik. *Zeitschrift für Wirtschafts- und Unternehmensethik, 2*(1), 8–33.

Wieland, J. (2012). *Die Entdeckung der Ökonomie: Kategorien, Gegenstandsbereiche und Rationalitätstypen der Ökonomie an ihrem Ursprung* (2nd ed.). Marburg: Metropolis.

Wieland, J. (2016). Philosophie der Firma: Eine Skizze. In W. D. Enkelmann & B. Priddat (Eds.), *Was ist? Wirtschaftsphilosophische Erkundungen. Definitionen, Ansätze, Methoden, Erkenntnisse, Wirkungen* (pp. 285–314). Marburg: Metropolis.

Williamson, O. E. (1975). *Markets and hierarchies*. New York, NY: The Free Press.

Williamson, O. E. (1985). *The economic institutions of capitalism: Firms, market, relational contracting*. New York, NY: The Free Press.

Williamson, O. E. (1996). *The mechanisms of governance*. Oxford, UK: Oxford University Press.

Williamson, O. E. (2005). The economics of governance. *The American Economic Review, 95*(2), 1–18.

The manufacturer's authorised representative in the EU is Springer
Nature Customer Service Centre GmbH, Europaplatz 3, 69115 Heidelberg,
Germany. If you have any concerns regarding our products, please
contact ProductSafety@springernature.com

Printed and bound by CPI Group (UK) Ltd, Croydon, CR0 4YY
05/10/2026
02228154-0007